"The liberalism of Warner and Palmer could be called 'adultism.' The other policies—of a statist right or a statist left or for that matter a statist middle—all treat adults as bad children or sad children. Poor things, poor things, they're waiting to be fed. On the contrary, adults are to be accorded the dignity of 'the equal presumption of liberty and citizen-based democratic political principles' … You need this lucid and eloquent book. Read it, right away. No time to waste …."

Deirdre N. McCloskey, *Distinguished Professor Emerita of Economics and of History, and Professor Emerita of English and of Communication, adjunct in classics and philosophy, at the University of Illinois at Chicago, USA*

"Read this book and you will be introduced to new perspectives on the power of local knowledge—rooted in human experience—to fuel sustainable development and to generate the socio-economic wealth of nations."

Vernon L. Smith, *Nobel Laureate in Economic Sciences*

"*Development with Dignity* is an outstanding contribution to the public discourse addressing the intimate relationships between universal rights, human dignity, and economic prosperity. Adam Smith's liberal plan of liberty, equality, and justice is restated and grounded in the latest research in the social sciences and humanities, and readers will learn of the power of entrepreneurship to improve lives for individuals as they are empowered to pursue productive specialization and realize social cooperation through mutually beneficial exchange. As a result, these individuals experience greater freedom and prosperity. Palmer and Warner have produced a must-read book dealing with the most fundamental and important question in the social sciences."

Peter Boettke, *George Mason University, USA*

T0373574

Development with Dignity

At a time when the global development industry is under more pressure than ever before, this book argues that an end to poverty can only be achieved by prioritizing human dignity.

Unable to adequately account for the roles of culture, context, and local institutions, today's outsider-led development interventions continue to leave a trail of unintended consequences, ranging from wasteful to even harmful. This book shows that increased prosperity can only be achieved when people are valued as self-governing agents. Social orders that recognize autonomy and human dignity unleash enormous productive energy. This in turn leads to the mobilization of knowledge-sharing that is critical to innovation and localized problem-solving. Offering a wide range of interdisciplinary perspectives and specific examples from the field showing these ideas in action, this book provides NGOs, multilateral institutions, and donor countries with practical guidelines for implementing "dignity-first" development.

Compelling and engaging, with a wide range of recommendations for reforming development practice and supporting liberal democracy, this book will be an essential read for students and practitioners of international development.

Tom G. Palmer is executive vice president for international programs at Atlas Network, where he holds the George M. Yeager Chair for Advancing Liberty. He is also a senior fellow at the Cato Institute.

Matt Warner is president of Atlas Network and the editor of *Poverty and Freedom: Case Studies on Global Economic Development* (2019).

Rethinking Development

Rethinking Development offers accessible and thought-provoking overviews of contemporary topics in international development and aid. Providing original empirical and analytical insights, the books in this series push thinking in new directions by challenging current conceptualizations and developing new ones.

This is a dynamic and inspiring series for all those engaged with today's debates surrounding development issues, whether they be students, scholars, policy makers, or practitioners internationally. These interdisciplinary books provide an invaluable resource for discussion in advanced undergraduate and postgraduate courses in development studies as well as in anthropology, economics, politics, geography, media studies, and sociology.

Global Development and Learning in the Age of Neoliberalism
Stephen McCloskey

The Diaspora's Role in Africa
Transculturalism, Challenges and Development
Stella-Monica N. Mpande

Post-Conflict Participatory Arts
Socially Engaged Development
Edited by Faith Mkwananzi and F. Melis Cin

Development with Dignity
Self-determination, Localization, and the End to Poverty
Tom G. Palmer and Matt Warner

For more information about this series, please visit: www.routledge.com/Rethinking-Development/book-series/RDVPT.

Development with Dignity

Self-determination, Localization, and the End to Poverty

Tom G. Palmer and Matt Warner

LONDON AND NEW YORK

Cover image: Dinesh Dixit, photo by Bernat Parera

First published 2022
by Routledge
2 Park Square, Milton Park, Abingdon, Oxon OX14 4RN

and by Routledge
605 Third Avenue, New York, NY 10158

Routledge is an imprint of the Taylor & Francis Group, an informa business

© 2022 Tom G. Palmer and Matt Warner

British Library Cataloguing-in-Publication Data
A catalogue record for this book is available from the British Library

Library of Congress Cataloging-in-Publication Data
Names: Palmer, Tom G., author. | Warner, Matt, author.
Title: Development with dignity : self-determination, localization, and the
end to poverty / Tom G. Palmer and Matt Warner.
Description: Abingdon, Oxon ; New York, NY : Routledge, 2022. |
Includes bibliographical references and index.
Identifiers: LCCN 2021041225 (print) | LCCN 2021041226 (ebook) |
ISBN 9781032135649 (hardback) | ISBN 9781032135632 (paperback) |
ISBN 9781003229872 (ebook)
Subjects: LCSH: Economic development–Moral and
ethical aspects–Developing countries.
Classification: LCC HD75 .P34 2022 (print) | LCC HD75 (ebook) |
DDC 338.9009172/4–dc23/eng/20211109
LC record available at https://lccn.loc.gov/2021041225
LC ebook record available at https://lccn.loc.gov/2021041226

ISBN: 978-1-032-13564-9 (hbk)
ISBN: 978-1-032-13563-2 (pbk)
ISBN: 978-1-003-22987-2 (ebk)

DOI: 10.4324/9781003229872

Typeset in Bembo
by Newgen Publishing UK

Contents

About the authors

Tom G. Palmer is executive vice president for international programs at Atlas Network where he holds the George M. Yeager Chair for Advancing Liberty. He is also a senior fellow at Cato Institute. Before joining Cato, he was a vice president of the Institute for Humane Studies at George Mason University. Until the pandemic he traveled extensively to work with NGOs promoting liberal democracy and locally led economic development, which he had been doing since before the end of the USSR and its empire. He has published in journals such as the *Harvard Journal of Law and Public Policy*, *Foreign Policy*, *Ethics*, *Critical Review*, *Global Policy*, *Eurasia Review*, and *Constitutional Political Economy*, as well as in publications such as *The Wall Street Journal*, *The New York Times*, *Die Welt*, *Caixin*, *Al-Hayat*, *Boston Review*, the *Los Angeles Times*, *The Washington Post*, *D Presse,* and *The Spectator of London*. He is the author of *Realizing Freedom: Libertarian Theory, History, and Practice* (Washington: Cato Institute, 2014), and the editor of a number of books on political, economic, and moral thought, most recently including (with William A. Galston) *Truth and Governance: Religious and Secular Views* (Washington: Brookings Institution Press, 2021). Palmer received his BA in liberal arts from St Johns College in Annapolis, Maryland, his MA in philosophy from The Catholic University of America, Washington, DC, and his doctorate in politics from Oxford University. He currently lives in Thailand with his husband.

Matt Warner is president of Atlas Network and the editor of *Poverty and Freedom: Case Studies on Global Economic Development*. He coined the term "the outsider's dilemma" to describe the challenge of helping low-income countries develop without getting in the way of their most viable paths to prosperity. Matt writes, speaks, and consults internationally on the topics of economics, institution building, nonprofit management, and impact philanthropy. His work has appeared in

Foreign Policy, Devex, The Hill, Cato Journal, Forbes, and *Econ Talk,* among others. Matt has a master's degree in economics from George Mason University and is certified by Georgetown University in organizational development consulting. He was a 2019–2020 Penn Kemble Fellow with the National Endowment for Democracy. Matt and his wife, Chrissy, an attorney, live in Vienna, Virginia, with their four children.

Foreword

Deirdre N. McCloskey

You need this lucid and eloquent book. Read it, right away. No time to waste. You need it especially urgently if you still believe, as many do nowadays, that the road to national enrichment is top-down stimulus spending, industrial planning, foreign aid, and the World Bank.

From wide and deep experience in poor countries, and wide and deep reading in politics and philosophy, Matt Warner and Tom G. Palmer know what they're talking about. Their talk is their title, taken from the anguished declaration by the mother of Mohamed Bouazizi, the Tunisian street vendor who in 2011 poured gasoline on himself and lit the fire to protest the undignified extortions of him by the police. She declared, as humans do, "Dignity before bread."

Not that bread is to be disdained. A woman with bread in her belly has at least that much out of the way and can turn to higher things, such as educating herself and clothing her kids and praying to her god. Still, humans over and over choose dignity over even bread. They scrimp for their children, they go over the top at the Somme, they risk their lives to protest the indignities imposed by tyrants. Dignity, Warner and Palmer observe, is much praised but little studied. They study here not the right-wing dignity of rank or the left-wing anti-dignity of charity, but the liberal dignity of human agency, "the modern conception of dignity [which] has made possible rapid innovation." And it makes possible more than innovation in bread. It makes for the dignity of the human spirit.

Applying such a concept to economic development is a large advance over the rightish and leftish polices of dependency, which reduce people to serfs and children. Instead, give Chinese citizens the minimal dignity of letting them start a business or move to Shanghai (yet do not give them a vote), and income per head commences growing at 10 percent per year. Give the same dignity, imperfectly, to Indian citizens (yet with a dignifying vote), and the result is only a little less enriching and more dignified.

One dignity is that right to vote. As southern Blacks in the United States could have told you in the 1960s, dignity is the main point—not the dubious proposition that voting always leads to good decisions. But another dignity is the right to work and buy and sell as you wish, voting with your pesos or rupees. In both cases you have the right to say "No," to vote for the other candidate or work at the other factory. In the late nineteenth century, a naïve European asked a free man in the Powder River country of Montana and Wyoming, "Who is your master?" The man replied, "He ain't been born yet." He had permission and therefore dignity, the right to say "No."

The liberalism of Warner and Palmer could be called "adultism." The other policies—of a statist right or a statist left or for that matter a statist middle—all treat adults as bad children or sad children. Poor things, poor things, they're waiting to be fed. On the contrary, adults are to be accorded the dignity of "the equal presumption of liberty and citizen-based democratic political principles."

It is an equality of *permission*, note. It's not the impossible goal of equality of outcome or opportunity that thoroughgoing socialism promises—yet does not deliver. In the very nature of such goals, it can't. After all, people differ gloriously in height, intelligence, imagination, beauty, the ability to hit a major league fast ball. Full equality would require chopping off the tall poppies. Never mind an alleged equality to be achieved of dollar income—if I am not as beautiful or creative as you, full equality has not been attained. Let us pour acid on your face or drive nails into your head. Then you and I will be equal. You see the problem.

But liberal permission, against traditional or statist hierarchies— the police leaning on Bouazizi for a daily bribe—is a promise we *can* keep. Permitting people to own and exchange their gifts for mutual advantage is the way of adultism. It's all Bouazizi wanted, to support his family, and to have the dignity of being a little businessman. And it's what the state denied him. States do it regularly, saying "No" to a Cuban who wants to raise and sell chickens privately, or saying "No" to a poor African American who wants to braid hair for a living. In an adult liberalism the right to say "No," as the tenth item in the US Bill of Rights puts it, is "reserved to the people."

People in poor countries experience deep indignities, which is why, our authors show, they remain poor. It has been repeatedly shown since 1776 that the ending of poverty comes from new ideas from dignified adults, not from state-led protectionism or internal improvements or New Deals from the bottom of the deck. The central peculiarity of the modern world is the slow demise of hierarchy in the face of the liberal—an adult idea of letting people, the sporting British say, "have a go." End slavery.

Liberate women, immigrants, gays. Letting people have a go has turned out to make for the first sustained economic growth in history, a Great Enrichment per person by a gob-smacking 3,000 percent. Yes, three *thousand* percent, 1776 to the present. Vaccines instead of bleeding. Airplanes instead of wagons. Dignity instead of subordination to the ancient hierarchies of lord, husband, and state functionary.

The Enrichment continues, and will if the life-enhancing policies of Warner and Palmer triumph, against the magical promise of the man on the white horse or the woman at the development office. The end and the purpose is dignity, but the *means* are also dignity. Put dignity first and the rest follows. So it has, 1776 to 2022.

The World Bank's current formula of "Add institutions and stir" does not work. (Nor did its earlier formula of "Add foreign aid and stir.") You can install a splendid tube-well in a Pakistani village, but if you don't get buy-in from the villagers so that they own the institution, as Warner and Palmer put it, the well becomes merely a decrepit monument. Warner and Palmer argue instead that "mere offices and laws do not suffice." "The rule of law ... rests on ethics." "Institutions may be [or at least may seem to be] the machinery by which commitment problems are solved, but such machinery only works as well as the norms of those who operate it."

The institutions, that is, are consequences, not causes. They are, as Warner and Palmer note, "built by participatory public life": owning the tube-well, having the experience of the New England town hall, being able to buy and sell and vote and walk the streets without being rousted by the police. Alexis de Tocqueville said so concerning the non-slave states of the United States that he saw in 1831 and said it again ternary years later about his own habitually statist country in *The Ancien Regime and the French Revolution*. In 1835 he wrote,

> Looking at the turn given to the human spirit in England by political life; seeing the Englishman ... inspired by the sense that he can do anything ... I am in no hurry to inquire whether nature has scooped out ports for him, or given him coal or iron.

That's right, and the real source of institutional success—the Englishman accorded liberty and dignity.

"What you feel is dignity," write Warner and Palmer about economic liberty. "You have become an owner, which means you are recognized as a bearer of rights and responsibilities." Earlier political philosophers such as Jefferson were correct in asserting that only people of property should be full citizens. What they misunderstood, though, is that in the world of the Great Enrichment, with the elimination of slavery, every person on the planet is a property owner because each person has, as Locke wrote, "a property in his own person," and, I would add, in her own person.

Crucially, Warner and Palmer make a powerful case that dignity is universal—not only, as non-European tyrants claim in extenuation of their assaults on human dignity, "Western." Democratic dignity should come first, cause and consequence, means and end. The notion, for example, that there is a "Chinese Model" in which undignified tyranny leads to better results than democratic liberalism is mistaken. China grew after 1978 by granting dignified permission to entrepreneurs, which is what had happened in the eighteenth century in Britain. It was not the centralization of Mao, which Xi Jinping is now busy reimposing, but exactly laissez-faire that did the trick. And will.

You are a generous, fair-minded, well-disposed person, I have no doubt. You wish the wretched of the earth to be raised up. Know, actually, that recently they have, not by the World Bank but by liberty and its dignity. In 1960, four out of the five billion people on the planet subsisted on a wretched $2 a day. Now the average world income has risen in the same prices to $45 a day. One billion out of the present seven billion languish still back at $2. Though a great improvement, the remnant is disgraceful.

I know you want to end the disgrace and bring the whole world to full human dignity. What then to do?

First, stop listening to the statists. Second, listen to Warner and Palmer.

Preface

Tom G. Palmer and Matt Warner

In our work with various think tanks, we have long observed a tradition of deferring to local priorities and vision. In part, that has been motivated by the importance we place on think tank independence, which is indispensable for credibility. Our commitment to independence has also influenced a global grant-making strategy that prizes diversity of funding among potential grantees. Even more importantly, though, we believe that local knowledge is critical for determining and navigating social change, particularly institutional change, throughout the communities we hope to see thrive. A couple of years ago, we started to take note of broader discussions among the economic development and international aid communities around the idea of "localization" as a key strategy for correcting power imbalances and for reforming an aid tradition that has come under scrutiny for underperformance, among other serious shortcomings.

That motivated us to become more engaged in those discussions. We hoped to learn as much as we could from the many organizations and experts who, in one way or another, are helping all of us take the challenge of localization seriously as we wrestle with its implications for development practice. At the same time, our own experiences over recent decades have taught us some practical lessons about pursuing localization effectively.

Last year, when so many of our obligations, travel and otherwise, were disrupted by the COVID-19 pandemic, we decided that we should devote some time to organizing what we had learned to date in the context of the generally encouraging, if not fully realized, efforts to "decolonize development." This book is the result. It sits at the intersection of development practice, economics, sociology, anthropology, and moral and political theory, all of which help to develop a unifying theme that we believe epitomizes localization in its most fundamental form: the dignity of the individual. Accordingly, we address very topical questions of economic development and of institutional and legal systems and we compare competing democratic and autocratic models of development.

Modern thinking about dignity is both central to development outcomes, as we argue, and increasingly relevant to discussions around reforming aid, as we document. We illustrate the importance of dignity throughout the book with examples of individuals whose own visions for development in their local context we hope will inspire deeper interest in and respect for the power of localization.

Ultimately, our ambition for this book is twofold. We want to shine a stronger light on local individuals and organizations whose work promises a better future for development practice. At the same time, we hope that by organizing the latest themes in development around the modern concept of human dignity, the global landscape of agencies, NGOs, academics, and think tanks focused on development might recognize the significance of this universal ideal and even find common ground in ways that transcend the ideological divides of the past. At the very least, we hope we have done justice to the many thoughtful contributions to the problems we examine and to the complexity and nuance of the local, idiosyncratic solutions we applaud.

Acknowledgments

In our line of work the value of shared learning is baked into the model. We would not feel the same level of curiosity and enthusiasm for the topics covered in this book were it not for the global network of friends who have given us so much insight into the solutions they are forging in their local communities. Specifically, interviews with Parth Shah gave us an inside look into the enterprising and dignified lives of street vendors in India. The tireless work of Aimable Manirakiza in Burundi has refuted the myth that big changes can only happen as a result of big budgets and foreign expertise. Arpita Nepal in Nepal showed us how bizarre and ill-fitting those foreign designs can be in the local context. We are also indebted to so many creative entrepreneurs for their insights and inspiration, notably including Rekha Dey, a visionary who sees big opportunities for bamboo construction, Verónica Cañales, whose determination to master the knowledge of the hardware trade is matched by her passion for delivering customer satisfaction, and Papa Coriandre, who has proven that great entrepreneurial talent will show up when economies are made more inclusive. Those on the frontlines of development have so much to teach us all if we are ready to learn.

Of course, we are grateful to the many great scholars and thinkers who have helped all of us understand ourselves and the world a little better. To know one personally and to call her a friend is particularly humbling, and we wish to express our heartfelt gratitude to Deirdre McCloskey for providing the generous foreword to this book and for patiently offering crucial feedback throughout the writing process. Similarly esteemed, we are grateful to Bill Easterly whose work has been of great influence on our thinking. We are also in debt to Simeon Djankov, Nouh El-Harmouzi, and Peter Boettke whose reviews of early drafts provided helpful suggestions and encouragement, and to Gurcharan Das for his writings and for invaluable conversations about the role of dharma and the importance— and the difficulty—of knowing and doing the right thing, without which neither democracy nor markets would provide the benefits at the core of development. So many patient teachers, notable among them the late Paul Heyne and Leonard Liggio, have helped us see the importance of the individual life stories that others generally pass over.

Our colleagues at Atlas Network motivate us every day with their integrity, their intelligence, and their unrelenting commitment to see the world improve, especially for those who have been denied opportunities. Brad Lips sets the standard for authenticity and generosity; Lyall Swim, for excellence in all we do; Amanda Ashworth, for her encouragement and expert guidance through the publication process; Casey Pifer, for keeping those on the frontlines of development foremost in our minds; and all the others on the team who exemplify hard work, dedication to the cause of helping others, and good cheer. Throughout the course of the book, we highlight the importance of accountability in various forms. No one provides this better for our own work than our board chair, Debbi Gibbs, who inspires us to be better every day. This is likewise the case for our past board chairs, Linda Whetstone and Dan Grossman, both of whom we continue to count as wise mentors.

There are so many who have generously supported our work and we hope the shared learning we offer throughout this book does justice to the faith they have placed in us. In particular, we would like to thank Heather Templeton Dill and Amy Proulx at the John Templeton Foundation for inspiring us to new heights and for fueling the work of so many frontline entrepreneurs who are working to make space for opportunity and prosperity for their communities in countries all over the world. We are also deeply and forever indebted to the late Donald G. Smith, whose legacy is honored by the attentive and thoughtful leadership of Julie Smith, Richard Greenberg, John Hartsel, and Scott Barbee. Our late friend George M. Yeager also provided generous investments in poverty reduction, as well as many fruitful conversations on political economy and social and economic change. Rob Granieri, Rebecca Dunn, and Phil Harvey have also been crucial supporters, among many others, all of whom we hope recognize their role in the successes of our partners.

We would also like to thank Colin Doran for data analysis, Marcus Amine and Dara Ekanger for editing support, and, at Routledge, Helena Hurd and Matthew Shobbrook for their encouragement, patience, and guidance throughout the publication process. Last but not least we owe a big thank you to our respective spouses, Sonram and Chrissy, who may be starting a support group soon for those living with overly distracted partners.

Introduction
Why dignity matters

On December 16, 2010, in the town of Sidi Bouzid in the hinterland of Tunisia at about 10 p.m., Mohamed Bouazizi, a young man who was the sole breadwinner for his extended family, borrowed $200 to buy wholesale vegetables. His plan was to sell them the next day from his street cart. The next morning, at about 10:30 a.m., the police approached him in the marketplace and began harassing him to extract a bribe. It was something he had experienced many times before. Bouazizi had been working this way to provide for his family since he was a teenager.

His close friend, Hajlaoui Jaafer, later said, "Since he was a child, they were mistreating him. He was used to it." Jaafer summed up Bouazizi's experience trying to earn a living this way: "I saw him being humiliated."[1] After demanding money that he did not have, the police then restrained him and proceeded to slap him, insult him, and spit on him. They dumped his goods into the street and took his most valuable asset, the scales he used to weigh his vegetables.

Without his scales and the sales he needed to repay his debts, Bouazizi faced ruin. Worse, state officials had rained indignities on him in public. He had been humiliated by unaccountable government officials—again. Having gathered up what he could, he went to the governor's office to try to get his scales back. No one would help him. They did not see him. He was invisible because, in their eyes, he had no dignity. He told them, "If you don't see me, I'll burn myself." They still refused to help. He left and returned soon after with a can of gasoline. Bouazizi stood in the street and doused himself with fuel. Before lighting himself afire, Bouazizi—a desperate man stripped of his goods, his capital, and his dignity—shouted, "How do you expect me to make a living?"[2] He died on January 4, 2011.

According to Mohamed Bouazizi's sister, Leila, "In Sidi Bouzid, those with no connections and no money for bribes are humiliated and insulted and not allowed to live."[3] A year after the terrible act, Bouazizi's mother reflected on the meaning of her son's death. She described twenty-three

DOI: 10.4324/9781003229872-1

years of humiliation and extortion, harassment, and oppression by officials "who do not let people like us live." She concluded of her son Mohamed's act:

> When he set fire to himself it wasn't about his scales being confiscated. It was about his dignity. Dignity before bread. Mohamed's first concern was his dignity. Dignity before bread.[4]

No one doubts the importance of bread. Agronomists work to improve our ability to secure nutrition from the soil, a science that has accelerated in recent years to heights previously unimagined.[5] Likewise, economists work to understand and to cultivate the best conditions for the production of food.[6] Agronomists focus on plants, soil chemistry, and so on, economists on human interactions and the institutions, rules, and procedures that govern them. Rarely addressed is one of the most important factors for human flourishing: dignity. Dignity is at the foundation of democratic liberty and of social and economic development. Hence our title: *Development with Dignity: Self-Determination, Localization, and the End to Poverty.* Dignity, development, and self-determination are inextricably tied together everywhere in the world, in rich countries and in poor, in East, North, West, and South, sometimes more tightly, sometimes more loosely, but the connection is always there.

Dignity is the indispensable foundation for democratic governance. It is the dignity of the citizen, secure in her or his rights, which are respected by the authorities and her fellow citizens, that protects the flourishing of the private person. Benjamin Constant famously contrasted "ancient liberty" with "modern liberty." Ancient liberty he characterized as a collective self-determination that was compatible with "the complete subjection of the individual to the authority of the community," whereas modern liberty is "individual liberty." The modern age, the age of improvement, trade, and development, is an age of individual liberty, but Constant warned us not to give up entirely collective self-determination, or public choice, by citizens.

> The danger of ancient liberty was that men, exclusively concerned with securing their share of social power, might attach too little value to individual rights and enjoyments.
>
> The danger of modern liberty is that, absorbed in the enjoyment of our private independence, and in the pursuit of our particular interests, we should surrender our right to share in political power too easily. The holders of authority are only too anxious to encourage us to do so. They are so ready to spare us all sort of troubles, except those of obeying and paying! They will say to us: what, in the end, is the

aim of your efforts, the motive of your labors, the object of all your hopes? Is it not happiness? Well, leave this happiness to us and we shall give it to you. No, Sirs, we must not leave it to them. No matter how touching such a tender commitment may be, let us ask the authorities to keep within their limits. Let them confine themselves to being just. We shall assume the responsibility of being happy for ourselves.

Could we be made happy by diversions, if these diversions were without guarantees? And where should we find guarantees, without political liberty? To renounce it, Gentlemen, would be a folly like that of a man who, because he only lives on the first floor, does not care if the house itself is built on sand.[7]

It is not only prudent, but dignified, to take one's place as an equal participant in democratic governance, as discussant, voter, or elected officeholder. Those who give up entirely the dignity of the citizen for the liberty of the private person will, in the end, lose both. Dignity demands not autocracy but democratic self-governance among free and equal citizens. Constant singles out democratic Athens as the exception to his general characterization of antiquity:

> There was in antiquity a republic where the enslavement of individual existence to the collective body was not as complete as I have described it. This republic was the most famous of all: you will guess that I am speaking of Athens.

The realization of democratic self-government, which was merely adumbrated in the example of Athens, is helpful to understanding the modern experience of development with dignity.

Tyrannies of minorities and majorities

Democratic governance rejects minority tyranny, for it requires the consent of the majority, ascertained in various ways, for collective decision-making. Democratic governance also rejects majority tyranny, because it requires the rule of law and legal protection of personal liberty. That is to say, it requires clear restrictions on the powers of both minorities and majorities. Without restraints grounded in constitutions, laws, and norms, democracies can become autocracies. Authoritarian populism, while rooted in majoritarianism, is corrosive of democracy, for once a minority has been declared "the enemy of the people" and silenced through restrictions on free speech, it is no longer possible even to know what majorities think or prefer. In democratic systems, minorities may become majorities through the change of opinions, but when people fear to express their reasons, what is assessed through voting is no longer authentic majority opinion, but fear.[8]

Writing of "modern constitutional democracies," Scott Gordon notes,

> They are "democratic" in the sense that there is wide participation by the general citizenry in the formation of public policy; but they are also "constitutional" in that they contain institutionalized mechanisms of power control for the protection of the interests and liberties of the citizenry, including those who may be in the minority.[9]

A key component of democratic government is the loyal opposition. When one party replaces the other in control of parliament or congress, the party or group formerly in charge of government shifts to become the loyal opposition. They don't take to the streets or blow up train stations because they lost the election. But such loyalty is impossible, or at least extremely unlikely, if the losers who now form the opposition fear that by losing an election, they risk losing everything: their goods, their property, their rights, and perhaps even their lives. Dignified acceptance of defeat is a central condition of democracy, and that happens only when the defeated know that their dignity before the law will be respected. Without a loyal opposition, you cannot have a democracy. Democratic politics does not rest on humiliating and destroying enemies, but on contesting the seats of power with opponents, with the various parties knowing that if they lose, they will not become "unpeople."[10]

Even the most authoritarian of dictators, Mao Tse-Tung, was forced to acknowledge the terrible consequences of undemocratic governance. In 1962, after the Great Famine had killed millions of people, he told a gathering of seven thousand cadres,

> Without democracy, you have no understanding of what is happening down below; the situation will be unclear; you will be unable to collect sufficient opinions from all sides ... top levels of leadership will depend on one-sided and incorrect material to decide issues.[11]

Though he never truly learned that lesson, the horrors he perpetrated should memorialize forever the severe limits of authoritarian development.

As the French statesman and historian François Guizot observed, it is humility—remembering that we may be wrong—that demands democratic liberties.

> At the very moment when it presumes that the majority is right, it does not forget that it may be wrong, and its concern is to give

full opportunity to the minority of proving that it is in fact right, and of becoming in its turn the majority. Electoral precautions, the debates in the deliberative assemblies, the publication of these debates, the liberty of the press, the responsibility of ministers, all these arrangements have for their object to insure that a majority shall be declared only after it has well authenticated itself, to compel it ever to legitimize itself, in order to its own preservation, and to place the minority in such a position as that it may contest the power and right of the majority.[12]

Economic development—prosperity—is not just a matter of more work, but of improvement. As Deirdre McCloskey has demonstrated, "Our riches did not come from piling brick on brick, or bachelor's degree on bachelor's degree, or bank balance on bank balance, but from piling idea on idea."[13] Improvements in human wellbeing do not come from multiplying opportunities for work, or doing more work, but from innovative changes, from substituting wheelbarrows for baskets, telegraphs for carrier pigeons. It requires innovation, tested through experience and tinkering, and that requires the liberty to experiment with one's own labor, time, and assets, in order to create additional value.[14] Development happens when people enjoy the dignity of being free to make their own choices precisely because this allows their own knowledge to be brought to bear on solving the problems of poverty. Development happens when people are treated as adults with the presumption of liberty, in which they are presumed free to take risks on their own, without asking permission from superiors. Their liberty is regulated, not by superior beings (whether parents, kings and queens, commissars and officials, or commissioners and presidents), but by the rule of law and the norms, or ethical consensus, that gives effect to the rule of law.

Moreover, securing equal liberty is itself an important constituent of development, as Amartya Sen has argued: "The freedom to enter markets can itself be a significant contribution to development, quite aside from whatever the market mechanism may or may not do to promote economic growth or industrialization."[15] Securing equal liberty enables many diverse individuals and groups to draw on their own unique knowledge and talents to engage in mutually beneficial cooperation and thereby to create shared prosperity. That is the *process* by which the aims of development are achieved. The "division of knowledge" inherent in that process rests on the recognition that everyone knows something that others don't know. That is one of the most violated principles in today's dominant development strategies, underappreciated, when not completely ignored. For that reason, we believe it is also the key to illuminating a better path forward.

Development is not measured solely by the availability of material goods, of instrumental goods; there are also goods that people value for their own sake. We value bread because it nourishes us. We value dignity for its own sake, not for the sake of something else. The connection between dignity, democracy, and development is, in general, reinforcing, as we will argue. Dignity is both an input and an output, a foundation for democratic liberty and prosperity and, in a virtuous circle, itself a product of democracy and development. Democracy and development have been extensively studied, but the role of dignity has received less attention. A significant exception to that has been the publication of economic historian Deirdre McCloskey's *The Bourgeois Era.*

Humiliation and indignity

As with many concepts, dignity may be understood by means of its negation, through the experience of humiliation and the suffering of indignities. That was the daily experience of Mohamed Bouazizi and of countless others like him. Such experiences of humiliation are well known among the world's poor—the majority in poor countries and the minorities in rich countries. You don't have to look far to see examples of it, even in wealthy countries. Being stopped by the police on a DWB—Driving While Black—is not merely inconvenient; it is an act of humiliation. Being arrested for selling cigarettes singly, rather than by the pack, is not merely annoying, but a humiliation and, in the case of Eric Garner, the occasion for his slow death by police strangulation.[16]

Being treated as a powerless supplicant at a state licensing bureau and then being denied the permission to open a business or carry on a trade is not merely costly; it is an indignity. The social consequences add up. In many developing countries, the size of the "shadow" economy—comprised of those left with no choice but to earn their livelihoods outside the formal market—is considerable, and it's one of the reasons they remain poor. As you are outside the law, it is difficult to enforce contracts peacefully, to collect debts, to insist on your legal rights, to transfer property titles, or to access the formal financial system and the lower interest rates legality makes possible. If you work in the "shadow" economy, you are highly unlikely ever to grow your business.

In Burundi, one of the poorest places on the planet, the right to join the formal market with the legal protections afforded a licensed business has been severely restricted by the bureaucracy, in the interests of the bureaucrats and of the established merchants and cronies. As a result, the system works only for the big players who are well connected and can afford to navigate the byzantine landscape of permissions and bribes. If you work in the "shadow" economy, you have little enough to pay bribes and high government fees. You certainly can't spend many months traveling around the country to various government offices to pay them or hire a lawyer to do so. You make money every day to survive. You tend to your business. So you stay out of the formal market and you remain mired in a legal environment where you are always vulnerable to the kind of abuse Mohamed Bouazizi faced.

It's the same harassment a man known as Papa Coriandre experienced most of his life in Burundi. His nickname comes from his business. He makes and sells products from coriander. In his own words, what follows is his story.

> *I come from a family of 11 children, and I am the oldest. I am married to one woman, and we have two children. We also have four other people that we take care of at my place. I had to find a way to support my family. I started selling coriander juice in my Buterere neighborhood. The coriander product has health benefits and is inexpensive compared to other consumer products in Burundi.*
>
> *When I started my business, I didn't have any official documents to sell my products. I had to work by monitoring the local authorities such as the police, the administrator, the intelligence services, and other competitors so that they could not catch me or report me to the police or the local administration. During this period, I couldn't really grow the business.*
>
> *I worked informally because the costs of registering a business were exorbitant if I calculated the official costs and other unofficial costs because registration took a long time with different departments. And there were agents demanding other unofficial fees from me.*
>
> *I remember it was around 5:00am when six police cars and other security services showed up. They arrested me with my wife, loaded all of my business products, and closed my business because I was working without a registration document. They threw me in jail. I spent several days there. That's when I thought about stopping my business because I saw that my life no longer made sense. I had just died a form of death in my own country as I tried to survive. Honestly, it was very hard.*
>
> *I think I decided to keep going through perseverance based on hope. In Burundi, we live hoping that tomorrow will be better even if we do not see that we will wake up in the morning. There were several reasons for taking the risk to continue. In Burundi, when you are the eldest of the family the culture calls on you to financially support the other members of the family so I also had my parents, uncles, and other members who were dependent on my business. I had to keep taking risks to survive in this country.*

It was in 2018 when it became easier and more affordable to register a business. My business grew when I started working legally. Starting a business in Burundi is easy and simple today. It costs only 30,000 frsbu [compared to 140,000 frsbu]. The process now takes less than four hours with a single document and an identity card.

We have gone from 2 to 139 employees. We went from 21 customers to 2,710 customers. We also created new products. We produce coriander soap, hand sanitizers, sesame, and coriander porridge for children and adults.

At the start, we used cooking pots. Today we have equipment that allows us to dry agricultural products in less than 5 hours, new bottles with the Coriandre brand, a new location and other equipment that allows us to produce our products in the shortest possible time.

At the beginning, we had a single point of sale in Bujumbura (Butere). Today, we are in 11 provinces of Burundi. We are in Bubanza, Cibitoke, Kayanza, Ngozi, Muramvya, Gitega, Mwaro, Makamba, Rumonge, Bujumbura-Rural and elsewhere.

I have acquired new skills on management, marketing, communication and other knowledge which helped me to have new skills in agricultural transformations which we use today. My business motto is speed, innovation, trust, and humility.

Me, as Papa Coriandre, this is where I come and where I go. I invite foreigners to come and see how my business continues to change the lives of people in my country through this business that we started with the innovation we created ourselves. My two lovely and intelligent children are now studying at one of the best schools here in Burundi.

Ninety percent of the population here are farmers. When they grow their produce, we buy it and they make money. After I process the agricultural products that I get from the farmers, I sell them the products they need while the other traders source to my company or elsewhere for the continuity of their business. We share knowledge and we form a chain against poverty and unemployment in our community.[17]

For years he managed a two-person operation, never able to grow without access to the legal system, and thus to the protection of his assets, to enforceable contracts, or even to legal recourse against police abuse. The institutions that governed Papa Coriandre and his business kept him and his country poor. That began to change when institutional reforms made access to business licenses more inclusive. The process was streamlined (i.e., many government officials were stripped of their power over licensure) and made less expensive. In the year prior to the changes, Burundi saw only a 5 percent increase in new business formation. Since the changes, that jumped to 49 percent, which included Papa Coriandre's business.

In the short time since he obtained a license, Papa Coriandre's business has grown to 139 employees. Papa Coriandre's business was recognized as a legal entity. He ceased being a legal "unperson" when his business ceased being a legal "unbusiness." Removal of a restriction, weakening of a system that denied him permission, permitted Papa Coriandre to carve his path out of poverty. Enduring development comes from the dignity of not having to beg permission from others, of not having to accede to their insistent demands for bribes, of not having to bow and scrape for permissions that should be presumed.

The story of Papa Coriandre underscores an important constituent element of dignity, which is the experience of activity, of being an active agent, of being treated as an adult, and not merely a passive recipient. One of the greatest of indignities is for adults to be addressed as children, as people of color were in some areas for so long, being called "boy" or "girl," rather than "man" or "woman." Having to humbly request permission to live one's life, to experiment with what is one's own, and to try and either succeed or fail is to be excluded from the dignity of adulthood.

The approach of "development agencies" worldwide, and of the agencies that distribute "foreign aid," has been one of frequent denial of their "clients'" agency. The tone was set clearly and unashamedly by economist John Kenneth Galbraith. In an interview with economist John Newark, Galbraith described the "accommodation of poverty" as "self-perpetuating" and "something which one must accept." Newark asked the key question: "A reasonable conclusion, I think, to draw from your focus on the equilibrium of poverty is that meaningful change must come from the outside. Is that true?" Galbraith answered: "Absolutely."[18]

Such was the common view that shaped "development economics," the inertia of which still drives much of current aid and development programs. We believe that Galbraith and generations of development economists who preceded and followed him have not only been in error but have inflicted enormous harm on the world's poor. Talk of a "poverty trap" from which the poor can only escape with expert guidance (and tax dollars) dispensed by foreign experts is humiliating. And when one failure followed another, the answer was more expertise and more power and more money.[19] The experts have patronized the poor, humiliated them, and perpetuated their poverty, in spite of their best intentions, because they have ignored the role that dignity plays in discovering enduring solutions. Rather than acting to remove people from an alleged "accommodation to poverty," treating people as patients to be ministered to from the "outside," as lacking control, agency, and responsibility for their own development, fosters learned helplessness.[20] It is at once humiliating and

misguided and more likely to lead to authoritarianism and the perpetuation of poverty than it is likely to spur democracy and development.

Well-meaning outsiders need to learn humility. That starts by acknowledging the "outsider's dilemma," meaning that those with valuable assets
or technical knowledge need to respect the knowledge that is uniquely
available only to those who are actually grappling with their own problems.
As most mature adults have learned, one cannot change others as much
as they can change themselves. Moreover, for development changes to
stick, they need to emerge as a function of the people they are meant to
serve. In his study of institutional change, sociologist W. Richard Scott
emphasizes the complexity with which specific institutions evolve.[21] Even
if democratic development is our common goal, there is no template an
outsider can use to install enduring institutions in other people's communities. While successful institutions may share some things in common
(and the study of successful institutions can provide reliable insights), each
maintains idiosyncrasies that reflect the particular people, their unique
histories, and the particular contexts in which they are working well.[22] It
is not only institutions, understood as rules written out in constitutions
or statutes or administrative regulations, but the ethical frameworks, the
norms, and the expectations that accompany them, that make possible
the functioning of the institutions; and while constitutions, statutes, and
administrative regulations can be copied, norms cannot.[23]

Development is accomplishment and it rests on accomplishments,
which in turn require the active participation of those who are—from
the outsider's perspective—"being developed." In fact, they are not
"being developed"; they are developing themselves. They are agents, not
patients. They have knowledge that "development experts" lack, knowledge of time and place that requires being there and then, as well as "tacit
knowledge" that cannot be recorded in spreadsheets or written down in
reports.[24] The presumption that what poor people lack is knowledge and
that outside experts have the knowledge they lack has caused enormous
harm to the poor, especially when backed up by force and by billions of
dollars extracted from foreign taxpayers. An early critic of development
economics, Polly Hill, insisted that outsiders should demonstrate humility
and seek to learn from others: "We must study the farmer, not patronize
him: we must assume that he knows his business better than we do." She
added that she was not saying that there were no knowledge disparities,
"I emphasize the word 'business,' for this is not to say that the farmer will
be unappreciative of skilled technical advice and help."[25] When outsiders
have skilled technical advice, they may offer it, but when they claim
knowledge of economic and social facts that is somehow superior to that
of people whose families have lived in a country or a region for many

generations, they are almost always wrong. The sad thing is that they rarely learn from their mistakes, because the costs do not fall on them, but on the people whom they humiliated and on the taxpayers from their home country, who were forced to finance the humiliation.

Those experiences of humiliation, which are so intimately interwoven with poverty, underdevelopment, well-meaning interventionism, domination, and tyranny, are not, however, inevitable. The cycle of humiliation, domination, and poverty has been broken, can be broken, and is being broken; breaking that cycle starts with the assertion and the affirmation of dignity.

Replacing humiliation with dignity

The hundreds of thousands of Tunisians who were inspired by Bouazizi's ghastly martyrdom and who poured into the streets to demand democracy were not moved merely by a demand for material wealth, although material wealth can be a very good thing. They marched for an end to a root cause of poverty, the humiliation they experienced at the hands of unaccountable power. They demanded dignity. To be sure, the record amply shows that respect for the dignity of the Mohamed Bouazizis of the world means more prosperity—more bread, but produced in dignity, for it is rarely the desire for more bread alone that moves people to risk their lives; it is the demand for dignity, for that which "is elevated above any price, and hence allows of no equivalent."[26] The recognition of secure rights under law generates prosperity, but while the material rewards take time to generate, dignity is delivered when the rights are recognized.

Visit a place, urban or rural, where people who have never enjoyed any legal title receive for the first time a deed of title and you will see what it means. On May 7, 2015, Mrs. Maria Mothupi, a ninety-nine-year-old resident of Ngwathe Municipality in South Africa, received for the first time a secure legal deed to her home. She was two years old when the 1913 Land Act banned ownership of land by black South Africans. Almost a century later, when she held in her hands the deed to her own home, she said that she could "sleep well now" because she finally had something to pass on to her children.[27] When Tom Palmer's family received secure legal title to farmland near the Mekong River, they were aglow. They could not be legally dispossessed and could live and farm without fear.[28]

When you get your own title deed, you don't just get the right to an asset's capital value, as determined by a present-value equation, in which the value is equal to the sum of all the future rents it will generate, discounted by the rate of interest. That's how appraisers and economists see things, and that's a helpful way to see them. But it's not how it feels when you hold that title. You experience being a legal agent. You are recognized as a person. When you buy or sell property, there is mutual recognition, for "contract presupposes that the parties entering into it recognize each other as persons and property owners."[29] What you feel is dignity. You have become an owner, which means you are recognized as a bearer of rights and responsibilities.[30]

Economic history and theory show us what happens when people enjoy well-defined and legally secure rights that can be transferred voluntarily through a tolerably efficient and fair legal system. People sow crops, tend to them, harvest them, and exchange them. People build houses, barns, and market stalls, start and grow businesses, build and install machinery, invest in research, deliver the mail, buy and sell, and do all the other things that raise living standards and real wages. They educate and inoculate themselves and their children. They live healthier and longer lives. They flourish.

The institutional foundations of prosperity are no mystery. Adam Smith noted that

> little else is requisite to carry a state to the highest degree of opulence from the lowest barbarism, but peace, easy taxes, and a tolerable administration of justice; all the rest being brought about by the natural course of things. All governments which thwart this natural course, which force things into another channel, or which endeavour to arrest the progress of society at a particular point, are unnatural, and to support themselves are obliged to be oppressive and tyrannical.[31]

Carrying a state to the highest degree of opulence takes time for it to yield enduring results. Respect for the dignity of a human being doesn't take time to yield results. The result is simultaneous with the act. Enjoying it takes no chains of abstract reasoning and no assessment of empirical evidence that it will generate knock-on benefits. It is its own reward. It is a part of a good life. People strive for it for its own sake. As Mrs. Bouazizi said, "Dignity before bread."

Dignity and liberty as universal claims are modern. Indeed, after the invention of agriculture in the various regions of the world, long experience of subjugation generated habituation to obedience, to lives lived in fear, to quivering at the anticipation of the lash—or, in more modern times, the late-night knock on the door. After five hundred years of hereditary slavery, some may even come to believe that it's simply their natural condition; in Mauritania, Fatma Mint Mamadiou told journalist

Elinor Burkett, "God created me to be a slave, just as he created a camel to be a camel."[32] For those who grew up without it, dignity with liberty may sometimes be an acquired taste.

Fortunately, such extreme situations have dwindled rapidly over the past two centuries, as the demand for dignity, democracy, and development has spread. Before the achievement of democratic liberty, however, comes the appreciation of dignity. It took time for the idea of dignity to become a universal aspiration, although the last two centuries have seen an astonishing acceleration in the spread of the idea. In the process of being universalized, the concept of dignity changed, not only in extent but in content, as we will show.

Recognition of dignity is the key to moving from poverty and degradation to that highest, or at least higher and higher, degree of opulence of which Adam Smith spoke. Dignity is the key to unlocking democracy and development, liberty, and prosperity. Amartya Sen challenged us to "assess the requirements of development in terms of removing the unfreedoms from which the members of the society may suffer."[33] It is to that task that this book is dedicated.

Notes

1   Yasmine Ryan, "The Tragic Life of a Street Vendor," *Al Jazeera*, January 20, 2011, www.aljazeera.com/features/2011/01/20/the-tragic-life-of-a-street-vendor/.

2   Bob Simon, "How a Slap Sparked Tunisia's Revolution," *CBS News*, February 22, 2011, www.cbsnews.com/news/how-a-slap-sparked-tunisias-revolution-22-02-2011/.

3   Lin Noueihed, "Peddler's Martyrdom Launched Tunisia's Revolution," January 29, 2011, www.reuters.com/article/uk-tunisia-protests-bouazizi/peddlers-martyrdom-launched-tunisias-revolution-idUKTRE70I7TV20110119.

4   Rania Abouzeid, "The Martyr's Mother: An Interview with Mannoubia Bouazizi," *Time*, December 14, 2011. http://content.time.com/time/speci als/packages/article/0,28804,2101745_2102138_2102239,00.html.

5   Hardly any of the agronomists who have made our lives possible will ever be known, but one stands out: Norman Borlaug, whose patient work to increase crop production was honored with a Nobel Peace Prize in 1970. The Nobel Committee acknowledged that "more than any other single person of this age, he has helped to provide bread for a hungry world," www.nobelprize. org/prizes/peace/1970/ceremony-speech/.

6   To understand how devastating the wrong policies can be in countries with enormous capacity to grow food, see Robert Conquest, *The Harvest of Sorrow: Soviet Collectivization and the Terror Famine* (Oxford: Oxford University Press, 1987); Anne Applebaum, *Red Famine: Stalin's War on Ukraine* (New York: Doubleday, 2017); and Frank Dikötter, *Mao's Great Famine: The*

History of China's Most Devastating Catastrophe, 1958–1962 (New York: Walker Publishing Co., 2010), among many other studies.

7　Benjamin Constant, "The Liberty of Ancients Compared with that of Moderns," https://oll.libertyfund.org/title/constant-the-liberty-of-ancients-compared-with-that-of-moderns-1819.

8　See Tom G. Palmer, "The Terrifying Rise of Authoritarian Populism," *Reason*, September 2019, https://reason.com/2019/07/14/the-terrifying-rise-of-authoritarian-populism/.

9　Scott Gordon, *Controlling the State: Constitutionalism from Ancient Athens to Today* (Cambridge, MA: Harvard University Press, 1999), p. 4.

10　See Mancur Olson, "Democracy, Dictatorship, and Development," *The American Political Science Review*, Vol. 87, No. 3, September 1993, pp. 567–576. As recent events indicate, what is important is not merely the formal rules governing the transfer of power but the norms governing the processes through which they are implemented. The losers respect those processes and the prevailing norms restrain them—and those they would suborn or threaten—from ignoring the objective outcomes of voting processes. Mere parchment barriers to tyranny without the character of citizens and holders of public office to respect them are as protective as the term implies.

11　Amartya Sen, *Development as Freedom* (New York: Anchor Books 1999), p. 182.

12　François Guizot, *The History and Origins of Representative Government in Europe* (1821; Indianapolis: Liberty Fund, 2002), Lecture 7, p. 63.

13　Deirdre McCloskey, *Bourgeois Equality: How Ideas, Not Capital or Institutions, Enriched the World* (Chicago: University of Chicago Press, 2016), p. xiii.

14　Numerous cases of such inventive tinkering, and of the interaction among multiple parties, often unknown to each other, can be found in Matt Ridley's *How Innovation Works, And Why It Flourishes in Freedom* (New York: HarperCollins, 2019).

15　Sen, *Development as Freedom*, p. 7.

16　Al Baker, J. David Goodman, and Benjamin Mueller, "Beyond the Chokehold: The Path to Eric Garner's Death," *The New York Times*, June 13, 2015, www.nytimes.com/2015/06/14/nyregion/eric-garner-police-chokehold-staten-island.html.

17　Based on an interview of Papa Coriandre conducted in Burundi July 2021 by Aimable Manirakiza. Printed with permission.

18　Interview of John Kenneth Galbraith by John Newark in *Aurora Online*, in *Interviews with John Kenneth Galbraith*, ed. James Ronald Stanfield and Jaqueline Bloom Stanfield (Jackson: University of Mississippi Press, 2004), p. 156.

19　For a stark example, see Jeffrey Sachs, Chandrika Bahadur, Guido Schmidt-Traub, Jeffrey D. Sachs, Margaret Kruk, and John McArthur, "Ending Africa's Poverty Trap," in *Brookings Papers on Economic Activity* 1 (Washington, DC: Brookings Institution, 2004), pp. 117–216. For a description of the actual working and the actual impact of Sachs's policies, backed by hundreds of millions of donor dollars, see Nina Munk, *The Idealist: Jeffrey Sachs and the Quest to End Poverty* (New York: Anchor Books, 2013).

20 See Martin E. P. Seligman, *Helplessness* (New York: W. H. Freeman and Company, 1975).

21 W. Richard Scott, *Institutions and Organizations: Ideas, Interests, and Identities* (Los Angeles: Sage Publications, 2014), p. 82.

22 See Daron Acemoglu and James Robinson, *Why Nations Fail* (New York: Crown Business, 2013).

23 See the criticism of Acemoglu and Robinson's approach by Deirdre McCloskey, *Bourgeois Equality*, pp. 136–137.

24 As Michael Polanyi explained in *The Tacit Dimension* (Chicago: University of Chicago Press, 1980), "We know more than we can say." F. A. Hayek, *Law, Legislation, and Liberty* (Chicago: University of Chicago Press, 1973), p. 77.

> Although still an unfamiliar conception, the fact that language is often insufficient to express what the mind is fully capable of taking into account in determining action, or that we will often not be able to communicate in words what we well know how to practice, has been clearly established in many fields.

25 Polly Hill, *Studies in Rural Capitalism in West Africa* (Cambridge: Cambridge University Press, 1970), p. 28.

26

> In the kingdom of ends, everything has either a **price** or a **dignity**. What has a price can be replaced with something else, as its *equivalent*; whereas what is elevated above any price, and hence allows of no equivalent, has a dignity.
>
> What refers to general human inclinations and needs has a *market price*; what, even without presupposing a need, conforms with a certain taste, i.e., a delight in the mere purposeless play of the powers of our mind, has a *fancy price*; but what constitutes the condition under which alone something can be an end in itself does not merely have a relative worth, i.e., a price, but an inner worth, i.e., *dignity*.
>
> (Immanuel Kant, *Groundwork of the Metaphysics of Morals*
> (Cambridge: Cambridge University Press, 2012),
> Prussian Academy Edition 4, pp. 434–435)

27 Eustace Davie, "Amendments to the Land Rights Bill Would Be a Great Injustice," *City Press*, August 24, 2020, www.news24.com/citypress/voices/amendments-to-the-land-rights-bill-would-be-a-great-injustice-20200824.

28 The energizing effect of secure and securely transferrable property title has long been known and has been documented effectively by, among others, Hernando de Soto, *The Mystery of Capital* (New York: Basic Books, 2000).

29 G. W. F. Hegel, *Philosophy of Right*, trans. T. M. Knox (Oxford: Oxford University Press, 1952; 1977), p. 57.

30 "Ownership," Tony Honoré, *Making Law Bind: Essays Legal and Philosophical* (Oxford: Oxford University Press, 1987).

31 Quoted from a now-lost manuscript by Dugald Stewart in "Account of the Life and Writings of Adam Smith, LLD," in Adam Smith, *Essays on Philosophical Subjects*, eds. W. P. D. Wightman and J. C. Bryce, Vol. 3 of the Glasgow Edition of the Works and Correspondence of Adam Smith (Indianapolis: Liberty Fund, 1982), p. 322.

32 Elinor Burkett, "'God Created Me to Be a Slave,'" *New York Times Magazine*, October 12, 1997:

> Ask Fatma Mint Mamadiou how old she is, and the Mauritanian woman turns her gaze shyly downward; she does not know when she was born. Ask her how many camels and sheep she tended, or how many bags of water she hauled every day, and her face turns to stone; she cannot count. Ask her whether she and the girls she grew up with in a village in the remote Brakna region were ever raped, and her features harden in puzzlement. She listens intently as the question is framed and reframed. Finally, she replies matter-of-factly, "Of course they would come in the night when the needed to breed us. Is that what you mean by rape?"

33 Sen, *Development as Freedom*, p. 33.

1 Dignity

Mainstream writers on development have recently begun to explore the importance of dignity in the design and delivery of aid. Preferences of recipients are regularly ignored and subjugated to the preferences of donors, which are often influenced by rent-seeking special interests, and the poor are regularly portrayed as objects of pity in "poverty porn," rather than as persons deserving of respect.[1] There is a growing awakening that the donor/recipient relationship can undermine one of the most important elements of human well-being: one's dignity. In March 2019, researchers at the Overseas Development Institute published the results of a simple exercise. They asked refugees who were receiving aid what dignity meant to them. They concluded that the meaning of dignity is both context and culturally specific, but that two concepts of dignity stood out: dignity as respect and dignity as self-reliance.[2] They quote one refugee as saying, "Working hard and earning your own livelihood is a big part of Rohingya identity and our idea of dignity."[3] Those types of explorations should prompt a widening of the focus to encompass not only the design and delivery of aid to those in need, but to address the centrality of dignity, not only to aid, but to development, which is not something that can be *delivered* to people, but is an achievement.

What is dignity? People contest the meaning and the proper uses of vitally important concepts all the time. We can ask, *What is dignity?*, as well as *What is equality?*, *What is justice?*, *What is liberty?*, *What is fairness?* Many central concepts in moral and political discourse are "essentially contested," meaning that although people deploy them, they contest their meaning as they do so.[4] Asking "What is equality?" may yield very different answers, even among those who profess to be in favor of equality. We can distinguish between a concept, such as "equality," and its competing conceptions, such as that "everyone should be equal before the law" or that "everyone should always have the same amount of wealth."[5]

DOI: 10.4324/9781003229872-2

Concepts can also evolve, which makes the task of extracting the meaning from usage a challenge, because the use of the concept may have changed over time, as the concept was applied to new situations or contexts. A particularly interesting and relevant case in point is the concept of "free man" in England's *Magna Carta* of 1215, the famous contract in which the King "granted, for us and our heirs for ever, all the liberties written out below, to have and to keep for them and their heirs, of us and our heirs," and that among those liberties was that

> no free man shall be seized or imprisoned, or stripped of his rights or possessions, or outlawed or exiled, or deprived of his standing in any way, nor will we proceed with force against him, or send others to do so, except by the lawful judgment of his equals or by the law of the land.[6]

So, who was a "freeman"? Every human being? All adult males? All adult landowners? As one scholar noted, the rights of a freeman, as well as the definition of a freeman, were broadened over time. "The rights declared in 1215/1225 applied to considerably fewer than ten percent of the inhabitants in England, Scotland, Wales, and Ireland."[7] Those rights and that appellation were later applied in the seventeenth century to all English subjects and later to subjects in the colonies. The history of liberty has been, to a large extent, the history of the extension of the concept of liberty to more and more categories of people, until it embraces all of humanity.

"Dignity" also has a history. In the Roman world, both the term and the concept were once applied to the wealthy and the powerful—senators, equestrians, consuls, emperors, the *res publica* itself. Now the concept applies to a poor and humble Moroccan vegetable merchant in the twenty-first century. The English *dignity* is derived from the Latin *dignitas*, and, like liberty, its scope has expanded and, with it, its content, for the original meaning was connected to class and social standing, whereas the modern derivative—dignity, as well as the equivalent or similar terms in many other languages—has come to be globally embraced, across cultures and countries, and applied to all.

In hierarchical societies the dignity of some excludes that of others. The term corresponds to "rank." In the modern world, when it comes to dignity, the have-nots want, not to dispossess what the haves enjoy, but to enjoy it in equal measure. Modern dignity is achieved not by clambering over others but by achieving and enjoying equality. As the modern figure, an inspiration to reformers of later centuries, Richard Rumbold, said in his last speech before he was brutally executed, "I am sure there was no man born marked of God above another, for none comes into the world with a saddle on his back, neither any booted and spurred to ride him."[8]

Everywhere that people are seized or imprisoned, or stripped of their rights or possessions, or outlawed or exiled, or deprived of their standing in any way, or proceeded against with force, all without the lawful judgment of their equals or by the law of the land, they yearn for dignity, and with it equal liberty and equality before the law. The modern forms of the indignity to which billions of people are subjected today include many that would have been familiar to the people of England in the time of King John: being forced to beg for permission to start a business, to transfer property rights, to make contracts on mutually agreeable terms, to trade across borders, and—to add insult to injury—having to wait for days, months, or years for permissions that can be refused on a whim (or without the payment of a bribe); being subjected to arbitrary power and even brutal violence; being dispossessed and lacking access to the law, which is reserved only for the rich, the powerful, and the connected.

A brief examination of the historical trajectory of the concept of dignity may help us to see how a concept that originated in a particular context, denoting the high statuses (dignity and rank often being used interchangeably) of certain persons, has come to have universal application, having been separated from rank and privilege.

Cicero's legacy

One of the most important texts in the history of moral and political thinking was written by the Roman orator, lawyer, and statesman Marcus Tullius Cicero. In the last year of his life, in the form of a letter to his son, Cicero laid out his mature thoughts on social and political life and on the duties of life, "For no part of life … can be free from duty. Everything that is honourable in a life depends upon its cultivation, and everything dishonourable upon its neglect."[9] Cicero's treatment of *dignitas* and its related idea of *decorum* (or seemliness) played a significant role in articulating and promulgating the conception of dignity that we will apply throughout this work.

Although *dignitas* is a term of comparison, Cicero transferred the focus from the comparison of the statuses of groups of persons (or of the state) compared to other persons or states and put it on the comparison of humans to non-rational beings. The dignity of a human being was rooted in rationality, albeit understood differently than it was understood by Immanuel Kant 1,803 years later. While applying the concept of dignity to all human beings, Cicero simultaneously recognized the numerical and material individuation that makes each of us unique. Cicero's reconceptualization of *dignitas* has echoed down the ages louder than its earlier and more restrictive meaning because of both Cicero's intellectual and persuasive powers and the outsized influence of his writings, which were copied by hand and which transmitted his ideas from the Classical World through the Dark and the Middle Ages to our own.[10]

Cicero's formulation has three key elements:

1   Dignity is universal because all humans share a common nature. ("One must understand that we have been dressed, as it were, by nature for two roles: one is common, arising from the fact we all have a share in reason and in the superiority by which we surpass the brute creatures."[11])

2   Dignity is individualized by the fact that we each possess "our own nature." ("The other, however, is that assigned specifically to individuals. For just as there are enormous bodily differences ... similarly, there are still greater differences in men's spirits." "We must act in such a way that we attempt nothing contrary to universal nature; but while conserving that, let us follow our own nature."[12])

3   Dignity is inherent to our common nature, but it also sets standards and goals for us. It requires effort to live a dignified life and we can fail to live up to our dignity by not acting in accordance with our two natures, our universal (human) nature and our individual nature. ("If we wish to reflect on the excellence and worthiness [*dignitas*] of our nature, we shall realize how dishonourable it is to sink into luxury and to live a soft and effeminate lifestyle, but how honourable it is to live thriftily, strictly, with self-restraint and soberly."[13])

Cicero's re-formulation of the concept of dignity brings with it a requirement of effort, of striving; we must act, in some ways and not in others, to qualify as dignified, as maintaining our dignity. That is also a necessary ingredient in the citizenship foundational to democracy and in the work and entrepreneurship and future orientation foundational to development.

Cicero also laid a foundation for human rights that was widely cited in succeeding ages and played a substantial role in the formulation of modern doctrines of human rights:

All men should have this one object, that the benefit of each individual and the benefit of all together should be the same. If anyone arrogates it to himself, all human intercourse will be dissolved. Furthermore, if nature prescribes that one man should want to consider the interests of another, whoever he may be, for the very reason that he is a man, it is necessary, according to the same nature, that what is beneficial to all is something common. If that is so, then we are all constrained by one and the same law of nature; and if that also is true, then we are certainly forbidden by the law of nature from acting violently against another person.[14]

Much more can be said about the philosophical formulations of the modern conception of dignity, as well as the social and economic influences, but a few more centrally important thinkers are important to the story.

For the highly influential philosopher Thomas Aquinas, personhood *per se* is both individuated (in contrast to the idea of collective or organic persons) and associated with "high dignity": "By some the definition of person is given as *hypostasis distinct by reason of dignity*. And because subsistence in a rational nature is of high dignity, therefore every individual of the rational nature is called a *person*."[15] Like Cicero, Thomas Aquinas not only focused on the rational nature and on the capacity for choice of rational beings, but on the fact that personhood—and hence dignity—attaches to individuals:

> The particular and the individual are found in the rational substances which have dominion over their own actions; and which are not only made to act, like others; but which can act of themselves; for actions belong to singulars. Therefore also the individuals of the rational nature have a special name even among other substances; and this name is *person*.[16]

The dignity that has transformed the modern world is not the haughty dignity of the Roman senator or man-at-arms, but the equal dignity that characterizes each individual and which validates self-control and respect of the rights of others, enterprise, innovation, and value creation. Indeed, as the early modern writer Giovanni Pico della Mirandola, put it in his famously influential *Oration on the Dignity of Man*, each individual is a choosing being, capable of choosing a life's path, for "we have been born into the condition of being what we choose to be."[17] A few saw that possibility, however dimly, but it did not become widely acknowledged as a legitimate aspiration and the foundation of just and stable social and legal orders until the late eighteenth century.

Dignity is far removed from the narrow idea of maximizing total utility, because it includes the capability to become what we choose to be. The economist Frank H. Knight criticized the idea that what liberty achieves is the solution of a mathematical or mechanistic problem of maximizing want satisfaction, as if human beings were merely aggregates of demand schedules. Of wants, Knight noted, "It is their essential nature to change and grow. ... The chief thing which the common-sense individual actually wants is not satisfactions for the wants which he has, but more, and *better* wants."[18]

Dignity is not a concept or a practice of exclusively Western provenance, of course, for similar chords can be heard in the music of other cultures and civilizations, but it has been the harmony of concepts that emerged in Europe that has come to blend with the melodies and harmonies of other civilizations. Various conceptions of dignity also play central roles in other great civilizations, but as a matter of historical record, dignity as a foundation for equal rights becomes central to the rise of liberalism, democracy, and widespread and shared prosperity in Europe first and elsewhere later.

The incipient radicalism of Cicero's conception of dignity was nourished in the early modern age, thanks in part to the widespread republication and readership of his book *On Duties*, quoted earlier. One influential figure who revived the Latin term *dignitas* to describe the equal rights and standing of all humans was the German lawyer and philosopher Samuel Pufendorf, who in 1673 expressed in elevated language the response to oppression of the offended and the oppressed who would validate their rights:

> There seems to him to be somewhat of *Dignity* in the Appellation of **Man**: so that the last and most efficacious Argument to curb the Arrogance of insulting Men, is usually, *I am not a Dog, but a Man as well as your self.* Since then Human Nature is the *same* in us all, and since no Man will or can cheerfully join in Society with any, by whom he is not at least to be esteemed equally as a Man and as a Partaker of the same common Nature: It follows that, among those *Duties which Men owe to each other*, this obtains the *second* Place. That *every Man esteem and treat another*, as naturally *equal to himself, or as one who is a Man as well as he.*[19]

We've heard in arguments precisely those words: "I'm not a dog, but a human being like you." Pufendorf well captured the common appeal of modern dignity. (And for those who consider dogs to be family members, as we do, one could change it to "I'm not just a thing.")

The revolutionary radical John Locke placed the dignity of human beings at the core of his defense of liberty and rejected the philosophy of subordination and humiliation that advocates of limitless power advanced. Humans enjoy the power of reason and choice, in contrast to non-rational beings, but are equal among each other. Locke asserted, against hierarchical absolutism, that "there cannot be supposed any such *Subordination* among us, that may authorize us to destroy one another, as if we were made for one another's uses, as the inferior ranks of Creatures are for ours."[20] Those themes had been advanced by the politically radical Levellers, who tied again the individual's "own nature" (to use Cicero's term) to the right of control over one's own life. In Richard Overton's words, "To every individual in nature is given an individual property by nature not to be invaded or usurped by any. For every one, as he is himself, so he has a self-propriety, *else could he not be himself.*"[21]

The writings of the later thinker Immanuel Kant are often given pride of place in the discussion of dignity (he used not the Latin *dignitas*, but the German *Würde*, which can also be understood as closer to English "worth," as in *würdig*, "worthy"). His voice was influential, but his argument, rather than being situated within the context of human sociality and empirical observation, as were those of Cicero, Thomas Aquinas, Pufendorf, Locke, and others whom we have cited, was built on a contestable metaphysical foundation. For Kant, the human will is completely unconditioned and outside of the realm of cause and effect. For that reason, we think it best to focus on the tradition, exemplified in the activity of the Levellers, which had greater social, economic, and political engagement, even if not developed at such great length as was Kant's.

We thus arrive at a conception of dignity that is radical, egalitarian, modern, and at the same time, aspirational. One that has found its way around the world and connected with deep roots in multiple cultures.

Aristocratic dignity extended, or the rise of the underclasses?

An alternate, albeit overlapping, account of the emergence of dignity has been presented by the legal theorist Jeremy Waldron, who also seeks to trace the emergence of dignity in social practice, rather than to deduce it as Kant did from transcendental philosophy, but who argues that universal dignity spread from the top, as it were, as a universalization of the status of those who held the whips, and not from the bottom, from those who toiled, tinkered, improved, and created value. Thus, "The modern notion of *human* dignity involves an upward equalization of rank, so that we now try to accord to every human being something of the dignity, rank, and expectation of respect that was formerly accorded to nobility."[22]

Waldron draws mainly on intuitions into what constitutes aristocratic or noble behavior, but there is some historical support for his thesis, as well. Sidney Painter argues that it was the relative independence of the feudal vassals, or nobles, that set the model for the liberties to which the other elements of society aspired:

> The medieval nobleman enjoyed extremely extensive freedom to act as an individual. The feudal corporation to which he belonged imposed little restraint on him. The church could control him far less than it could other men. Even the state recognized him as especially privileged. Naturally the status of the noble was the envy of the other classes. Essentially the rights and liberties for which the middle and lower classes struggled throughout the seventeenth, eighteenth, and nineteenth centuries were those enjoyed by the nobles of the middle ages. Obviously the conception of individual freedom and the desire to possess it came from many sources and arose in many different legal environments, but the legal and political institutions which secured this freedom in western Europe and America were those forged by the feudal aristocracy. During the period when most men were closely controlled by corporate organizations the nobles retained and nurtured the concept of individual liberty.[23]

Although Waldron's account is rich with insights, we believe it fundamentally misses an even more important part of the story: The social transformation from below that laid the foundations for the modern world. It was not merely theorists who led the way, but the theorists of dignity who followed the practices that were more often emerging, not from ruling circles, but from those on the margins of the political order. As Walter Ullman noted,

> If one wishes to understand why and how it came about that from the late thirteenth century the individual gradually emerged as a full-fledged citizen, it would seem profitable to look at two rather practical facets of medieval society: on the one hand, the manner in which those far away from the gaze of official governments conducted their own affairs and, on the other hand, the feudal form of government which was practiced all over Europe.[24]

While Waldron argues that "the older notion [of dignity] is not obliterated; it is precisely the resources of the older notion that are put to work in the new,"[25] a far more powerful influence was the rising up from previously excluded populations, who "brought with them," new modes of treating others. In fact, that influence obliterated "the older notion" of superiority over others to replace it with universalized and individualized dignity.

Waldron seems to express a markedly Anglo-centric view, as England (especially) has a history of people acquiring wealth and then using it to integrate themselves into the upper class. British class distinctions, which persist to this day, are remarkably porous, for many enter the upper classes through wealth, fame, or even the acquisition of the proper accent. That experience is not at all universal and even in Britain, the process entailed the aristocracy accommodating itself to the "lower orders" who increasingly had the wealth older aristocrats coveted. So while there is evidence of "upper class" mores and bearing becoming more widely embraced by those "moving upward," there is a stronger case to be made that the characteristics of self-control that Waldron attributes to aristocrats emerged among the "calculating" merchants, artisans, mechanics, tradesmen, and laborers—the growing "middle classes," whose mores increasingly replaced the more commonly characteristic impulsive, haughty, arrogant, dissolute, and violent behavior of the idle "nobility."

According to Waldron, "self-control" and "self-command" are essentially aristocratic.

> This one might imagine as quintessentially aristocratic virtue, a form of self-command distinguished from the behavior of those who need to be driven by threats or the lash, or by forms of habituation that depend upon threats and the lash. But if it is an aristocratic virtue, it is one that law now expects to find in all sectors of the population.[26]

Identifying the aristocratic classes intimately with self-control is, in the face of sociological evidence, implausible. For one thing, the aggressive, impulsive, and violent behavior of the nobles had to be controlled by the actions of the revolutionary urban associations of craftsmen and merchants, as Max Weber notes: in the communes of Italy special officers were elected "to protect the *popolani* [the people of the city], to prosecute nobles and to execute sentences against them, and to supervise the observance of the *ordinamenti* [ordinances]."[27] It was the urban creators, the "bourgeoisie," who had to restrain the uncontrolled aristocratic predators, not the other way around.

Another attitude, which emerged among the disdained "tradesmen," mechanics, laborers, and merchants, was expressed rather tartly by Thomas Paine:

> The more aristocracy appeared, the more it was despised; there was a visible imbecility and want of intellects in the majority, a sort of

je ne sais quoi, that while it affected to be more than citizen, was less than man. It lost ground from contempt more than from hatred; and was rather jeered at as an ass, than dreaded as a lion. This is the general character of aristocracy, or what are called nobles or nobility, or rather no-ability, in all countries.[28]

Those of no-ability were not models of social cooperation.

Being at the top of a hierarchical and extractive system and having a "noble bearing," as Waldron describes it, entails the possibility, if not the practice, of lording it over others and being able to express without accountability one's impulses of rapine, cruelty, sadism, and abuse. The ability to humiliate others is inherent in the "noble bearing" of what were once termed "titled knaves." When all are held to be equal in rank, that is, when ranks and castes no longer constrain us, those at the top lose their special status, which is not one of self-control, but of unaccountable control over others. Waldron tries, strangely, to connect aristocracy with "self-control," but self-control is not a prominent feature of warrior classes, nor of their privileged descendants, but of those who work to satisfy the needs of others through voluntary exchange. As Benjamin Constant noted,

> A man who was always the stronger would never conceive the idea of commerce. It is experience, by proving to him that war, that is the use of his strength against the strength of others, exposes him to a variety of obstacles and defeats, that leads him to resort to commerce, that is to a milder and surer means of engaging the interest of others to agree to what suits his own. War is all impulse, commerce, calculation.[29]

The self-control that Waldron attributes to aristocrats, which then trickled down to the rest of the population, in fact emanated from below, as Norbert Elias observed:

> As the interdependence of people increases with the increasing division of labour, everyone becomes increasingly dependent on everyone else, even those of high social rank on those people who are socially inferior and weaker. The latter become so much the equals of the former that they, the socially superior people, can experience shame-feelings even in the presence of their social inferiors. It is only in this connection that the armour of restraints is fastened to the degree which is gradually taken for granted by people in democratic industrial societies.[30]

It was the aristocrats, "those of high social rank," who adopted the "armour of restraints" that emerged from the industrious and not the other way around. Waldron has it backward.

Finally, the extraction of rents, aka exploitation, by non-productive aristocrats was well noted by the champions of modern dignity. In his criticism of British foreign policy, with its colonialism and imperialism, the Liberal M. P. John Bright informed his constituents that the empire was basically a system of welfare payments to the British aristocracy, whose sons were sent off to be viceroys and administrators and officers of a global empire:

> The more you examine this matter the more you will come to the conclusion which I have arrived at, that this foreign policy, this regard for "the liberties of Europe," this care at one time for "the Protestant interests," this excessive love for the "balance of power," is neither more nor less than a gigantic system of out-door relief for the aristocracy of Great Britain.[31]

Bourgeois dignity

The economist and historian Deirdre McCloskey calls the conception of dignity that has emerged in modern democratic societies "bourgeois dignity," and she argues that it is responsible for the "Great Enrichment"— the explosion of widespread and shared prosperity, as shown (and experienced) in the measured increases in the income, longevity, education, nutrition, health, and generally the standards of living of billions of people over the past two centuries. Those increases are mirrored by the stunning fall in the percentages and (over recent decades, as human population has grown) in the absolute numbers of humans who suffer in poverty.[32] The transformation was not merely the psychological transformation in the self-perception of, say, entrepreneurs, but in the respect more widely accorded to one another in society. As the Great Enrichment was not a matter of capital accumulation, but of innovation, what is notably important is the respect accorded to those who tinker, who experiment, who dissent, who innovate.

With the spreading knowledge of the Great Enrichment, which has been accelerated by telephony and the internet, yearning for the dignity that made that enrichment possible has also spread the world over. The yearning for dignity expresses a common need that is deeply rooted in the human psyche. It also sets in motion a virtuous circle, reinforcing the rule-governed *democratic* political frameworks and the dynamic and prosperous developing economies that, in turn, reinforce human dignity.

Dignity received and dignity accorded are both important, the former for providing support for democratic liberty and the latter as instantiating the liberty to create value and propel enrichment.

But why start with dignity and not with democracy or development? Human motivations are complex, as are explanations of complex transformations, but dignity seems to have a special place in the Great Enrichment. So powerful is the pull of dignity, of the craving for recognition, that it seems to demonstrate more transformative power than either the search for prosperity, which is considered by many grand theorists to be *the* motive power of historical change, or even of other central moral/political goods with which it is connected, such as justice, liberty, equality, and fairness.[33] Dignity seems as close to a universal value as one can find.

Dignity, McCloskey argues, "is a sociological factor," meaning that it resides both in how one views oneself and how one is viewed by others.[34] She argues for the central role of dignity in explaining the astounding Great Enrichment of modern prosperity and progress, which did not merely double income over a hundred years, but increased it by thirty, forty, or more times over two hundred years. We will show the contours of that Great Enrichment in the next chapter; here we focus on its sociological foundation in dignity.

McCloskey argues that the universalization of dignity, as a phenomenon of the early modern period and after, is responsible for that historically unprecedented modern explosion of development. While the institutions of political liberty are certainly good and necessary conditions for modern shared prosperity, they are not sufficient, for without dignity—the "sociological factor" of respect—for the innovator, the tinkerer, the inventor, the entrepreneur, one would not see the innovation that drives accelerated economic growth. What has made the modern world so dazzlingly prosperous compared to all previous ages of humanity is what McCloskey calls

> "trade-tested betterment"—or if you want a single word, "improvement" or "betterment" or even "innovism"—understood as the frenetic bettering of machines and procedures and institutions after 1800, supported by a startling change in the ethical evaluation of the betterings.[35]

A remarkable characteristic of bourgeois dignity is the ability of the person to shape her or his own identity through choices. It was by "careers open to talent" and the joining of voluntary associations that, with the growth of the communes and trade, one achieved one's own identity.[36] The playwright, essayist, celebrated wit, and reformer Voltaire compared the rapidly developing England of his day with France and dryly noted that

> in France the Title of Marquis is given gratis to any one who will accept of it; and whosoever arrives at Paris from the midst of the most remote Provinces with Money in his Purse, and a Name terminating in ac or ille, may strut about, and cry, Such a Man as I! A Man of my Rank and Figure! And may look down upon a Trader with sovereign Contempt; whilst the Trader on the other Side, by thus often hearing his Profession treated so disdainfully, is Fool enough to blush at it. However, I cannot say which is most useful to a Nation; a Lord, powder'd in the tip of the Mode, who knows exactly at what a Clock the King rises and goes to bed; and who gives himself Airs of Grandeur and State, at the same Time that he is acting the Slave in the Ante-chamber of a prime Minister; or a Merchant, who enriches his Country, dispatches Orders from his Compting-House to Surat and Grand Cairo, and contributes to the felicity of the world.[37]

Voltaire ridiculed the pretentions to dignity of aristocrats and celebrated the dignity of entrepreneurs and merchants. It was that celebration of the dignity of value creators, no matter how "humble" their birth, that transformed the world and that continues to transform it. That dignity is systematically denied to billions of people now through more modern forms of privilege, such as what the French call *le capitalisme de copinage*, or cronyism: the subsidies and monopolies handed out to the privileged friends of those in power; the restrictions on the poor to own property, to get a job, to start a business, and to truck, barter, and exchange one thing for another; the paperwork demanded and the permissions delayed and denied.

Becoming the person one wanted to become depended not on the display of allegedly aristocratic virtues or merely showing a patent of nobility, but on the rejection of class distinctions and privileges of birth. The replacement of status by contract also entailed the emergence of enhanced role complexity.[38] As Georg Simmel noted,

> The groups with which the individual is affiliated constitute a system of coordinates, as it were, such that each new group with which he becomes affiliated circumscribes him more exactly and more unambiguously. To belong to any one of these groups leaves the individual considerable leeway. But the larger number of groups to which an individual belongs, the more improbable it is that other persons will

exhibit the same combination of group-affiliations, that these particular groups will "intersect" once again [in a second individual].[39]

The liberty to affiliate, to combine with others, and to experiment
allows individuals to mobilize the knowledge that each and every
human being uniquely possesses, notably "the knowledge of the particular circumstances of time and place," knowledge that is systematically
overlooked or disregarded by outside "experts."[40]

The sense of dignity that characterizes the modern world is a rejection of the shame of work, of the labor upon which Waldron's aristocrats
looked with disdain. Thus, as the Finnish cleric Anders Chydenius
observed in his influential 1765 tract "The National Gain," his famous
defense of the dignity and liberty of the common people:

> In Västergötland, handicrafts and weaving are diligently pursued: there
> an old man is not ashamed to sit at a spinning-wheel; knives, bowls,
> plates, ribbons, bells, scissors and other wares are available there at
> more favourable prices than elsewhere. What is the cause of that?
> Inhabitants of that province have the right to travel wherever they
> wish to sell their wares. There the town of Borås has for a long time
> past been permitted to practise peddling throughout the kingdom.
> That means freedom to go from farm to farm, buying goods and
> selling one's own to others.[41]

Dignity entails no shame felt in creating value through work, innovation,
or buying and selling, and no shame is accorded to those who work,
innovate, or buy and sell. It is a mentality at odds with aristocratic mores,
although so attractive that those aristocrats who changed their attitudes,
abandoning aristocratic "rank," managed to flourish along with those on
whom they otherwise would have looked with disdain.

Dignity is vital to the emergence and maintenance of democracy and
development, we would add, because the condition of people with liberty, but without an awareness of their dignity, is quite fragile, for it takes
something more than a desire for bread to stand up for one's rights. The
disdain—the negation of dignity—experienced by people who are regularly seized or imprisoned, or stripped of their rights or possessions, or
outlawed or exiled, or deprived of their standing in any way, or proceeded
against with force, all without the lawful judgment of their equals or by
the law of the land—that's what burns the most. Those who labor; who
truck, barter, and exchange one thing for another; who save money and
loan it out; who tinker, innovate, and undertake new ventures; who combine things in ways before unknown; and who step out of traditional

roles, have historically—for most of human existence—been humiliated. That humiliation, that denial of dignity, has been a harm of great consequence not only to them but also to the billions of others who would have benefited from the enormous surpluses ordinary people are capable of creating when not humiliated. The historian of medieval economics A. R. Bridbury described the disdain accorded to traders in Europe in the Middle Ages and asked whether "social disapprobation acted as a brake upon enterprise and effectually constrained merchants who might otherwise have thrown themselves uninhibitedly into their work, with incalculable consequences for market forms and marketing techniques."[42]

The social anthropologist Polly Hill, in her studies of West African economic relations, noted three typical assumptions about West African economic behavior among those foreigners who sought to study them: "that it was the expatriate trader who taught the West African, if only by example, the elementary facts of economic life"; "that the basic fabric of economic life was so simple as to be devoid of interest to economists"; and

> that, given the complexities associated with "tribalism" (local land tenure, kinship and inheritance, communal work systems, and so forth), indigenous economies operate on too small a scale, or on too local a basis, to be of interest to economists—and are anyway incomprehensible.[43]

Those demeaning assumptions continue to inform much "expertise" regarding economic development.

Hill undermines those assumptions in her work, noting, for example, of Ghanaian cocoa famers that,

> the farmers, as businessmen, were unimpressed by the colonial administration and undertook their own development expenditure to provide better links between the cocoa forests and their homeland: before 1914 the Akwapim farmers had hired contractors to build three bridges over the river Densu (being businessmen they recouped their expenses by charging tolls), and a little later they invested at least £50,000 in the building of motorable access roads to Akwapim.[44]

To return to dignity by means of its negation, humiliation, very few people deliberately seek to be humiliated by others.[45] People seek recognition by others as moral agents. The philosopher G. W. F. Hegel, not generally known for the transparency of his thought, argued that "Self-consciousness exists in and for itself when, and by the fact that, it so exists for another; that is, it exists only in being acknowledged."[46] The acts of theft, of violence, of enslavement represent an annulment of the dignity of the other, and it is that indignity that generally burns hotter and causes far more harm than the immediate loss of value. It is the rejection of humiliation that overturns systems that perpetuate oppression and poverty. As Mrs Bouazizi told us, it's dignity that drives democratic liberty, or "dignity before bread."[47]

"Bourgeois dignity" draws our attention usefully to a great historical transformation over the past two centuries, despite the unfair disdain which characterizes the common use of the term "bourgeois."[48] Another term, which captures the political/democratic dimension of dignity, and which overlaps in usage with "bourgeois dignity" is "civic dignity." (The term *civil society* in English is generally used to translate *bürgerliche Gesellschaft* from German.) "Civic" roots the term in the practice of deliberative governance, and thus in legal rights and in mutual recognition of moral agency.[49]

Dalit dignity

The history of dignity on which we draw has been limned primarily with a European brush, but it has roots in other cultures. There are studies available of dignity's historical role and development in Hindu, Buddhist, Jewish, Christian, Islamic, and other contexts as well.[50]

The modern growth of trade across the globe has awakened and frequently drawn forth from indigenous roots the yearning for dignity that we document in this book. In the Indian subcontinent there are millions of people who are known as "Dalits." When we were growing up, the term used—now considered toxic and hateful—was "untouchable." Their status was that of constant humiliation and concomitant oppression and poverty. After independence, statesmen who were moved by ideas of equality created government programs to raise up Dalits, but they had little impact, at least partly because they did not respect the dignity, the agency, of Dalit people themselves.

Following the dramatic reforms of 1991 that opened many markets, restrained the "License Raj" that had strangled economic growth,[51] and freed Dalits to enter into businesses, the status of Dalits has improved more than, not merely the previous half-century, but the previous thousand or more years. There are now Dalit chambers of commerce and Dalit millionaires.[52] Universities that previously would not have allowed a Dalit to enter the grounds now seat Dalits on their boards of directors and solicit them for funding. Why? Because they grasped and realized their dignity. Through their own enterprise, they became wealthy and, unsurprisingly for anyone who is visited by the development officers of her or his alma mater, their ability to donate transformed disdain into respect.

The Dalit writer Chandra Bhan Prasad has worked successfully to defend the dignity of Dalit people across India. His task has been to take on one of the world's most entrenched systems of humiliation. And it is working. If it can work to liberate Dalits to rise up, find their voices, and achieve their prosperity, it can work anywhere. It is a struggle that is far from won, for those who wish to defend privilege resort, not only to their own capacity for violence but to that of government. Thousands of Dalits have been beaten, stoned, or lynched for standing up for themselves, for riding horses, for entering markets and competing with "upper caste" people, for wearing nice clothes.[53] Thus, in the 2020 pandemic flight from Delhi, Dalits were singled out for persecution and expulsion by the authorities. On April 17, 2020, in an interview on *Roundtable India*, Pushpendra Johar and Chandra Bhan Prasad discussed the treatment of Dalits during the pandemic:

> JOHAR: I remember reading it and I found it quite powerful when you wrote that those trying to flee the government in Delhi— their dignity is the first casualty, physical trauma they can still overcome over time. It is the dignity that these governments are taking away from people.
>
> PRASAD: Yes. It is dignity. And that is where the enemy demonizes its opponents. Undermining dignity is the biggest thing in warfare. I could just stand at my gate and see how fearful these guys are, they were fearful of us, that they may catch something from our societies. They are running away from everybody who is slightly well dressed. Who created this fear? Why should citizens be under fear in their own country without committing a crime? But the government thought that by fleeing Delhi they are committing a crime. This is unthinkable in any civilized society.[54]

That struggle of Dalits for dignity mirrors in many details the struggles of populations in other countries, including Europe and the Americas, struggles that are often still ongoing to one or another degree. The self-liberation of the Dalits from oppression and poverty is a process; it is incomplete, but it *is* happening. Our focus in the chapters that follow is on how to continue the progress that has been made, to extend it to others who have been left behind or excluded, and to allow all to realize their dignity and to live freely in the enjoyment of democracy and development.

Notes

1   See, for examples, the studies at https://dignityproject.net/; Editorial Board, "Foreign Aid Is Having a Reckoning," *The New York Times*, February 13, 2021, www.nytimes.com/2021/02/13/opinion/africa-foreign-aid-philanthropy.html; Nathalie Dortonne, "The Dangers of Poverty Porn," *CNN Health*, December 8, 2016, edition.cnn.com/2016/12/08/health/poverty-porn-danger-feat/index.html; Irina Mosel and Kerrie Holloway, "Dignity and humanitarian aid in displacement," *Humanitarian Policy Group Report*, Overseas Development Institute, March 2019; Jeremy Shapiro, "Exploring Recipient Preferences and Allocation Mechanism in the Distribution of Development Aid," *The World Bank Economic Review*, Vol. 32, No. 3, October 2020, pp. 749–766.

2   Mosel and Holloway, "Dignity and humanitarian action in displacement," p. 6.

3   Mosel and Holloway, "Dignity and humanitarian action in displacement," p. 7.

4   See W. B. Gallie, "Essentially Contested Concepts," *Proceedings of the Aristotelian Society*, Vol. 56, 1956, pp. 167–198.

5   Ronald Dworkin, "The Jurisprudence of Richard Nixon," *The New York Review of Books*, Vol. 18, No. 8, May 1972, pp. 27–35.

6   English Translation of Magna Carta, published July 28, 2015, British Library, www.bl.uk/magna-carta/articles/magna-carta-english-translation.

7   William F. Swindler, "Runnymede Revisited: Bicentennial Reflections on a 750th Anniversary," *Missouri Law Review*, Vol. 41, No. 2, Spring 1976, p. 153.

8   "Last Speech of Colonel Richard Rumbold, at the Market Cross at Edinburgh, with Several Things That Passed, at His Trial, June 26, 1685," in *A Complete Collection of State Trials and Proceedings for High Treason and Other Crimes and Misdemeanors, from the Earliest Period to the Year 1783*, compiled by T. B. Howell (London: T. C. Hansard, 1816), Vol. XI, pp. 879–881, 881.

9   Cicero, *On Duties*, eds. M. T. Griffin and E. M. Atkins (Cambridge: Cambridge University Press, 1991), I, 3, p. 3.

10 *On Duties* (*De Officiis*) was the third book to be produced in Europe by printing press after the introduction to Europe of moveable type and the first classical text to be so printed. Handwritten copies were, compared to other books, already more widely available across Europe.

11 Cicero, *On Duties*, I, 107, p. 42.

12 Cicero, *On Duties*, I, 110, p. 43.

13 Cicero, *On Duties*, I, 106, pp. 42–43. Cicero obviously reflects the prevailing mores of his age, notably regarding "manliness" as the standard of dignity, but it takes little or no effort to abstract from the gendered nature of the description. What emerges is an exhortation to live well and to exercise self-control.

14 Cicero, *On Duties*, II, 26, pp. 109–110.

15 St. Thomas Aquinas, *Summa Theologica*, trans. Fathers of the English Dominical Province (Westminster, MD: Christina Classics, 1981), Pt. 1, Q. 29, Art. 3, Reply to Objection 2, Vol. I, p. 158.

16 Aquinas, *Summa Theologica*, Pt. 1, Q. 29, Art. 1, "I answer that," Vol. I, p. 156 (Original emphasis in the English translation). Thomas also advanced greatly

the understanding of the uniqueness of each and every human person. In his rebuttal to the "Latin Averroists" who argued that you and I can both know the same thing because we share a collective intellect, he presented an array of arguments on behalf of individualism, including the importance of individuation to moral philosophy:

> If … the intellect does not belong to this man in such a way that it is truly one with him, but is united to him only through phantasms or as a mover, the will will not be in this man, but in the separate intellect. And so this man will not be the master of his act, nor will any act of his be praiseworthy or blameworthy. That is to destroy the principles of moral philosophy. Since this is absurd and contrary to human life (for it would not be necessary to take counsel or to make laws), it follows that the intellect is united to us in such a way that it and we constitute what is truly one being.
>
> (Thomas Aquinas, *On the Unity of the Intellect Against the Averroists* (Milwaukee: Marquette University Press, 1968), Chap. II, par. 82, p. 57)

Finally, Thomas pioneered the application of individual rights to social order in his commentaries on the Roman law, in which he reconciled "objective right," or justice, with "subjective right," or the claims of right of individuals and groups:

> It would seem that lawyers have unfittingly defined justice as being the steady and enduring will to render unto everyone his right. For, according to the Philosopher (Nicomachean Ethics, V, i.), justice is a habit which renders a man apt to do what is just, and which causes them to act justly and to wish what is just … I answer that, The aforesaid definition of justice [Justinian's Institutes, 1.1] is fitting if understood aright. For since every virtue is a habit that is the principle of a good act, a virtue must needs be defined by means of the good act bearing on the matter proper to that virtue. Now the proper matter of justice consists of those things that belong to our intercourse with other men … Hence the act of justice in relation to its proper matter and object is indicated in the words, Rendering to each one his right, since, as Isidore says (Etym. X), a man is said to be just because he respects the rights (ius) of others.
>
> (Aquinas, Summa Theologica, IIa, IIae, Q. 58, Vol. III, p. 1429)

17 Giovanni Pico della Mirandola, *Oration on the Dignity of Man* (Washington, DC: Regnery Gateway, 1956), pp. 11–12.
18 Frank H. Knight, *The Ethics of Competition, and Other Essays* (New York: Harper and Brothers, 1935), p. 22. James M. Buchanan, one of Knight's students, later wrote that:

> man wants liberty to become the man he wants to become. He does so precisely because he does not know what man he will want to become in time. Let us remove once and for all the instrumental defense of

liberty, the only one that can possibly be derived from orthodox economic analysis. Man does not want liberty in order to maximize his utility, or that of the society of which he is a party. He wants liberty to become the man he wants to become.

> (James M. Buchanan, "Natural and Artifactual Man," in
> The Collected Works of James M. Buchanan, Vol. I, *The
> Logical Foundations of Constitutional Liberty* (Indianapolis,
> IN: Liberty Fund, 1999), pp. 246–259)

19 Samuel Pufendorf, 1673, *The Whole Duty of Man, According to the Law of Nature*, eds. Ian Hunter and David Saunders (Indianapolis, IN: Liberty Fund, 2003), I, 7, p. 100. (Original emphasis in the English translation)
    Pufendorf also writes of "the Dignity which Nature bestowed upon him," p. 101.
20 John Locke, *Two Treatises of Government*, ed. Peter Laslett (Cambridge: Cambridge University Press, 1988), II, 6, p. 271. He quotes Richard Hooker on what is necessary for "a Life, fit for the Dignity of Man," (II, 15, p. 277). See, for an illuminating study of Locke's views on subordination and enslavement, and correction of recent misstatements and historical errors, Holly Brewer, "Slavery, Sovereignty, and 'Inheritable Blood': Reconsidering John Locke and the Origins of American Slavery," *American Historical Review*, Vol. 122, No. 4, October 2017, pp. 1038–1078.
21 Richard Overton, "An Arrow against All Tyrants," in *The English Levellers*, ed. Andrew Sharp (Cambridge: Cambridge University Press, 1998), p. 55. As Colonel Thomas Rainborough insisted in the Putney debates of 1647,

> For really I think that the poorest he that is in England hath a life to live, as the greatest he; and therefore truly, sir, I think it's clear, that every man that is to live under a government ought first by his own consent to put himself under that government; and I do think that the poorest man in England is not at all bound in a strict sense to that government that he hath not had a voice to put himself under.
>
> (A. S. P. Woodhouse, ed., Puritanism and Liberty: Being
> the Army Debates (1647) from the Clarke Manuscripts
> with Supplementary Documents (London: J. M. Dent &
> Sons, Ltd., 1992), p. 53)

22 Jeremy Waldron, *Dignity, Rank, and Rights* (Oxford: Oxford University Press, 2012), p. 33.
23 Sidney Painter, "Individualism in the Middle Ages," in Sidney Painter, *Feudalism and Liberty: Articles and Addresses*, ed. Fred A. Cazel Jr. (Baltimore: The Johns Hopkins University Press, 1961), p. 259. On the other hand, see Robert von Keller, *Freiheitsgarantien für Person und Eigentum im Mittelalter, eine Studie zur Vorgeschichte moderner Verfassungsgrundrechte* (Heidelberg: Carl Winters Universitätsbuchhandlung, 1933), which argued that the rights asserted by nobles were often modeled on the claims that were being, or had already been, successfully asserted by urban populations. See esp. pp. 75–77.

24 Walter Ullman, *The Individual and Society in the Middle Ages* (Baltimore: The Johns Hopkins Press, 1966), p. 54. The distance from power and the fracturing of political power created a remarkably competitive political order, within which the nobodies of the time could maneuver and find space to become somebodies.

25 Waldron, *Dignity, Rank, and Rights*, p. 33.

26 Waldron, *Dignity, Rank, and Rights*, p. 53.

27 Max Weber, *Economy and Society* (Berkeley, CA: University of California Press, 1978), Vol. II, p. 1304. See pp. 1301–1307 (Original emphasis).

28 Thomas Paine, "Rights of Man, Part I," in *Political Writings*, ed. Bruce Kuklick (Cambridge: Cambridge University Press, 1989), p. 111.

29 Benjamin Constant, "The Liberty of the Ancients Compared with that of the Moderns," in *Political Writings*, ed. Biancamaria Fontana (Cambridge: Cambridge University Press, 1988), p. 313.

30 Norbert Elias, *The Civilizing Process* (Oxford: Blackwell Publishing, 2000), p. 117. See also Christine Dunn Henderson, "On Bourgeois Dignity: Making the Self-Made Man," in *Dignity: A History*, ed. Remy Debes (Oxford: Oxford University Press, 2017), pp. 275–276:

> Trade between individuals or nations who differ requires that the trading partners forsake going to war to settle those differences, and that they be willing to tolerate different ways of life, beliefs, and values for the sake of the mutual advantage gained through commerce.

Adam Smith wrote of "the virtues of self-denial, of self-government, of that command of the passions which subjects all the movements of our nature to what our own dignity and honour, and the propriety of our own conduct require," Adam Smith, *The Theory of Moral Sentiments* (first published in 1759; Indianapolis, IN: Liberty Fund, 1982), Part I, Chap. 5, p. 23.

31 John Bright, Speech at Birmingham Town Hall, October 29, 1858, in *Selected Speeches of the Right Hon. John Bright, M.P., on Public Questions* (London: J. M. Dent & Co., 1907), p. 204, available at oll-resources.s3.us-east-2. amazonaws.com/oll3/store/titles/1658/0618_Bk.pdf.

32 See https://ourworldindata.org/extreme-poverty for data, evidence, and visual presentation of the dramatic and continuing fall in poverty.

33 Francis Fukuyama argues that it is the search for recognition of the "inner self's worth or dignity" that drives most contemporary political conflicts. Francis Fukuyama, *Identity* (London: Profile Books, 2018).

34 Deirdre McCloskey, *Bourgeois Dignity: Why Economics Can't Explain the Modern World* (Chicago: University of Chicago Press, 2010), p. 11.

35 Deirdre McCloskey, *Bourgeois Equality: How Ideas, Not Capital or Institutions, Enriched the World* (Chicago: University of Chicago Press, 2016), p. 93.

36

> The crucial point about both guilds and communes was that here individuation and association went hand in hand. One achieved liberty

by belonging to this kind of group. Citizens, merchants, and artisans pursued their own individual goals by banding together under oath.

(Anthony Black, *Guilds and Civil Society in European Political Thought from the Twelfth Century to the Present* (Ithaca: Cornell University Press, 1984), p. 65)

37 Voltaire, *Letters Concerning the English Nation*, ed. Nicholas Cronk (Oxford: Oxford University Press, 1999), p. 43.

38 The legal historian Sir Henry Sumner Maine described well "the movement of the progressive societies" as "a movement from Status to Contract," Henry Sumner Maine, *Ancient Law* (first published in 1861; Brunswick: Transaction Publishers, 2003), p. 170. On role complexity, see Rose Laub Coser, *In Defense of Modernity: Role Complexity and Individual Autonomy* (Stanford, CA: Stanford University Press, 1991). On self-control, role complexity, and individuality, see Norbert Elias, *The Society of Individuals* (New York: Continuum, 2001), p. 129.

> [T]he development of society towards a higher level of individualization in its members opens the way to specific forms of fulfillment and specific forms of dissatisfaction, specific chances of happiness and contentment for individuals and specific forms of unhappiness and discomfort that are no less society-specific. The opportunity individuals now have to seek the fulfillment of personal wishes on their own and largely on the basis of their own decisions, carries with it a particular kind of risk. It demands not only a considerable amount of persistence and foresight; it also constantly requires the individual to pass by momentary chances of happiness that present themselves in favour of long-term goals that promise more lasting satisfaction, or to juxtapose these to short-term impulses. Sometimes they can be reconciled, sometimes not. One can take a risk. One has the choice. More freedom of choice and more risk go together.

39 Georg Simmel, "The Web of Group Affiliations," in *Conflict and The Web of Group Affiliations*, trans. Kurt H. Wolff and Reinhard Bendix (respectively) (New York: The Free Press, 1955), p. 140.

40 F. A. Hayek, "The Use of Knowledge in Society," *American Economic Review*, Vol. XXXV, No. 4, September 1945, pp. 519–530.

41 Anders Chydenius, "The National Gain," in *Anticipating the Wealth of Nations: The Selected Works of Anders Chydenius (1729–1803)*, eds. Maren Jonasson and Pertti Hyttinen, trans. Peter C. Hogg (London: Routledge, 2012), p. 155.

42 A. R. Bridbury, "Markets and Freedom in the Middle Ages," in *The Market in History*, eds. B. L. Anderson and A. J. H. Latham (London: Croom Helm, 1986), pp. 79–119, 85.

43 Polly Hill, *Studies in Rural Capitalism in West Africa* (Cambridge: Cambridge University Press, 1970), pp. 6–7.

44 Hill, *Studies in Rural Capitalism in West Africa*, p. 28.

45 We set aside unusual proclivities; it seems that people with erotic fixations on humiliation don't generally seek it out outside of certain settings.

46 G. W. F. Hegel, *The Phenomenology of Spirit*, trans. A. V. Miller (Oxford: Oxford University Press, 1977), p. 111.

47 Rania Abouzeid, "The Martyr's Mother: An Interview with Mannoubia Bouazizi," *Time*, December 14, 2011. http://content.time.com/time/speci als/packages/article/0,28804,2101745_2102138_2102239,00.html.

48 Marxists use the term to refer to a particular and distinctive "class" of people. In some texts, Marx used the term to refer to those innovative entrepreneurs who organize productive enterprises and invest in wealth creation, and in others, he used it to refer to those who cluster around the state, who live off of taxation, who lobby to prohibit competition and restrict the freedom to trade, in brief, to those who invest, not in creating wealth, but in securing the power to redistribute or destroy the wealth of others, and to keep markets closed, the poor in their place, and society under their thumbs. In the words of the historian Shirley Gruner, "Marx felt he had got a grip on reality when he found the 'bourgeoisie' but in fact he had merely got hold of a very slippery term," Shirley M. Gruner, *Economic Materialism and Social Moralism* (The Hague: Mouton, 1973), pp. 189–190. Many intellectuals associate "bourgeois" with standards of taste and decorum they consider beneath them, unaware of how much they owe to bourgeois innovations in making art and culture available to the masses, including the intellectuals who disdain them. See, among many examples, Witold Rybczynski, *Home: A Short History of an Idea* (New York: Penguin Books, 1986).

49 The terms "bourgeois" and "civil" in modern European languages are historically rooted in the "early town community"; Anthony Black lists terms used for towns in the high Middle Ages as "*civitas, commune, communitas, universitas civium/burgensium, urbani, burgensis populus, universi cives*, and the vernacular *commune* (French and Italian), Gemeinde, burgh," Black, *Guilds and Civil Society*, p. 49. Hans Planitz notes that "the expression burgenses was at first used only if the city was not a civitas, and civitas was at first only the old episcopal seat ('Bischofsstadt')," Hans Planitz, *Die Deutsche Stadt im Mittelalter: Von der Römerzeit bis zu den Zünftkämpfen* (Graz, Austria, and Köln: Böhlau, 1954), p. 100. In Karl Marx's anti-Semitic tract "On the Jewish Question," the term for "civil society" is *Bürgerliche Gesellschaft*; his attacks on "bourgeois society" are attacks on "civil society." In *The Communist Manifesto*, Marx and Engels adopted the French term *bourgeoisie*, itself derived from *bürgerlich*, and used it to refer to a sociological/economic "class" of people. For discussion of the confusion that Marx introduced, see Tom G. Palmer, ed., "Classical Liberalism, Marxism, and the Conflict of Classes," in *Realizing Freedom* (2nd ed.; Washington, DC: Cato Institute, 2014), pp. 321–341.

50 See especially the studies in Remy Debes, *Dignity: A History* (Oxford: Oxford University Press, 2017) and Marcus Düwel, Jens Braarvig, Roger Brownsward, and Dietmar Mieth, eds., *The Cambridge Handbook of Human Dignity: Interdisciplinary Perspectives* (Cambridge: Cambridge University Press, 2015).

51 For an account of the partial liberalization that freed millions from the License Raj and allowed hundreds of millions to lift themselves out of poverty, see Gurcharan Das, *India Unbound: The Social and Economic Revolution from Independence to the Global Information Age* (New York: Anchor Books, 2002).

52 Swaminathan S. Anklesaria Aiyar, "The Unexpected Rise of Dalit Millionaires," *The Economic Times*, July 31, 2011, economictimes.indiatimes.com/ swaminathan-s-a-aiyar/the-unexpected-rise-of-dalit-millionaires-swaminathan-s-anklesaria-aiyar/articleshow/9429337.cms?utm_source= contentofinterest&utm_medium=text&utm_campaign=cppst and "Capitalism's Assault on the Indian Caste System: How Economic Liberalization Spawned Low-caste Dalit Millionaires," Cato Institute Policy Analysis, No. 776, July 21, 2015, www.cato.org/sites/cato.org/files/pubs/ pdf/pa776.pdf.

53 One means of humiliating others, and of exalting oneself and one's social group above them, is by prohibiting people from consuming, and especially from dressing, "above their station," either through formal sumptuary laws or through brutality, lynchings, and mob violence. India is rapidly going through a transformation, in which Dalits wear clothes that others consider above their station, but it is a transformation through which other societies have also passed. See T. H. Breen, "The Meaning of Things," in *Consumption and the World of Goods*, eds. John Brewer and Roy Porter (London: Routledge, 1993).

54 "The Dignity of the Underclass is the first casualty: Chandra Bhan Prasad," *Round Table India*, April 29, 2020, roundtableindia.co.in/index.php?option= com_content&view=article&id=9894:the-dignity-of-the-underclass-is-the-first-casualty-chandra-bhan-prasad&catid=118&Itemid=131.

2 Dignity and innovation

Imagine a very poor country. The average life expectancy is forty-four years, sixteen years fewer than in the Democratic Republic of the Congo. Indoor plumbing is considered a luxury. More than one out of four children (28 percent) die before the age of five. Forty-three percent of "gainful workers ten years and older" work just to grow food, and that doesn't count the almost universal use of the labor of children younger than ten years of age on farms, also known as "chores." Nearly 10 percent of the working population ten years or older provide domestic and personal services for those considered wealthy by the standards of that society. No one has a cell phone, not even a radio or a television.

That's the world Tom's grandparents were born into, then and now one of the richest countries in the world.[1] Depending on your age and where you live, your grandparents (or perhaps your grandparents' parents or grandparents) were born into such a world, too. Tom's grandparents had significantly higher life expectancies and enjoyed substantially greater material comfort than did their grandparents. The world was getting better for most people. His parents had more material welfare and education than their parents enjoyed, although his father was temporarily paralyzed by polio as a teenager, something against which Tom was vaccinated as a child. Of course, during periods of war, exceptionally brutal dictatorship, and other calamities, life got worse, but when they ended, progress (for those who survived the violence) typically started again. The result has transformed the world. The last decades have seen the greatest escape from poverty ever experienced in the history of our species.

The shock of the global COVID-19 pandemic and the fall in trade, tourism, travel, and other industries have paused, even reversed partially, years of progress. Hundreds of millions of people have been plunged back into poverty. And yet, as the pandemic subsides, the world is almost certain to recover and growth will begin again. Resilient economic systems respond faster, better, and more equitably to such shocks. The progress

DOI: 10.4324/9781003229872-3

and the improvements have been uneven, with some becoming richer earlier or at faster rates than others, and yet many have started well behind and overtaken wealthier societies. Even with all of its unevenness, the Great Enrichment, to use Deirdre McCloskey's phrase to describe the four- or five-generation period that precedes us today, has become almost universal, as it reaches more and more of the world's population.[2]

There was a time, however, not that long ago (think Tom's grandparents' great grandparents), when life expectancy and living standards were not improving. Before the vast expansion of trade, before the stunning increase in innovation, before the Great Enrichment, life plodded along for most people with little change in life expectancy or living standards from generation to generation. Something changed at the end of the eighteenth century and the beginning of the nineteenth century. The Great Enrichment increased per-capita income by fully a factor of 30 times, an astonishing 3,000 percent. It was not a slow and steady process, with each generation a bit wealthier than the one before it. Considering the great scope of human history, it came quite suddenly.

What changed? Those who talk about "capitalism" assert, in "left-wing terms" and in "right-wing terms," that it's all about "capital." Getting rich is about accumulating capital, all sides claimed. That's not a bad description of how you or Matt or Tom could become richer—earn and save and accumulate and you'll have more money, i.e., more purchasing power. You'll be richer. It's how the development establishment has described development for many years. As the influential development theorist W. Arthur Lewis put it, "The central fact of economic development is rapid capital accumulation."[3] That, we now know, is not the case. We're not talking about enrichment by theft or by the accumulation of a little bit, say, a doubling or tripling of income; income increased by not a factor of two or three, but by a factor of thirty. *Individuals* will get richer if they engage in rapid capital accumulation, to be sure, but that does not explain why *entire societies* become vastly richer, as evidenced by consumption per capita exploding by a factor of thirty. The piling up of Grand Canals and silk spinning machinery and new paddy fields and literate court officials made China a little richer, but the diminishing returns inherent in such activities unless they are radically innovative means that a Great Enrichment was not in the cards.

The story of the Great Enrichment—of the escape from mass poverty—is not the story of increasing capital accumulation, but the story of innovation. Adding another windmill to the stock of windmills did not generate a steam engine. Without novelty in design, even adding steam engines faces sharply diminishing returns. We measure the power of engines in horsepower, but the internal combustion engine was not created by adding another horse to the team pulling the plow or the carriage. Capital accumulation through work and saving is a fine thing, but it's certainly not the difference between how people lived in 1790 or 1890 and how they live now.

Stealing is also a means for some to become wealthy. A bank robber who gets away with a million dollars is a million dollars richer. But society isn't. In fact, the efforts both to perpetrate and to foil robberies—and the harm suffered in their perpetration—make societies in the aggregate poorer than they would be without robbers. Nor are modern societies rich because they robbed other societies through colonialism. Like domestic robbery, colonialism made some people rich—the colonial administrators, the suppliers of weapons and ships, the favored few who enjoyed grants of monopoly, but the mass robbery of colonialism negatively affected at least two groups: the taxpayers and conscripts of the colonizing state and the dispossessed (and often taxed and conscripted) of the colonized country. As economic historians Lance E. Davis and Robert A. Huttenback showed in their study of the economics of British imperialism, "The British as a whole certainly did not benefit economically from the Empire. On the other hand, individual investors did."[4]

The injustice of colonialism has been acknowledged for some decades; its general harm to both colonized and colonizers has received less attention. Adam Smith identified the principles of imperialism:

> Folly and injustice seem to have been the principles which presided over and directed the first project of establishing those colonies; the folly of hunting after gold and silver mines, and the injustice of coveting the possession of a country whose harmless natives, far from having ever injured the people of Europe, had received the first adventurers with every mark of kindness and hospitality.[5]

Smith's account of the injustice has been widely accepted, but his argument that the imperial system impoverished, rather than enriched, the subjects of the colonizing state deserves more attention.

> In the system of laws which has been established for the management of our American and West Indian colonies, the interest of the home-consumer has been sacrificed to that of the producer with a more extravagant profusion than in all our other commercial regulations. A great empire has been established for the sole purpose of raising up a nation of customers who should be obliged to buy from the shops of our different producers, all the goods with which these could supply them. For the sake of that little enhancement of price which

this monopoly might afford our producers, the home-consumers have been burdened with the whole expence of maintaining and defending that empire. For this purpose, and for this purpose only, in the two last wars, more than two hundred millions have been spent, and a new debt of more than a hundred and seventy millions has been contracted over and above all that had been expended for the same purpose in former wars. The interest of this debt alone is not only greater than the whole extraordinary profit, which, it ever could be pretended, was made by the monopoly of the colony trade, but than the whole value of that trade or than that whole value of the goods, which at an average have been annually exported to the colonies.[6]

Plundering other countries merely added to the sum of stuff available to the plunderers, but that wouldn't have translated into the life-transforming innovations that account for the differences between 1890 and today, or between 1790 and 1890. Filling ships with elephant ivory or gold or cotton stolen or coercively extracted from others won't make communications faster by introducing the telegraph, the telephone, or the internet, nor will it introduce the flush toilets that have transformed homes and allowed people to walk down urban streets without having chamber pots emptied on their heads. Indeed, in many cases the imperial nations ended up poor, as well.

For example, Portugal and Spain in 1800 were among the poorest countries in Europe despite centuries of imperialism, exhausted by the expenditure of blood and treasure to support imperialism. Russians today were not made wealthier by the impoverishment of the subjugated peoples of the Soviet Empire, who suffered through the imposition of communism via Russian imperialism. They all suffered from folly and injustice.

Innovation enriches

To understand the astonishing transformation of the world in the modern age, let's return to the paragraph that opens this chapter. The dramatic improvements since Tom's grandparents were born were because of the creation of new products and services that had not existed before. If the difference were merely a matter of increased saving rates (something that did not happen, by the way, because savings rates often fell as incomes rose) or capital accumulation, Tom would merely have more of the same things that his grandparents' generation had enjoyed. That would have been a good thing, but it would not have accounted for the differences between Tom's standard of living and that of his grandparents. More horses and kerosene lamps are generally better than fewer, but that's not the difference in income and living standards between 1890 and today. Innovation, not increased savings or accumulation of more stuff, and certainly not stealing goods from others, accounts for the modern world.

Some would attribute all that innovation to advances in science, or to the scientific revolution, or to investments in research. And surely scientific advances do play a role, as does investment in research, but innovation involves much more than invention, which conjures images of brilliant scientists shouting "Eureka!" as they rush from the lab with world-transforming discoveries, or of obscure lone geniuses in garages suddenly unleashing marvelous disruptions on the world, or, finally, of vast research complexes pushing out inventions, one after the other being spit out on the conveyor belt. Scientists discover and inventors invent and researchers research, to be sure, but discoveries and inventions and research aren't by themselves innovations.

An invention that isn't engineered, manufactured, marketed, and distributed isn't an innovation. Many scientific discoveries and many inventions are of little or no economic significance, which is not to say that they are uninteresting or unimportant. They just aren't innovations. Many innovations are "obvious" (at least in hindsight) improvements to existing products and processes, or adaptations, repurposing, or even copying what others have done in other markets. The last is the advantage that lower-income countries have in "catching up" to wealthier countries, because people there can copy what people did earlier in wealthier countries and try them out at home. The leapfrogging of landline telephone technology into cell-phone telephony by many lower-income countries is an obvious case in point. As Matt Ridley demonstrates in his romp through the history of innovations, innovation is not to be confused with invention; innovation is typically gradual and not "disruptive"; often it is not understood in its significance until long after it is first introduced; and innovation is more commonly a network phenomenon involving multiple persons than it is the act of a lone genius.[7]

A system of innovation—not to be confused with discovery or invention or research—is closely bound up with the dignity and the associated liberty to step out of one's "station," to go beyond the circumstances of one's birth, to imagine the world otherwise, to experiment, to be bold, to be persistent, to defy convention, to go against the grain, and to submit new products, services, and procedures to the market test for customers to take up or to pass over—or just lighting out for a different city, region, or country. Ordinary people innovate in this sense when they move to a new job.

In 1947, the English historian T. S. Ashton, after arguing for falling interest rates as a cause of industrial advances, observed that

> inventors, contrivers, industrialists, and entrepreneurs—it is not easy to distinguish one from another at this period of rapid change—came from every social class and from all parts of the country. ... Lawyers, soldiers, public servants, and men of humbler station than these found in manufacture possibilities of advancement far greater than those offered in their original callings. A barber, Richard Arkwright, became the wealthiest and most influential of the cotton-spinners; an innkeeper, Peter Stubs, built up a highly esteemed concern in the file trade; a schoolmaster, Samuel Walker, became the leading figure in the north of England iron industry.[8]

Old barriers of class and standing were falling, and barbers and innkeepers were becoming rich by trying new things and introducing new processes and products.

Ashton went on to note the prominence in the change of "the rise of groups which dissented from the Church by law established in England" and suggested that the key was because "the Nonconformists constituted the better educated section of the middle classes."[9]

We now are able to take a wider view than Ashton, whose focus was Britain during a period of seventy years, and we can see that the indispensable ingredient in innovation is not better educated middle classes, which is to denigrate neither education nor the middle classes, but the rising dignity and liberty that members of all classes of people enjoyed. (The indispensable ingredient is the dignity that provides the foundation for people's insistence on the presumption of liberty to innovate.) Investment in education has many justifications, but such investment is far from a sufficient condition for economic growth.[10] There are many governments of poor countries that have invested in education and that have failed to provide opportunities for their increasingly schooled populations to create wealth. Egypt has seen gross enrollment ratios in tertiary educational institutions rise between 2011 and 2018 from 26.8 to 38.9 percent, while per capita GDP fell from $2,792 to $2,537.[11] Longer-term comparisons tend to be inconclusive regarding the impact of educational expenditures *per se* on economic growth; when not combined with suitable conditions propitious for innovation, they tend to generate an increasingly educated, but unemployed, workforce, as in Egypt.[12]

Education is as likely to be the effect, rather than the cause, of innovation and rising prosperity; people who are prosperous are more likely to send their children to school rather than to the fields or the workshops.

It's far from a necessary or sufficient condition for development. The rise of subjugated populations, such as the Dalit people of India discussed previously, could be, at best, only partly accounted for by increased education, for many of the most successful entrepreneurs have come from among those with the least access to education, and generally not the best. Many poor people acquire valuable education through the school of enterprise, when they are allowed to do so. Kalpana Saroj was taken from school and married off as a child bride but is now a centimillionaire in Mumbai, where she is chairperson of Kimani Tubes. She remarked of her movement from poverty to wealth,

> I learnt everything about being an entrepreneur from the ground up through this business—sourcing raw materials, the art of negotiating, identifying market trends and, above all, holding my own among a sea of crooks trying to take advantage of me.[13]

Ashton's focus on "manufacture" also reflects a historically limited understanding of the Great Enrichment, one that is typical of studies focusing on the Industrial Revolution. Economic growth is not reducible to the establishment of manufacturing facilities. Indeed, the focus on "manufacture" as the key to growth doomed many countries in the twentieth century to failure. One example is "import substitution," which was applied to Latin America at the suggestion of economist Raul Prebisch, which resulted in many Latin American countries having wretchedly unproductive "manufacturing." It left the people poor.[14] A more famous example is Soviet Communism. The logic of Soviet economic growth policy was, roughly, *Britain and then the US and then Germany became rich when they established great factories, complete with smoke and noise, that employed huge numbers of people. If we build factories with thousands of workers and lots of smoke and noise, we, too, will become rich.*

And it would all be so easy, as Lenin explained

> *All citizens* become employees and workers of a *single* nationwide state "syndicate." All that is required is that they should work equally, do their proper share of work, and get equally paid. The accounting and control necessary for this have been *simplified* by capitalism to the extreme and reduced to the extraordinarily simple operations—which any literate person can perform—of supervising and recording, knowledge of the four rules of arithmetic, and issuing appropriate receipts.[15]

Somehow, that didn't work. Instead of increasing the well-being of the people, it generated what Michael Polanyi called the system of "conspicuous production," in which "targets are produced in place of *commodities* and the consumer is despoiled for the sake of serving the rulers' prestige."[16]

Notes

1 "Life Expectancy (from Birth) in the United States, from 1860 to 2020," compiled by Aaron O'Neill, February 3, 2021, www.statista.com/statistics/1040079/life-expectancy-united-states-all-time/; *Report of the Statistics of Agriculture of the United States, Eleventh Census: 1890, Part II: Comparative Occupation Statistics* (Washington, DC: Government Printing Office, 1895), p. 93, www2.census.gov/library/publications/decennial/1940/population-occupation/00312147ch2.pdf; "Child Mortality Rate (under Five Years Old) in the United States, from 1800 to 2020," compiled by Aaron O'Neill, March 19, 2021, www.statista.com/statistics/1041693/united-states-all-time-child-mortality-rate/; there are no census data on indoor plumbing until the 1940 census, when only 55 percent of homes had "Complete plumbing facilities … defined as hot and cold piped water, a bathtub or shower, and a flush toilet," www2.census.gov/programs-surveys/decennial/tables/time-series/coh-plumbing/plumbing-tab.txt.
2 McCloskey's pioneering historical, economic, and cultural research is a primary intellectual inspiration for this work. Among her many learned essays and books, her trilogy on the "Bourgeois Era" stands out for reformulating the issues of economic development in both descriptive and moral terms. See Deirdre McCloskey, *Bourgeois Ethics* (Chicago: University of Chicago Press, 2006); *Bourgeois Dignity* (Chicago: University of Chicago, 2010), and *Bourgeois Equality* (Chicago: University of Chicago Press, 2016).
3 W. Arthur Lewis, "Economic Development with Unlimited Supplies of Labor," *The Manchester School*, Vol. 22, May 1954, pp. 139–192; cited in William R. Easterly, *The Elusive Quest for Growth* (Cambridge, MA: MIT Press, 2002), Kindle Edition, locations 511–512.
4 Lance E. Davis and Robert A. Huttenback, *Mammon and the Pursuit of Empire: The Economics of British Imperialism*, abridged edition (Cambridge: Cambridge University Press, 1988), p. 267. As they explain further,

> In the Empire itself, the level of benefits depended upon whom one asked and how one calculated. For the colonies of white settlement, the answer is unambiguous: They paid for little and received a great deal. In the dependent Empire, the white settlers, such as there were, almost certainly gained as well. As far as the indigenous population was concerned, while they received a market basket of government commodities at truly wholesale prices, there is no evidence to suggest that, had they been given a free choice, they would have bought the particular commodities offered, even at the bargain-basement rates.

5 Adam Smith, *An Inquiry Into the Nature and Causes of the Wealth of Nations*, eds. R. H. Campbell and A. S. Skinner, textual ed. W. B. Todd, vol. II of the

Glasgow Edition of the Works and Correspondence of Adam Smith (Indianapolis: Liberty Fund: 1981), IV.vii, "Of Colonies," p. 588.

6 Smith, *Wealth of Nations*, IV.viii, "Conclusion of the Mercantile System," p. 661.

7

> Most innovation is a gradual process. The modern obsession with disruptive innovation, a phrase coined by Harvard professor Clayton Christensen in 1995, is misleading. Even when a new technology does upend an old one, as digital media has done to newspapers, the effect begins very slowly, gathers pace gradually and works by increments, not leaps and bounds.
> (Matt Ridley, *How Innovation Works: And Why It Flourishes in Freedom* (New York: Harper Collins, 2020), p. 9)

8 T. S. Ashton, *The Industrial Revolution: 1760–1830* (1948; Oxford: Oxford University Press, 1976), pp. 13–14.

9 Ashton, *The Industrial Revolution*, p. 15.

10 Nor are they even necessary, as economic historian David Mitch argues. See "The Role of Education and Skill in the British Industrial Revolution," in *The British Industrial Revolution: An Economic Perspective*, ed. Joel Mokyr (2nd ed., Boulder: Westview Press, 1999), pp. 241–279.

11 Egyptian gross enrollment ratio in tertiary education, http://uis.unesco.org/en/country/eg, accessed May 20, 2021; Egyptian GDP per capita, https://data.worldbank.org/indicator/NY.GDP.PCAP.CD?locations=EG, accessed May 10, 2021.

12 The official unemployment rate among Egyptians with upper secondary school educations was 35.5 percent in 2017, www.statista.com/statistics/1028359/egypt-unemployment-by-educational-status/.

13 Rakhi Chakraborty, "Dalit child bride to $112 million CEO: The wonder story of Kalpana Saroj," *YourStory*, February 24, 2015, https://yourstory.com/2015/02/kalpana-saroj/amp/.

14 The succeeding history of failed attempts to "protect" infant industries, jump-start industries, and so on is presented in a series of case studies by Arvind Panagariya, *Free Trade and Prosperity: How Openness Helps Developing Countries Grow Richer and Combat Poverty* (Oxford: Oxford University Press, 2019).

15 V. I. Lenin, *The State and Revolution* (Peking: Foreign Languages Press, 1973), pp. 120–121 (Original emphasis).

16 Michael Polanyi, "Toward a Theory of Conspicuous Production," in *Society, Economics, & Philosophy: Selected Papers*, ed. R. T. Allen (New Brunswick: Transaction Publishers, 1997), pp. 165–182, 181.

3 Dignity and enterprise

The attempt to replicate rising incomes by building factories is an example of "cargo cult" thinking applied to economics. Physicist Richard Feynman described such thinking in a commencement address at the California Institute of Technology,

> In the South Seas there is a cargo cult of people. During the war they saw airplanes land with lots of good materials, and they want the same thing to happen now. So they've arranged to imitate things like runways, to put fires along the sides of the runways, to make a wooden hut for a man to sit in, with two wooden pieces on his head like headphones and bars of bamboo sticking out like antennas—he's the controller—and they wait for the airplanes to land. They're doing everything right. The form is perfect. It looks exactly the way it looked before. But it doesn't work. …
>
> Now it behooves me, of course, to tell you what they're missing. But it would be just about as difficult to explain to the South Sea Islanders how they have to arrange things so that they get some wealth in their system. It is not something simple like telling them how to improve the shapes of the earphones.[1]

Unfortunately, a great deal of development advice, backed up by huge sums of money, has focused on the equivalent of telling people how to improve the shapes of their wooden earphones.

When the focus was on "industrialization," by which was meant big factories, the advice was to build factories and steel mills and so on, like they have in England, in America, in Germany, and in Japan. Then the wealth will arrive. Such cargo cult thinking was pioneered in the USSR and copied in India and in other countries. Whether imposed through sheer terror, as in the USSR, or through infusions of "foreign

DOI: 10.4324/9781003229872-4

development aid," or through taxing farmers to divert their incomes to allegedly more worthy and more valuable economic activities, it failed.

Tom recalls meeting officials at the Ministry of Planning in then Communist Poland, where he was told that Poles should not mine and export copper, because the "countries that turn the copper into pots and pans and other manufactured goods will get all the benefit"; "Poland," the planners averred, should instead invest in factories to turn copper into manufactured goods, like pots and pans. It was Prebisch's "import substitution" idea again. Even in the late 1980s, it was hard for many people to let go of the conviction that factories were the only route to wealth. That thinking, we're sad to report, continues, but now it's the internet ("Just install Wi-Fi in the schools—like they have in America and Denmark and Korea—and the country will take off!"), and in the future it will be something else. It's cargo cult thinking, with as much chance of success as the industrious builders of airstrips in the jungles of the South Seas.

There is no truth to the claim that the only thing that makes countries rich is manufacturing. New Zealand became prosperous when they abandoned attempts to force industrialization (again through "import substitution" and "domestic content" policies[2]) and allowed farmers and fishers to innovate, to import and export, and to submit their products to the market test.[3] The growth of call centers and the outsourcing of data processing in India did not fit with the cargo cult model, but it brought prosperity to many millions in India and delivered valuable services to many more millions inside and outside of India. Such unplanned innovation, quite against the model of "industrial policy," made possible a dynamic and successful IT industry that has enabled people from villages where their parents labored under the sun for a few rupees a day (and sometimes owned only one pair of pants for their children, meaning that only one child could be outside the family hut at a time) to commute to work in air-conditioned offices where they labor on computers and, in their homes, plan their children's educations and trips abroad.

Like many in the field of development economics, we're leading up to institutions as being a key in the transformation of poverty into prosperity, but with a twist. Too many who would reject cargo cult thinking in cases of manufacturing actively embrace it when it comes to institutions. Create a securities and exchange commission landing strip and a stock market will be sure to touch down. Erect a central bank air traffic control tower and a complex financial system will land. Translate the French *Code Civil* (or the German *Bürgerliches Gesetzbuch* or some other law book) and a well-functioning legal system will spot you and deliver the rule of law and vast wealth. Such thinking—all of which has been promoted in the name of development—is just the next stage in cargo cult thinking, but instead of improving the shape of the earphones, they've shifted their attention to the runway or the air traffic control tower.

Medical improvements that cut child mortality rates and increased life expectancy came from sanitation, vaccination, antibiotics, surgical procedures, and more—all innovations. New and better forms of plumbing—among them Thomas Kennedy's introduction in 1888 of an improvement to the now-familiar flush toilet system of swirling water,[4] which was soon improved on by George B. Howell's introduction of the water closet reservoir[5]—improved "indoor plumbing" and made it available to many more people, an innovation that has improved life generally.

Tom remembers using an outhouse, a hole in a wooden seat over a bucket inside a wooden shed, when visiting his grandparents (or, in the case of Tom's husband's relatives in Thailand, the forest). Indoor plumbing contributed enormously to sanitation and longevity. Farm machinery, improved seeds, fertilizers based on fixing nitrogen from the air, and many other innovations have greatly reduced the percentage of the labor force needed solely to produce food and have enabled people to leave the farms and to become aerospace engineers, bus drivers, airplane mechanics, bioengineers, and website designers—all professions that did not exist when Tom's grandparents were born—or to swell the ranks of hairstylists, literature professors, bartenders, high school teachers, construction workers, electricians, grocery store workers, and landscapers. Electronic banking, mutual funds, ATMs, and much more have made it easier for the majority of people to access funds as needed, to save, and to invest their savings in more resilient and diversified forms than were previously available, or that were available only to the already rich.

As labor incomes grew, the rich bought machines, rather than hiring personal servants, to wash their clothes and dishes. Labor became the input that rose in price as other prices plummeted, which has certainly proven advantageous to those of us who live from our labor, rather than from inherited lands or financial capital, though a dollar bought more goods and services for them, too. Those innovations of washing machines and dishwashers and so much more became available to more and more people so that almost every household in wealthy countries has at least a clothes-washing machine, and with the washing machine came greater leisure time, and much more, besides.[6] Radios, televisions, and cell phones had to be not only invented but iteratively adapted for successful commercialization, including marketing, manufacturing, and distribution; that is to say, they became *innovations*. Like the bicycle and the auto, they all started as toys for the rich but soon became tools for the poor.

Even the poorest countries in the world today enjoy medical care, dental care, immunization, communication, and travel opportunities, and countless conveniences unavailable (and even unimaginable) when Tom's grandparents were born. Take dental care as an example. Not many people in middle-income countries today would opt for the dental care available to even the richest people in the richest countries in the world thirty years ago; astonishing innovations have radically transformed dental care—innovations such as painless dentistry, implants, 3D printing, and dental sealants cured by blue light. And consider the history of lighting. As the Nobel economist William Nordhaus showed, the amount of labor needed to produce lighting fell from 50 hours per 1,000 lumen hours to 41.5 hours from about 9000 BCE to CE 1750. But consider that in the fifty years from 1750 to 1800 it fell from 41.5 hours to 5.4 hours, far more than in the preceding 10,750 years. By 1890, when Tom's grandparents were born, it had fallen to 8 minutes. From that time to 1992 (when Nordhaus stopped measuring) it had fallen to just over 4 seconds.[7] It's not merely that there's a lot more light, as in more street lighting; it's *better* light—it's available whenever we want it, any place we want it, and even in multiple changing colors, such as new types of lightbulbs that are programmable, Wi-Fi-connected, and voice-activated.[8]

And yet those dramatic changes in living standards—and countless others—are very rarely appreciated. In some ways it's good news that all those improvements are just taken for granted. When older people mention how things have changed since they were young, eyes typically roll and the story turns into "I had to walk to school every day … in the snow … uphill … and both ways!" Eye-rolling aside, it's a fact that for most people in most countries, including the poorest, the material conditions of life have greatly improved over the past century, as they have in fact over the past decade. But for millennia before, they did not improve at all. By today's standards, life for the vast majority of people was short and characterized by soul-crushing suffering. We so often see the past through rose-colored glasses because most of the documents left to us were written by, and were written about the lives of, the richest and most powerful people of their day, not by or about the mute, inglorious masses who toiled, suffered, and died in anonymity, their lives undocumented, uncelebrated, forgotten.

Historians Nathan Rosenberg and L. E. Birdzell Jr. put it well:

> If we take the long view of human history and judge the economic lives of our ancestors by modern standards, it is a story of almost unrelieved wretchedness. The typical human society has given only a small number of people a humane existence, while the great majority have

lived in abysmal squalor. We are led to forget the dominating misery of other times in part by the grace of literature, poetry, romance, and legend, which celebrate those who lived well and forget those who lived in the silence of poverty. The eras of misery have been mythologized and may even be remembered as golden ages of pastoral simplicity. They were not.[9]

Even as living standards for the masses of people rose over the past two centuries, the myths of golden ages of past prosperity were not dispelled by the lived experiences of millions and millions of people whose lives had become much richer than those of their parents. Myths of golden ages of lost prosperity, virtue, and bliss have been with us since the Iron Age or before. Even in the midst of the most astonishing rise in living standards in world history, in the mid-nineteenth century, as the improvement was becoming increasingly evident to anyone who was paying attention, historian Thomas Babington Macaulay noted that

> it is now the fashion to place the Golden Age of England in times when noblemen were destitute of comforts the want of which would be intolerable to a modern footman, when farmers and shopkeepers breakfasted on loaves the sight of which would raise a riot in a modern workhouse, when to have a clean shirt once a week was a privilege reserved for the higher class of gentry.

Macaulay presciently recognized that the way of life of his own generation would later be considered unbearable by even the poorest of the next century.

> We too shall, in our turn, be outstripped, and in our turn be envied. It may well be, in the twentieth century, that … numerous comforts and luxuries which are now unknown, or confined to a few, may be within the reach of every diligent and thrifty workingman. And yet it may then be the mode to assert that the increase of wealth and progress of science have benefited the few at the expense of the many.[10]

Many today continue to believe that "the increase of wealth and progress of science have benefited the few at the expense of the many." But that is not the case. Recall that when Tom's grandparents were born, the life expectancy at birth for the United States was 44. The world average in 2018 (the most recent year for which data are available) was 73. The lowest in the world was in the impoverished Central African Republic, at 53. The highest was that of Hong Kong (85); followed by Switzerland, Japan, and Macao (84); and then by Spain, Singapore, Sweden, Liechtenstein, Norway, South Korea, Italy, Israel, France, Faroe Islands, and Australia (83). Some of those in the highest rank today were among the lowest not very long ago. Unsurprisingly, life expectancy is strongly correlated with per capita income, with the average for high-income countries (81) being seventeen years higher than for low-income countries (64). That gap, by the way, has narrowed dramatically over the years.[11]

After the eye-rolling at explanations of how much more convenient and commodious life is at present when compared to the fairly recent past, the second dismissal of growing prosperity asserts that it is unequal. That's followed by the claim that the wealth of one country or group is due solely or overwhelmingly to injustices done to others, whose poverty is the cause of the wealth of others. It is true that rates of economic growth vary widely among countries; although claims of growing inequality are contestable, some countries have seen faster-rising incomes than others. The latter claim, that the rising incomes of some nations are due to lesser rises in others, is false. Innovations are not like slices of a fixed pie, such that if one slice is bigger, another must be smaller. In fact, the rising innovations in one country are almost sure to be shared—and with increasing rapidity—in others. Innovations make the pies not only bigger, but better, with new toppings and ingredients.

Innovation and entrepreneurship

It's widely agreed that any understanding of economic growth must include an appreciation of the role of the "entrepreneur," the one who undertakes an enterprise. Being an "entrepreneur" does not connote being a member of any particular social class or ethnic group—it's a characteristic of human activity that can be isolated and studied as an "ideal type." A poor woman exercises it when she sets up a stall in the local open market. A poor man exercises it when he realizes that he can make more money for his family by working in a gold mine in South Africa. It's not only the Edisons and Fords, or the Bezos, Musks, Ibrahims, and Mas, who are the entrepreneurs. We all exercise entrepreneurship to one degree or another. It's not an ascriptive characteristic but a feature of human activity.

It's a shame that wealth creation comes under the term "economics," which calls to mind, unsurprisingly, the behavior of "economizing." Entrepreneurship is so much more than "economizing," that is, allocating scarce resources among competing uses. Economizing assumes known uses and known quantities of known resources. That's just calculation. You can hire an MBA to do it or just buy yourself a calculator. Entrepreneurship is what humans need to deal with unknown uses of unknown quantities of unknown resources, as well as unknown wants and unknown ideas. As economist and rabbi Israel Kirzner notes, "To discover ... unexploited opportunities requires alertness. Calculation will not help, and economizing and optimizing will not of themselves yield this knowledge."[12] Entrepreneurship is a faculty that deals with uncertainty, risk, novelty, and surprise. It can be mundane and every-day, like noticing that something sells at a higher price in the neighboring town than it does here, meaning one can get on a bicycle and try to buy low and sell high, or revolutionary, like envisioning delivery straight to your living room of any of thousands of movies of your choice, anytime you desire.

One of the first systematic studies of the entrepreneur identified entrepreneurship with the bearing of uncertainty and risk. In the mid-eighteenth century Richard Cantillon, an Irish banker who was working in Paris, wrote an essay on the nature of commerce. One can surmise that Cantillon was living in Paris when he noted of city people in his *Essai sur la Nature du Commerce en Général* that

> except for wine, families rarely stock provisions. In any case, most of the city's inhabitants live on a day-by-day basis and yet, as the largest consumers, are not in a position to stock commodities coming from the country. For this reason several urban dwellers emerge as merchants or entrepreneurs to buy the country's produce from those who bring it, or have it brought on their account. They pay a certain price for it depending on the place where it is bought, in order to resell it, either wholesale or retail, at an uncertain price.[13]

Cantillon did not identify the entrepreneur with any particular social class or occupation. On the contrary, he identified not only wine merchants but also drapers and farmers as entrepreneurs, because they face uncertainty when buying at a certain price to sell at an uncertain price: "The farmer is an entrepreneur who, without any certainty about what advantages he will derive from the enterprise, promises to pay the owner a fixed sum of money for his farm or land" and "The draper is an entrepreneur who buys cloth and materials from the manufacturer at a certain price to sell at an uncertain price, because he cannot predict the quantity that will be consumed."[14]

Thus, the entrepreneur bears uncertainty. She buys at a certain price to sell at an uncertain price, but one that she hopes will be higher than she paid. That differential between price paid and price received is profit, if positive, and loss, if negative. Some people may be more alert to those potential differentials than others. They may also perceive what "can be" and not merely "what is." It's an exercise of entrepreneurship to imagine combining wheels with luggage in order to make pulling or pushing luggage easier than, well, "lugging" it. (The story of wheels on luggage is, in fact, rather more complicated than just a "Holy Smokes! Why didn't anyone think of that before?!" moment, as science writer Matt Ridley documents in his book *How Innovation Works*.[15])

Of course, alertness to profit opportunities is not limited to mutually beneficial wealth-creating activities but also characterizes what economists call rent-seeking and other people might call legalized theft, corruption, and looting. Economist William Baumol distinguished between productive entrepreneurship and entrepreneurship that is *un*productive or even destructive. Bandits and predatory rulers have engaged in plenty of entrepreneurship over the years (we even witness it now in real time, as hackers continue to improve their "ransomware" and similar harmful activities), but to the detriment of aggregate wealth. The gains to successful hackers are invariably less than the harm suffered by their victims and by those buying anti-virus programs and security to avoid their predation. In Baumol's words,

> This type of entrepreneurial undertaking obviously differs vastly from the introduction of a cost-saving industrial process or a valuable new consumer product. An individual who pursues wealth through the forcible appropriation of the possessions of others surely does not add to the national product. Its net effect may be not merely a transfer but a net reduction in social income and wealth.[16]

Notice the promise implicit in the distinctions Baumol draws:

> If reallocation of entrepreneurial effort is adopted as an objective of society, it is far more easily achieved through changes in the rules that determine relative rewards than via modification of the goals of the entrepreneurs and prospective entrepreneurs themselves.[17]

Permissionless innovation, a.k.a. the presumption of liberty, is based on dignity

Not even the most totalitarian and violent government is able to impose its will to stifle human creativity if it lacks ideological legitimation of some sort.[18] Innovation can be stifled most easily when two conditions are met. First, there are entrenched and powerful parties whose interests could be harmed by an innovation. Occupational guilds often opposed innovations for just such reasons, as historian Sheilagh Ogilvie has documented.[19] Second, there is a general distrust of, and hostility toward, innovators, entrepreneurs, and merchants. Thus, Baumol distinguishes rules that impede earning wealth from the "social disgrace" that impedes the earning of wealth, which he illustrated via the distinction between the treatment of commerce in the Roman world, which was generally undertaken by freed slaves, who were considered to be lacking in dignity, and the treatment of commerce in the modern world, which has been associated with a rise in the dignity of entrepreneurs, innovators, and merchants.[20] Eliminating the "social disgrace"—the indignity—accorded to innovators, entrepreneurs, and merchants is a key step toward validating their liberty and, with that liberty, putting their energies, insights, and daring at the service of humanity.

The key to understanding the presumption of liberty is to distinguish it from what many consider the natural background: the presumption of power. On the one hand, there is the presumption of power that the medieval guilds had come to exercise, which meant that it was presumed that someone had the legitimate authority to deny permission and that those who wished to trade or innovate had to petition for it. On the other hand, there is the presumption of liberty, which holds that the person who intends to exercise her liberty is presumed to have unhindered permission to do so, unless there is a sufficient reason to restrict or forbid it. The burden of proof is on the one who would restrict liberty, not on the one who would exercise it.[21] Harm to the rights of others and negative externalities, such as pollution, quickly come to mind as reasons that could rebut the presumption of liberty, but, as John Stuart Mill explained, there is no "right" to protection from lawful competition, only against force or fraud.

Economist and political philosopher Anthony de Jasay described the presumption of liberty as meaning "that any act a person wishes to perform is deemed to be permissible—not to be interfered with, regulated, taxed, or punished—unless sufficient reason is shown why it should not be permissible."[22] Jasay explained the presumption of liberty as a "consequence of the difference between two means of testing the validity of a statement—namely, falsification and verification."[23]

The presumption of liberty and the presumption of innocence in court are grounded on the same epistemic limitations we all face. No one is so wise as to be endowed with the foreknowledge of all possible outcomes and their significance. In previous ages, of course, kings claimed to rule by asserting divine right, or racial superiority, or some other characteristic that placed them above all the rest, that elevated their dignity above ours. The modern age is an age of equality in dignity and, with it, the presumption of liberty. To uphold dignity is to provide a foundation for liberty, while to uphold liberty is to make possible the assertion of dignity.

It was the change in the status of those who took the route of entrepreneurship, of becoming innovators, i.e., the change in the presumptions governing them, that has made possible the modern world, a world in which, despite the lingering distrust and hatred of those who seem to conjure wealth out of nothing via exchange and innovation, figures such as Kalpana Saroj and Steve Jobs are widely—if not universally—respected, rather than almost universally hated and feared, as in ages past. Recall Voltaire's description of the French aristocrats flouting their titles and looking "down upon a Trader with sovereign Contempt." The bigger problem was that so many traders were "fool enough to blush at it."[24]

It is when those who trade and innovate are "fool enough to blush at it" that the interests opposed to innovation, and thus to general prosperity, triumph, and societies are kept poor. The dignity of enterprise, whether the enterprise of engaging in or facilitating trade or of introducing innovations, is the key to widespread and shared prosperity.

Gurcharan Das, former CEO of Procter and Gamble India, commentator on the Vedic texts, economic historian, author, and distinguished public intellectual, offers a trinity of dignity, liberty, and dharma (or virtue) as central to the free and prosperous society.

> Dignity is a sociological fact while liberty is an economic and political concept. Middle-class Indians won some dignity when they won political independence in 1947; they gained some more when they attained economic liberty in 1991; but only now, twenty years later, have they begun to feel the full meaning of dignity after the economic rise of India. ... Liberty without dignity is self-despising; dignity without liberty makes for status without hope.[25]

Gains from trade and innovation

Voluntary exchange and arbitrage create value by moving goods and services from where they are valued less to where they're valued more. Willing parties to exchanges expect to benefit, or they wouldn't exchange. It follows that greater opportunities for such exchange create greater wealth, or, as Adam Smith put it, "The Division of Labour is Limited by the Extent of the Market."[26] The greater the network, the greater the gains available to trade. Smith focused on the division of labor, to which David Ricardo added the insight of comparative advantage, or how parties to exchange specialize in producing those goods and services for which the differing cost of production (understood as what a producer must forego in order to produce the good) increases the sum of the joint product, making possible greater shared gains from trade. That's a somewhat awkward way of saying that the number of oranges and apples available to the people of Minnesota and Florida is much greater if Minnesotans give up trying to grow oranges, the growing of which would require *not* growing a great many apples, and Floridians give up growing apples, which are similarly hard to grow in Florida, and instead grow oranges. The number of both oranges and apples will be greater and there will be more for all.

Realizing gains from trade and from reallocation of productive labor and capital goes some way toward explaining economic growth, but as Deirdre McCloskey has taught us, it doesn't go very far at all toward explaining the staggering increase in per capita wealth over the past two centuries.[27] For that, we need innovation. Indeed, a great deal of the gains from trade arises from the introduction of new products, services, ideas, technologies, and processes, which for our purposes count as innovations. Smithian and Ricardian gains from trade have existed since time immemorial, but the stupendous gains of the modern age are recent. They arise from innovation. Something changed to make innovation a prime driver of human betterment.

Innovations can be disruptive to the expectations of members of society. The train and the horseless carriage disrupted the world of transportation and sent many a maker of saddles, stirrups, and bridles looking for other work, to which they were now able to travel much faster and more comfortably by train, bus, or car. The Austrian economist Joseph Schumpeter added to our understanding of entrepreneurship by supplementing the ideas of uncertainty and alertness with the element of novelty, of the untried, of innovation. Thus,

> The function of entrepreneurs is to reform or revolutionize the pattern of production by exploiting an invention or, more generally, an untried technological possibility for producing a new commodity or producing an old one in a new way, by opening up a new source of supply of materials or a new outlet for products, by reorganizing an industry and so on.[28]

Innovation isn't reducible merely to the inspired inventions that so capture the imagination. Most of the significant or impactful innovations in human history have been embedded in or have induced cascades of changes. The innovation of wireless communication—often dated to Guglielmo Marconi's transmission in 1910 of a Morse code message from Britain to Canada—was a product also of numerous preceding innovations in the electromagnetic transmission of messages, among which Marconi's stands out. It, in turn, made possible the cascades of innovations that we know as television, the internet, microwaves, radar, and all of the innovations that have followed each one of those, from communication to entertainment to transportation to medicine and many other fields.

Not only is innovation rarely, if ever, reducible to the "Eureka" moment of the discoverer or inventor, but, in fact, innovation can be introducing to a new market a product or process already in use elsewhere, or putting it to new use, or combining it with another product or process, or adapting it to become a component of something else. A great many valuable innovations consist of variations on existing products and processes, leading Matt Ridley to conclude that "most innovation consists of the non-random retention of variations in design."[29]

Continuing the Great Enrichment and extending it to more and more people requires maintaining and extending culture(s) of dignity. It's not just a matter of passing the right statutes and administrative regulations. The law is far more than ink on paper. It is implemented through norms. The norm of the presumption of innocence has saved many an innocent person from being burned alive or stoned to death. The norm of the presumption of liberty has saved many an innovation from the pyre and from the endless mazes of bureaucracy that have replaced the pyre in modern times. It is dignity that provides the bridge between norm and law, for it is the dignity of the individual that moves her to insist on the presumption of the liberty to innovate.

Wealth-generating innovation (as also Baumol's "productive entrepreneurship") is not the act of the rare genius but a complex system. It works when a critical mass of the population accepts the presumption of liberty, and those with interests in stifling innovation and trade lack the power and the ideological legitimacy to stifle innovation and trade.[30]

Notes

1 Adapted from the commencement address given in 1974 at the California Institute of Technology (Caltech), https://calteches.library.caltech.edu/51/2/CargoCult.htm.

2 As New Zealand businessperson Alan Gibbs observed of his television importation business,

> We'd go to Japan and say to JVC, "We want to buy your TVs in pieces." They'd say, "Why? No one else does." We'd reply that we are required to assemble them in New Zealand. "Oh," they'd say, "do you have lots of cheap labour? Why would you do this? No other small countries do." We'd agree, but that's the rules in New Zealand. "Our government requires us to make them here if we want to sell them." "But," they'd say, "this costs a lot of money; we make thousands of televisions a day, pieces

come from all over the place; to send you the pieces we'll have to disassemble the sets, it will cost a premium." We said, "It doesn't matter what it costs; it's the only way to bring them in. This nonsense will no doubt be dropped one day, and you'll have your brand in place." So they'd sell us the pieces, minus the few components made in New Zealand, put them in a box with instructions on how to put them together; they'd charge 10 per cent more than they would for a ready-to-go TV, then we'd have to build a factory, hire people, make an assembling line, find finance for the stock. There was no real New Zealand content, no added value, as all the extra unnecessary labour was being paid for by New Zealand customers, who paid twice the price for their electronic goods. It was a total dead loss.

(Quoted in Paul Goldsmith, *Serious Fun: The Life and Times of Alan Gibbs* (Auckland, NZ: Random House, 2012), Kindle Edition, locations 2080–2090)

3 For a brief description of the process of abandoning "import substitution" and attempts to force industrialization, see Bill Frezza, *New Zealand's Far-Reaching Reforms* (Guatemala City: Universidad Francisco Marroquin Antigua Forum, 2015), https://static1.squarespace.com/static/53506678e4b0337f7ff65f95/t/57e15fdf2e69cf0a7550c583/1474387983903/New+Zealands+Far+Reaching+Reforms.pdf.

4 United States Patent Office, SIPHON WATER-CLOSET. SPECIFICATION forming part of Letters Patent No. 376,002, dated January 3, 1888, https://patentimages.storage.googleapis.com/1c/a3/7b/fbd4c1442f3a47/US376002.pdf.

5 United States Patent Office, WATER-CLOSET RESERVOIR SPECIFICATION forming part of Letters Patent No. 520,358, dated May 22, 1894, https://patentimages.storage.googleapis.com/79/ee/08/af64b275951719/US520358.pdf.

6 It is well worth watching the TED talk with the late Hans Rosling on the washing machine: "Hans Rosling and the Magic Washing Machine," www.gapminder.org/videos/hans-rosling-and-the-magic-washing-machine. When he was a boy, Tom's mother bought a washing machine that was a mechanical washtub with a hand-cranked wringer above it; he was rewarded for good behavior by being allowed to crank the handle and wring out the excess water, after which his mother would hang the washing to dry. Now Tom has an automatic electrical clothes dryer with a setting for "wrinkle free."

7 William D. Nordhaus, "Do Real-Output and Real-Wage Measures Capture Reality? The History of Lighting Suggests Not," in *The Economics of New Goods*, eds. Timothy F. Bresnahan and Robert J. Gordon (Chicago: University of Chicago Press, 1996), pp. 27–70, numerical values cited on pp. 46–47.

8 Deirdre McCloskey notes the even more astonishing significance of Nordhaus's calculations when one considers the *quality* of the goods consumed, which makes them in many ways difficult, if not impossible, to compare. Deirdre McCloskey, *Bourgeois Dignity: Why Economics Can't Explain the Modern World* (Chicago: University of Chicago Press, 2010).

9 Nathan Rosenberg and L. E. Birdzell Jr., *How the West Grew Rich: The Economic Transformation of the Industrial World* (New York: Basic Books, 1986), p. 3.

10 Thomas Babington Macaulay, *The History of England from the Accession of James II* (Philadelphia, PA: E. H. Butler and Co., 1849), pp. 291–292. As Macaulay noted in his "Southey's Colloquies,"

> If we were to prophesy that in the year 1930 a population of fifty millions, better fed, clad, and lodged than the English of our time, will cover these islands, that Sussex and Huntingdonshire will be wealthier than the wealthiest parts of the West Riding of Yorkshire now are, that cultivation, rich as that of a flower-garden, will be carried up to the very tops of Ben Nevis and Helvellyn, that machines constructed on principles yet undiscovered will be in every house, that there will be no highways but railroads, no travelling but by steam, that our debt, vast as it seems to us, will appear to our great-grandchildren a trifling encumbrance, which might easily be paid off in a year or two, many people would think us insane.
>
> (Thomas Babington Macaulay, "Southey's Colloquies," in *Critical and Historical Essays* (New York: Dutton, 1967), Vol. 2, pp. 187–224, 223)

11 Life expectancy at birth (total years), https://data.worldbank.org/indicator/SP.DYN.LE00.IN?name_desc=false. In 1990, the gap between the average life expectancy of high-income countries and of low-income countries was twenty-four years.

12 Israel Kirzner, *Competition and Entrepreneurship* (Chicago: University of Chicago Press, 1973), p. 41.

13 Richard Cantillon, *Essay on the Nature of Trade in General*, trans. Antoin E. Murphy (1755; Indianapolis: Liberty Fund, 2015), p. 25.

14 Cantillon, *Essay on the Nature of Trade*, pp. 24, 25.

15 See the section "Was wheeled baggage late?" in Matt Ridley, *How Innovation Works: And Why It Flourishes in Freedom* (New York: HarperCollins, 2020), pp. 170–172.

16 William J. Baumol, "Entrepreneurship: Productive, Unproductive, and Destructive," *Journal of Political Economy*, Vol. 98, No. 5, 1990, pt. 1, pp. 893–921, 904.

17 Baumol, "Entrepreneurship," pp. 893–921, 916.

18 As Estienne de la Boetie observed in 1576,

> I should like merely to understand how it happens that so many men, so many villages, so many cities, so many nations, sometimes suffer under a single tyrant who has no other power than the power they give him; who is able to harm them only to the extent to which they have the willingness to bear with him; who could do them absolutely no injury unless they preferred to put up with him rather than contradict him.
>
> (Etienne de la Boétie, *The Discourse of Voluntary Servitude*, trans. Harry Kurz (1942; Indianapolis: Liberty Fund, 2011), p. 5, https://oll-resources.s3.us-east-2.amazonaws.com/oll3/store/titles/2250/Boetie_Discourse1520_EBk_v6.0.pdf)

19

Guilds were not intrinsically either technophilic or technophobic. Rather, guilds provided a set of institutional mechanisms that their members could use to deal with the promise and the threat of innovations. Whether an innovation was opposed or accepted in a guilded industry depended on its distributional effects—whether it threatened a weak guild but benefited a strong guild, threatened a craft guild but benefited a group of merchants, threatened guild employees but benefited guild masters, threatened old masters but benefited young ones, threatened poor but numerous masters but benefited rich but isolated ones, threatened artisan members of the guild but benefited merchant members. It also depended on the institutional tools available to different interest-groups: which guild factions controlled the guild's finances, how receptive the legal system was to guild litigation, how responsive different levels of government were to guild petitions, whether jurisdictional enclaves created guild-free zones.

(Sheilagh Ogilvie, *The European Guilds: An Economic Analysis* (Princeton: Princeton University Press, 2019), p. 571)

In his *Eloge* on Jean Claude Marie Vincent de Gournay, his friend and student Anne Robert Jacques Turgot noted that Gournay understood the folly of imposing monopolies and "standards" on the market that consumers did not, in fact, demand. As Turgot put it, Gournay "was astonished to see that a citizen could neither make nor sell anything without having bought the right to do so at a great expense in a corporation," that is, that one had to first purchase from a monopolistic guild the right to undertake a trade and offer goods to willing customers.

He was far from imagining that this piece of stuff, for not being conformable to certain regulations, might be cut up into fragments of three ells length, and that the unfortunate man who had made it must be condemned to pay a penalty, enough to bring him and his family to beggary.

(Jacques Turgot, "Elogue de Gournay," in *Western Liberalism: A History in Documents from Locke to Croce*, eds. E. K. Bramsted and K. J. Melhuish (London: Longman, 1978), p. 305)

20

If the rules are such as to impede the earning of much wealth via activity A, or are such as to impose social disgrace on those who engage in it, then, other things being equal, entrepreneurs' efforts will tend to be channeled to other activities, call them B. But if B contributes less to production or welfare than A, the consequences for society may be considerable.

(Baumol, "Entrepreneurship," pp. 893–921, 898)

Joyce Appleby identifies the Netherlands as central to the modern vindication of the dignity of entrepreneurship. "The Dutch have been willing to nurture this complex social organization of the market by protecting the individual initiative on which it throve." *Economic Thought and Ideology in Seventeenth-Century England* (Princeton, NJ: Princeton University Press, 1978), p. 96.

21 For the significance of the presumption of liberty in modern political thought, see George H. Smith, *The System of Liberty* (Cambridge: Cambridge University Press, 2013), esp. pp. 16–21.

22 Anthony de Jasay, "Liberalism, Loose or Strict," *The Independent Review*, Vol. IX, No. 3, Winter 2005, pp. 427–432.

23 Jasay, "Liberalism, Loose or Strict," p. 430.

24 Voltaire, *Letters Concerning the English Nation*, ed. Nicholas Cronk (Oxford: Oxford University Press, 1999), p. 43.

25 Gurcharan Das, *India Grows at Night: A Liberal Case for a Strong State* (New Delhi: Penguin Books, 2012), pp. 171–172.

26

> As it is the power of exchanging that gives occasion to the division of labour, so the extent of this division must always be limited by the extent of that power, or, in other words, by the extent of the market. When the market is very small, no person can have any encouragement to dedicate himself entirely to one employment, for want of the power to exchange all that surplus part of the produce of his own labour, which is over and above his own consumption, for such parts of the produce of other men's labour as he has occasion for. There are some sorts of industry, even of the lowest kind, which can be carried on no where but in a great town. A porter, for example, can find employment and subsistence in no other place. A village is by much too narrow a sphere for him; even an ordinary market town is scarce large enough to afford him constant occupation. In the lone houses and very small villages which are scattered about in so desert a country as the Highlands of Scotland, every farmer must be butcher, baker and brewer for his own family. In such situations we can scarce expect to find even a smith, a carpenter, or a mason, within less than twenty miles of another of the same trade. The scattered families that live at eight or ten miles distance from the nearest of them, must learn to perform themselves a great number of little pieces of work, for which, in more populous countries, they would call in the assistance of those workmen.
>
> (Adam Smith, *An Inquiry Into the Nature and Causes of the Wealth of Nations*, eds. R. H. Campbell and A. S. Skinner, textual ed. W. B. Todd, vol. I of the *Glasgow Edition of the Works and Correspondence of Adam Smith* (Indianapolis, IN: Liberty Fund, 1981), I.iii, "That the Division of Labour is Limited by the Extent of the Market," p. 31)

27 McCloskey, *Bourgeois Dignity*, pp. 174–177.

28 Joseph A. Schumpeter, *Capitalism, Socialism and Democracy* (London: Taylor & Francis 2003), p. 132, Kindle Edition Location 2866.

29 Ridley, *How Innovation Works*, p. 227.

30 Historian Johan Norberg cites some examples of attempts by rulers to suppress innovations in *Open: The Story of Human Progress* (London: Atlantic Books, 2020), pp. 166–188.

4   Dignity and democracy

"Development comes first and democracy comes after," according to a commonly held thesis. That thesis holds that democracy may be an outcome of development, but democracy is not a valuable input into development. Those who advance such a view generally don't deny the desirability of democracy *per se*, although some do, but they either don't see democracy as compatible with development, at least at low levels of income, or they see the relationship between democracy and development as a tradeoff. Some argue that below certain levels of per capita income, democracy even undermines development, until some threshold of income is reached and democratic development becomes self-sustaining.

The "technocratic model of development, characterized by low levels of political participation, high levels of investment (particularly foreign investment) and economic growth, and increasing inequalities" was described succinctly by Samuel Huntington and Joan Nelson: "This model assumes that political participation must be held down, at least temporarily, in order to promote economic development, and that such development necessarily involves at least temporary increases in income inequality." According to Huntington and Nelson, "a conflict exists between the expansion of political participation and rapid economic growth."[1] Again, the focus is on investment, particularly foreign investment, as the core mechanism of economic growth.

According to Fareed Zakaria's reading of economic history, "One might conclude that a country that attempts a transition to democracy when it has a per capita GDP of between $3,000 and $6,000 will be successful."[2] Others, advocates of the "developmental state," have argued for the economic advantages of strong—and even authoritarian—executives, of "politically insulated" governments, of coherent, meritocratic, or Weberian bureaucracies, and even of dictatorships, the last of which allegedly "can overcome collective action problems inside and

DOI: 10.4324/9781003229872-5

outside the government that hinder the formulation of coherent policy, override both rent-seeking and populist pressures, and thus push the economy onto a more efficient growth path."[3] Such developmental states allegedly promote capital accumulation and efficient investment, which their advocates mistakenly consider to be the "core mechanisms that determine long-run growth":

> What is the underlying theory that would justify a focus on the efficacious state as one that was centralized, internally coherent, and politically insulated? The answers trace back to the core mechanisms that generate long-run growth: on the one hand accumulation, on the other the capacity to steer investment into sectors that are dynamically efficient.[4]

Seen in that light, democracy might be considered one of the rewards of economic development, but it is neither a constitutive element of development nor even a contributor to it.

We see the matter differently. Democratic governance contributes to creating the framework of innovation and competition that drives development and poverty reduction. Understanding both the problem of development *and* the problem of governance entails recognizing "the problem of what is the best way of utilizing knowledge initially dispersed among all the people."[5] The price system of a market economy is a vastly more efficient means of utilizing such dispersed knowledge than is economic dictatorship, and democratic governance is a more efficient—not to mention a more just—means of utilizing the dispersed knowledge of citizens than is autocracy. If the use of the state for rent-seeking is restrained, then letting people "have a go," as McCloskey put the economic engine of liberalism, is powerfully enriching.

Indeed, discussion and bargaining in exchange both rest on efforts to persuade, as Adam Smith noted:

> If we should enquire into the principle in the human mind on which this disposition of trucking [i.e., of trading] is founded, it is clearly on the natural inclination every one has to persuade. The offering of a schilling, which to us appears to have so plain and simple a meaning, is in reality offering an argument to persuade one to do so and so as it is for his interest.[6]

Like the presumption of liberty, democracy is bolstered by dignity, albeit with a different emphasis: not the dignity of managing one's own affairs that is associated with the presumption of liberty—to worship as one chooses, to live as one pleases, to innovate, and exchange ("bourgeois dignity," to use McCloskey's term), but the dignity of being entitled to engage in deliberation about the *res publica*, about matters that concern the entire polity, and to vote either directly on laws and public measures or for representatives who then vote on laws and public measures. It is the dignity of counting as an agent with a legitimate interest when authentically public goods are chosen and secured. The most important public good of all is the provision of peace and security for the lives, liberties, and possessions of the people, for such a framework of law and voluntary cooperation makes possible the other goods produced and consumed, whether publicly or privately. The legal framework and the security from being plundered are, moreover, authentic public goods, because they are both non-rivalrous in consumption—your enjoyment of security and liberty does not diminish my ability to enjoy it—and excludable only at some cost.[7]

Much hinges, of course, on what one means by democracy. Voting is not alone sufficient to characterize a political system as democratic. Voting is a means to the revelation of majority—or supermajority—preferences regarding those matters that are on the agenda of public choice. Some of the most oppressive dictatorships in history have been proclaimed "democracies" by their dictators. They seek to validate their claims to be democratic by holding public rituals, such as plebiscites and parliaments, that resemble the procedures of democracies, but no one should be fooled into thinking that the Democratic People's Republic of Korea or the now-defunct German Democratic Republic has ever been a democracy. A *necessary* element of democracy is also the protection of a core set of individual rights. The mechanism of voting, the rituals of which can be, and usually are, copied by modern autocratic states, is not sufficient to make a polity democratic, nor is a proclamation of democratic intentions or aspirations.

When terms such as justice, equality, and democracy are deployed in appraising political regimes, it helps to clarify just what one means in order to avoid talking past one another.[8] As W. B. Gallie noted, among "essentially contested concepts," the term democracy "has steadily established itself as the appraisive political concept par excellence."

> If we want to see just what we are doing, when we apply a given appraisive concept, then one way of learning this is by asking from what vaguer or more confused or more restricted version (or ancestor) our currently accepted version of the concept in question has been derived. Commonly we come to see more precisely what a given scientific concept means by contrasting its deductive powers with

those of other closely related concepts: in the case of an appraisive concept, we can best see more precisely what it means by comparing and contrasting our uses of it now with other earlier uses of it or its progenitors, i.e., by considering how it came to be.[9]

Our stipulation of democracy as entailing the protection of a core set of individual rights, realized in some system of the separation of powers, and political organizations that can be held to account through some system of majoritarian or supermajoritarian voting, is justified by both its history and by its logical requirements.

Democratic governance is both an important aspect of modern dignity, and it provides the legal and political framework for the presumption of liberty within which innovation flourishes. Written constitutions and statutes, of course, are of little or no value if the norms of democratic governance are absent. Written statutes are of no use when people are unwilling to follow them.

The 1936 Soviet Constitution spells out various guarantees of rights. Article 125 enumerated guarantees of freedom of speech, freedom of the press, freedom of assembly, including the holding of mass meetings, and freedom of street processions and demonstrations. Article 128 guaranteed that "the inviolability of the homes of citizens and privacy of correspondence are protected by law."[10] Without the inculcation of norms of courage, justice, respect, equality—core elements of modern dignity—formal institutions or written frameworks are dead letters.

Sustainable democracy

Fareed Zakaria has argued that, just as there can be liberal democracies, there can also be "illiberal democracies" and "liberal autocracies."[11] Bertrand de Jouvenel and J. L. Talmon even famously wrote of "totalitarian democracy," mainly to describe the Jacobin horrors of the Terror.[12] To delineate such combinations as political types, however, one would have to do more than show that a democratic polity has implemented an illiberal policy or that an autocratic polity has implemented a liberal one. One has to show that those are stable combinations, i.e., that the two terms cohere and persist, rather than merely that they temporarily coexist.

Stipulating that democracy is entirely a matter of determining the preferences of the majority and then translating those preferences into state policy is utterly inadequate as a definition of a type of political regime, because even pure majoritarianism requires a means to determine what the preferences of the majority are. Just how does one ascertain what the preferences of the majority are? An "illiberal democracy" that suppresses dissent; imprisons critics; monopolizes the media of expression; punishes with imprisonment, exile, or death the losing aspirants to office; and so on would be unable to determine just what the preferences of the majority actually were. An "illiberal democracy" would fail to meet even the minimal criterion of democracy because when the population lives in fear of censorship or worse, widespread preference falsification would make it impossible to know whether the people were

1   expressing preferences for policies and outcomes when voting or responding to polls or attending rallies; or
2   publicly affirming the party line out of fear, which is one reason why such allegedly democratic autocracies are often remarkably brittle and can collapse so swiftly, as happened, for example, in the case of the "German Democratic Republic."[13]

The term democracy is frequently used carelessly, meaning that the differing parties merely talk—or shout—past each other. Does it mean

1   the majority of the population (usually limited by some criteria of age, place of birth, parentage, residence, etc.) makes decisions about all those issues on which they wish to make decisions; or
2   citizens enjoy substantive liberties, notably freedom of speech and assembly and the right to vote for their political agents, and also substantial individual civil rights, generally including freedom of religion, freedom of exit, procedural rights to due process of law, secure rights of property and contract, and so on?

The two are incompatible. The second is contrary to the clause in the first that specifies "all those issues on which they wish to make decisions," because the second stipulation removes from the agenda of public choice those matters that are considered substantive liberties essential to the maintenance of democracy. Without the second stipulation—that the citizens enjoy the liberty to express their views and the rights of property through which such expression is realized—a political system cannot determine the preferences of the majority, which are not features like weight, that can be posited independently of their measurement. Many human preferences are determined in expressing them. When expressing preferences and registering the expressions of others, preferences often change, which is precisely what happens in free discussions.

Democracy is not a machine for registering preferences encoded in the people and capable of being tabulated independently of their actions in order to generate a social welfare function. Democracies are political systems that enable people to deliberate about the public good in order to live together peacefully and to resolve their differences through deliberation and collective decision-making processes that are expected to be fair to all. As the economist and philosopher Frank Knight put it, democracy is a system of "government by discussion."

The term liberal democracy is something of a useful redundancy because it is a conceptual requirement of democracy that it entail at least a core element of liberal protections of individual rights. (It remains a *useful* redundancy, however, because it reminds us of the importance of equal rights for all, something that democracies approximate to greater or disastrously lesser degrees.) Liberal democracies embed a range of limited majoritarian decision-making procedures concerning matters of public good within a restricted agenda of public choice, which restriction makes possible democratic discussion and deliberation about public good, including securing the general presumption of liberty. A majoritarian system that suppressed or exterminated those holding minority viewpoints would cease to be democratic and would, as time passes, lose any claim even to being majoritarian, as the means of ascertaining majority preferences would be eliminated. Minorities may become majorities, but only if their freedom to persist in advancing their views are respected: "The whole justification of democracy rests on the fact that in course of time what is today the view of a small minority may become the majority view."[14]

The majority principle and the principle of discussion are both necessary. The point is not to maximize a hypothesized collective welfare function but to negotiate social peace and harmony among multiple agents, each with her specific interests and unique knowledge. In response to worries about so-called voting paradoxes, economist and philosopher James Buchanan embraced majority rule in a free society

> precisely because it allows a sort of jockeying back and forth among alternatives, upon none of which relative unanimity can be obtained. Majority rule encourages such shifting, and it provides the opportunity for any social decision to be altered or reversed at any time by a new and temporary majority grouping. In this way, majority decision-making itself becomes a mean through which the whole group ultimately attains consensus, that is, makes a genuine social choice. It serves to insure that competing alternatives may be experimentally and provisionally adopted, tested, and replaced by new compromise alternatives approved by a majority group of ever-changing composition. This is democratic choice process, whatever may be the consequences for welfare economics and social welfare functions.[15]

The loyal opposition

Sustainable democracies require a most important institution, one that is nurtured through the sustained experience of democratic deliberation. That institution is the loyal opposition. In a democracy, when one party replaces the other in control of parliament or congress, the party or group formerly in charge of government shifts to become the loyal opposition. An opposition that is loyal to the constitutional order of their democratic polity and that has lost an election doesn't blow up train stations, assassinate election officials, or even (an unlikely possibility) invade the Capitol building to halt the peaceful transfer of power. Such loyalty is impossible, or at least extremely unlikely, if the losers who form the opposition fear that by losing an election, they risk losing everything: their goods, their property, their liberties, and perhaps even their lives. A loyal opposition is impossible without limitations on the power of the party that has won to punish those who lost.

Without a loyal opposition, you cannot have a democracy. In the absence of limits on state power, no government that is currently in power can afford to relinquish those unlimited powers, which would then be exercised by their enemies. That is one of the problems facing the dictatorship of Vladimir Putin in Russia, who claims to preside over a "managed democracy." He knows that, having shut down critical media; imprisoned, exiled, and poisoned his rivals; and resurrected a police state, he can never afford to relinquish the levers of power. He is riding a tiger. He is unlikely ever to allow a free election, because he fears what would happen to him if he were to lose. The usual way that such autocratic figures leave their presidential palaces is feet first, whether peacefully or violently.

Reliable elections to determine majority preferences require the protected liberties of speech and casting votes (without which the formation, expression, and tabulation of majority preferences are not possible) and some division of powers, minimally in the form of independent authoritative bodies with powers that are not themselves matters of immediate public choice.[16] Such bodies are necessary to supervise elections and to certify their outcomes. Again, merely setting up such a body does not guarantee that it will work. The US presidential election of 2020 demonstrated the importance of the norms of democratic integrity. Had a handful of election officials in several states obeyed the titular leader of their party, rather than follow the requirements of the law, the democratic order would have been overturned. Mere offices and laws do not suffice. Such bodies may include independent electoral commissions and—to supervise them—an independent judiciary, that is, a judiciary that is not easily subject to punishment or removal by the elected branches. Democratic polities require the rule of law, which is a necessary ingredient for both sustainable economic development and for sustainable democracy, and the rule of law, in turn, rests on ethics.

Thus, to quote the insightful Mancur Olson at some length,

> The conditions that are needed to have the individual rights needed for maximum economic development are exactly the same conditions that are needed to have a lasting democracy. Obviously, a democracy is not viable if individuals, including the leading rivals of the administration in power, lack the rights to free speech and to security for their property and contracts or if the rule of law is not followed even when it calls for the current administration to leave office. Thus, the same court system, independent judiciary, and respect for law and individual rights that are needed for a lasting democracy, are also required for security of property and contract rights.[17]

The same institutions and especially the norms that sustain democracy make development possible. They institutionalize respect for human dignity and they secure the frameworks for development.

Democratic development

We stressed in Chapter 2 the importance of innovation to development, of the presumption of liberty to innovation, and of dignity to the presumption of liberty, but innovation is not the only necessary foundation for development. Substantial security of property and a reasonably reliable legal system to secure rights and to adjudicate disputes among rights holders, as well as with government itself, are also contributing conditions. They just aren't sufficient.

A sustainable democracy requires that many matters be removed from the agenda of public choice; that is, it requires that it be liberal. Significant among the matters that are *not* on the agenda of public choice are those that are designated as rights, which may be enumerated in documents or unenumerated and embedded in norms and customary law. The rights to freedom of speech and to criticism of government are generally included among the rights essential to a democracy, but such rights do not exhaust the requirements of sustainable democracy.

Many who have argued for autocratic developmental states concede that autocracies run the risk of truly ruinous outcomes but focus on cases in which at least relatively soft autocracies might be credited with fostering economic development. (The practice common in previous decades of extolling the economic leadership of Lenin, Mussolini, Stalin, and Hitler has fallen out of fashion.) Looking at large numbers of regimes, rather than focusing on anecdotes, suggests that the alleged "upside" of rolling the dice on democracy or autocracy is not worth the effort.

William Easterly and Steven Pennings have subjected the thesis of the positive value of leadership generally to careful examination and comparison with the evidence and have concluded that

> despite starting with a model where "leaders matter" for growth, our main finding is that it is surprisingly difficult to confirm statistically significantly positive or negative leader growth effects for individual leaders. That is, knowing leaders matter for growth *in general* is very different from knowing *which* leaders matter for growth. We confirm significant positive or negative leader effects for less than 50 out of around 750 leaders with a tenure of at least 3 years (around 6% of leaders). Many of these are little known, forgotten, or surprising stars or villains. Autocrats are surprisingly under-represented in the set of statistically significant leaders, mostly because autocratic countries also have more noisy growth processes which make it difficult to isolate true leader effects.[18]

Of course, all political figures, whether democratic or autocratic, claim credit for anything good during their terms and blame anything bad on enemies, outsiders, saboteurs, and so forth. There's nothing new about that. What is remarkable is how many people attribute episodes of economic growth, not to trends already underway, or to other factors, but exclusively to "leadership." Politicians are always happy to accept the compliment.

Notes

1 Samuel Huntington and Joan Nelson, *No Easy Choice: Political Participation in Developing Countries* (Cambridge, MA: Harvard University Press, 1976), pp. 23, 24. An alternative approach emphasizes decentralized decision-making. Contrast Huntington's and Nelson's approach with that of Grace Goodell, who stresses active political involvement within a multiplicity of "fields of interaction," which "spring forth out of repeated dealings between people, and their regularity and intensity can be charted by actual observations," Grace Goodell, "The Importance of Political Participation for Sustained Capitalist Development," *European Journal of Sociology*, Vol. 26, No. 1, May 1985, pp. 93–127, 100.

If it is those who are active within a field of interaction who determine what is reasonable, hence determine law, these people themselves assure predictability in two ways: by providing *feedback* which defines the norm (often simply by objecting to new behavior), and by serving as *watchdogs* against the arbitrariness of coordinating or governing mechanisms.

(p. 103)

2 Fareed Zakaria, *The Future of Freedom: Illiberal Democracy at Home and Abroad*, rev. edn. (New York: W. W. Norton & Company, 2007), p. 61. The implications of Zakaria's claim are unclear; if a democracy might fail and become an autocracy, would that be a good reason not to embrace democracy?

3 Stephen Haggard, *Developmental States* (Cambridge: Cambridge University Press, 2018), p. 48. "In contrast to the property rights and 'rule of law' approach, the developmental state literature emphasized strong—and even authoritarian—executives and coherent, meritocratic, or 'Weberian' bureaucracies." p. 6.

4 Haggard, *Developmental States*, p. 45.

5 F. A. Hayek, "The Use of Knowledge in Society," in *Individualism and Economic Order*, ed. Hayek (Chicago: University of Chicago Press, 1980), pp. 78–79, Kindle Edition Location 1162.

6 Adam Smith, *Lectures on Jurisprudence,* eds. R. L. Meek, D. D. Raphael, and Peter Stein (Indianapolis, IN: Liberty Classics, 1982), p. 352.

7 Public good refers to goods that are publicly consumed and enjoyed; the term should not be assumed to apply to whatever a public body decides is good, which might entail sacrificing the many for the private enjoyment of the few, i.e., providing private goods at the expense of others. Paul Samuelson contrasts "private consumption goods" with "collective consumption goods $(X_{n+1}, \ldots, X_{n+m})$ which all enjoy in common in the sense that each individual's consumption of such a good leads to no subtraction from any other individual's consumption of that good," from "The Pure Theory of Public Expenditure," *Review of Economics and Statistics*, Vol. 36, No. 4, November 1954, pp. 387–389. Mancur Olson, *The Logic of Collective Action* (Cambridge, MA: Harvard University Press, 1965): "A common, collective, or public good is here defined as any good such that, if any person X_i in a group $X_1, \ldots, X_i, \ldots, X_n$ consumes it, it cannot feasibly be withheld from the others in that group," p. 14.

8 See W. B. Gallie, "Essentially Contested Concepts," *Proceedings of the Aristotelian Society*, Vol. 56, 1955, pp. 167–198.

9 Gallie, "Essentially Contested Concepts," p. 198.

10 1936 Constitution of the USSR, www.departments.bucknell.edu/russian/const/1936toc.html, www.departments.bucknell.edu/russian/const/36cons04.html#chap10.

11 Zakaria, *The Future of Freedom*, p. 16.

12 Bertrand de Jouvenel, *On Power: Its Nature and the History of Its Growth* (Boston: Beacon Press, 1962), pp. 254–282; J. L. Talmon, *The Origins of Totalitarian Democracy* (New York: W. W. Norton & Co., 1970).

13 Systematic preference falsification has been studied by Timur Kuran in his study *Private Truths, Public Lies: The Social Consequences of Preference Falsification* (Cambridge, MA: Harvard University Press, 1997).
14 F. A. Hayek, "Individualism: True and False," in *Individualism and Economic Order*, ed. Hayek (Chicago: University of Chicago Press, 1980), pp. 29–30, Kindle Edition Location 452. He continues,

> I believe, indeed, that one of the most important questions on which political theory will have to discover an answer in the near future is that of finding a line of demarcation between the fields in which the majority views must be binding for all and the fields in which, on the contrary, the minority view ought to be allowed to prevail if it can produce results which better satisfy a demand of the public. I am, above all, convinced that, where the interests of a particular branch of trade are concerned, the majority view will always be the reactionary, stationary view and that the merit of competition is precisely that it gives the minority a chance to prevail. Where it can do so without any coercive powers, it ought always to have the right.

15 James Buchanan, "Social Choice, Democracy, and Free Markets," *Journal of Political Economy*, Vol. 62, April 1954, pp. 114–123, reprinted in The Collected Works of James Buchanan, Vol. I, *The Logical Foundations of Constitutional Liberty* (Indianapolis, IN: Liberty Fund, 1999), pp. 89–102, 97. Buchanan considers the impossibility theorem associated with Kenneth Arrow to be not a weakness of democratic processes, but a strength:

> The definition of democracy as "government by discussion" implies that individual values can and do change in the process of decision-making. Men must be free to choose, and they maintain an open mind if the democratic mechanism is to work at all. If individual values in the Arrow sense of orderings of all social alternatives are unchanging, the discussion becomes meaningless. And the discussion must be considered as encompassing more than the activity prior to the initial vote.
>
> (p. 99)

16 That is not to say that the powers and membership of such bodies is not a matter of public choice at all, for while the membership in such bodies may be appointed for lengthy—even life—tenures, their initial selection, at least, remains a matter of public choice. Such selection procedures may be staggered with popular elections and those selected may rely to a large degree on the "Weberian bureaucracies" that advocates of the developmental state extol, but with the function, not of allocating capital, but of supervising election processes.
17 Mancur Olson, "Democracy, Dictatorship, and Development," *American Political Science Review*, Vol. 87, No. 3, September 1993, pp. 567–576, 569.
18 William Easterly and Steven Pennings, "Shrinking dictators: how much economic growth can we attribute to national leaders?" Paper presented

at Annual Bank Conference on Development Economics 2018: Political Incentives and Development Outcomes, June 25–26, 2018, Washington, DC, p. 26, https://pubdocs.worldbank.org/en/265381528721163955/EP2018 MayLeadersFinal.pdf. See also William Easterly, "Benevolent Autocrats," NYU Development Research Institute, DRI Working Paper No. 75, 2011, https://wp.nyu.edu/dri/2011/05/31/publications-benevolent-autocrats/.

5   Indignity of autocracy

Morton H. Halperin, Joseph T. Siegle, and Michael M. Weinstein examined the economic records of both democracies and autocracies, using data from the Polity IV Project and the World Bank, to address the thesis that democracy hinders growth at low incomes. They found that from the period from 1960 to 2005 (their study came out in 2010),

> despite the wide acceptance of the prevailing wisdom, democracies have, on average, out-performed autocracies on virtually every aspect of development considered. When a full sample of countries is considered, democracies have realized consistently higher levels of economic growth than autocracies during the past five decades.[1]

As they note, that is not very surprising, given that most wealthy countries are democracies, but the more interesting comparison was to take seriously the claims for autocratic governance of low-income countries. They found not only that low-income autocracies were more likely to have disastrous outcomes, but that "democracies, even low-income democracies, outperform autocracies in economic growth, in part because that growth is steadier and less prone to sudden, sharp dips. Their superior track record spares the poor much suffering."[2]

By updating the numbers in the Halperin, Siegle, and Weinstein study through 2018, and by more consistently comparing data, we also found a robust advantage for democracies over autocracies. For example, Halperin et al. took the democracy or autocracy score for 2008 and applied it to all previous years, but some countries shifted in or out of democracy or autocracy during the decades studied, so we adjusted the scores for each country year by year and matched the democracy and autocracy scores for each year with GDP growth rates for that year.[3] In addition, Halperin et al. used gross national income (GNI) data,[4] whereas we used gross domestic product (GDP) data, because GNI includes foreign aid

DOI: 10.4324/9781003229872-6

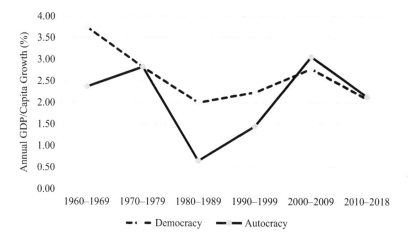

Figure 5.1 Median GDP growth rates for democracies and autocracies, global.

Data Source: The democracy/autocracy data were derived from the Polity IV database, www.systemicpeace.org/inscr/p4v2018.xls. GDP growth rates were taken from the World Bank's World Development Indicators, https://data.world bank.org/indicator/NY.GDP.PCAP.KD.ZG.

The democracy score used was the country's democracy score for that year. That is unlike in Halperin et al., where the authors selected the 2008 score as the democracy/autocracy score for all years. The democracy/autocracy data were derived from the Polity IV database, www.systemicpeace.org/inscr/p4v2018.xls. The same scores as Halperin et al. used were used to define democracy and autocracy, that is, 0 to 2 on the Polity IV = autocracy and 8 to 10 = democracy. GDP growth rates were taken from the World Bank's World Development Indicators, https://data.worldbank.org/indicator/NY.GDP.PCAP.KD.ZG.

and remittances from abroad, which occlude the actual productive economic activity in the country, whereas the GDP measure "represents the sum of value added by all its producers."[5]

When comparing the median GDP growth rates for democracies vs. autocracies from 1960 to 2018, one finds a strong advantage for democracies over autocracies, the latter of which exhibit greater variation. There is no global autocratic advantage.[6] The normal human bias toward assuming that some agency must be behind phenomena seems to guide people naturally to ascribing whatever happens in a country to its "leaders."

Halperin et al. then ran the data excluding East Asian countries, on the grounds that "the phenomenal growth experience of the East Asian Tigers noticeably skews the observed authoritarian growth rate."[7] When

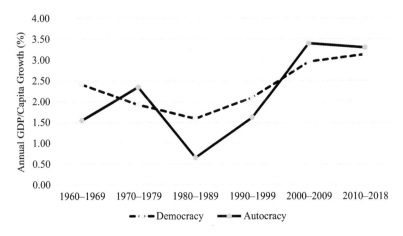

Figure 5.2 Median GDP growth rates for low-income democracies and autocracies.

Data Source: The democracy/autocracy data were derived from the Polity IV database, www.systemicpeace.org/inscr/p4v2018.xls. GDP growth rates were taken from the World Bank's World Development Indicators, https://data.world bank.org/indicator/NY.GDP.PCAP.KD.ZG.

The method for Figure 5.2 is the same as that for 5.1, except that the $2,000 GDP per capita cut-off used by Halperin et al. to focus on low-income coun-tries was adjusted to constant 2010 dollars ($2,532 GDP per capita) and the data were adjusted for each year so that some countries dropped out of the ranking as incomes rose above the cut-off. Moreover, whereas Halperin et al. changed their method from the earlier edition of the study and used both the Polity IV index and the Freedom House Index when running their low-income country analysis (*The Democracy Advantage* [New York: Routledge, 2010], Kindle Edition, location 4326), for the sake of consistency we used only Polity IV scores for every comparison.

we updated the data, we found that removing East Asian countries removed five democracies and eight autocracies, with the result that the remaining low-income autocracies have more consistently fallen further behind low-income democracies.

Democratic corrections

A major advantage of democracy is the institutionalization of means of correcting disastrous policies. Another advantage over autocracy is the relatively greater likelihood of making credibly consistent commitments

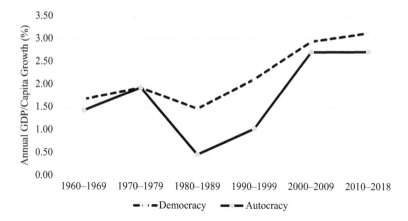

Figure 5.3 Median GDP growth rates for low-income democracies and autocracies, excluding East Asia.

Data Source: The democracy/autocracy data were derived from the Polity IV database, www.systemicpeace.org/inscr/p4v2018.xls. GDP growth rates were taken from the World Bank's World Development Indicators, https://data.world bank.org/indicator/NY.GDP.PCAP.KD.ZG.

not to confiscate investments, which commitments encourage longer-term investments, long-term contractual arrangements, and other positive ingredients of sustainable economic growth. Such credible commitment is also conducive to market-tested improvements, the drivers of economic growth. Democracies tend to be better able to overcome the problem of so-called time-inconsistency in decision-making. The problem of time-inconsistency in decision-making arises when, having made a commitment at one point, an agent later finds it not in her interest to fulfill it, notably when, having already secured the advantages of making the commitment, the agent has to undergo the costs of fulfilling that commitment. It's easy to promise at time T to do something at time $T + 1$, but when time $T + 1$ comes around, having already gotten the benefit from the promise at time T, one may feel less inclined to fulfill the commitment. A promise to respect another in the morning may be easy to say in the evening, in the throes of passion, but less easily carried out the next morning. The problem is that the incentive not to perform later what might be promised now makes itself felt at the start, because without a means of securing credible commitment not to confiscate their investments and assets, investors and traders will abstain from making long-term plans. The problem of time-inconsistency is faced not only by governments but by all parties engaged in any of a wide variety of interactions over time.[8]

Institutional economists, such as Douglass North and Barry Weingast, have argued that solutions to those problems are key to long-term economic growth.[9] A credible commitment necessarily entails limits on political power, for if the power is unlimited, it cannot make commitments. It is worth emphasizing again that, while such credible commitments not to confiscate assets are necessary to growth, they are not sufficient to realize an ongoing Great Enrichment, for which the liberty to innovate is indispensable. We would add that, while institutions may be the machinery by which commitment problems are solved, such machinery only works as well as the norms of those who operate it.

It is, of course, possible to cherry pick among the hundreds of autocracies in recent history to find a few that stumbled on some mechanisms of commitment. Ronald J. Gilson and Curtis J. Milhaupt identify three candidates for what they term "benevolent dictators," but their analysis provides no guidance for the decision of whether autocracy or democracy is preferable. They define an "economically benevolent" autocracy as one "whose leaders' utility functions rank long-term growth in GDP more highly than growth in their Swiss bank accounts, and thus use the power of the state to pursue national economic transformation."[10] They limit themselves to three allegedly benevolent dictatorships: Chile under Augusto Pinochet, South Korea under Park Chung-Hee, and China under Deng Xiaoping and his successors; they presume that the commitments made by those regimes were superior to those available to counterfactual democratic regimes; and they suggest, unconvincingly we believe, that the commitment mechanisms they identify offer useful guidance to "developing democracies." Despite the striking title, what their attempt succeeds in doing at best (as they acknowledge) is to identify pre-commitment techniques that might be available to democratic majoritarian coalitions, as well.[11] It is worth noting that Chile, which is identified by Gilson and Milhaupt as having benefited from a "benevolent dictator," has experienced higher rates of economic growth and more rapidly increasing standards of living than other Latin American countries but has had during the decades since a very low public understanding of economic policies, ranking 64 out of 74 countries, as shown in a newly developed measurement of "economic mentality" derived from the World Values Survey and the European Values Survey, the Global Index of Economic Mentality. This score is lower than Tajikistan, Zimbabwe, Nigeria, Nicaragua, and other countries with much lower rates of economic growth.[12]

Gilson and Milhaupt focus on a vitally important matter, which is how long-term and long-distance economic relations can emerge out of localized, kin-based, or similar limited-range relational exchanges, in which parties to economic exchange can credibly commit to fulfilling their obligations, but only within the limits of locality, kin, or similar circumscribed groups. Exchanges may take place with outsiders, but they tend to be limited to spot transactions. Mere willingness to haggle over prices in a bazaar is not a sufficient condition for the Great Enrichment. Bazaar economies, in which almost all transactions are spot transactions (that is, cash or barter for goods), with the transfers taking place simultaneously, are signs of institutional and normative underdevelopment, rather than promising signs of an exceptionally market-friendly mentality.

The extension of trust beyond small circles of kin or neighbors is a central element of the emergence of modern dignity and is made possible through the general liberal revaluation and associated institutional mechanisms, such as suretyship and reputation, the last now facilitated among an entire globe of complete strangers by credit bureaus and credit card companies, among other systems. Allegedly benevolent dictatorships have few, if any, lessons to share with democracies. Choosing three regimes from among hundreds, as Gilson and Milhaupt do, and then isolating commitment mechanisms conducive to investment, offers no support to autocratic regimes in general, as they acknowledge, and provides little guidance to developing democracies.

Liberal democratic norms and institutions provide their own vehicles for extending networks of trust and for solving—or at least ameliorating—the problem of time-inconsistency in decision-making, the latter by making the set of beneficiaries more likely (which is not to say certain) to be more inclusive. Some separation of substantial economic and political holdings (never entirely realized) diminishes incentives for winner-take-all struggles for power *and* wealth. The former El Salvadoran finance minister and World Bank division chief Manuel Hinds distinguishes one-dimensional societies ("Everything is reduced to a single dimension, the political one" that "turns political conflicts into all-or-nothing affairs") from multi-dimensional societies ("Economic and political power remain separate and independent from each other").[13]

Multi-dimensional societies are more likely than one-dimensional societies to be hospitable to innovative creation of value. If the holders of political authority also allocate or own the bulk of the wealth, they are more likely to oppose value-creating innovations, which typically erode the value of existing firms and capital. Consider as a recent example the ferocious opposition from taxicab companies to companies providing ride-sharing apps, which generated headlines worldwide such as "Europas Taxifahrer streiken gegen Uber," "Taxis contre Uber," "Alvo de críticas de taxistas, Uber abre escritório em São Paulo," and "Cab companies unite against Uber and other ride-share services."[14]

The gains of innovation are likely to be widely dispersed, while the losses from the introduction of innovations are likely to be concentrated on existing producers, who generally exercise much greater political power than do unorganized potential consumers who would stand to gain from innovations; when the political decision-makers are also the economic decision-makers, the concentration of losses on their heads means that innovation is far more likely to be stymied.

Democratic majorities are less likely to be rapacious than autocrats, because the majority also produce and own wealth they stand to lose, in addition to what might be gained through redistribution. As Mancur Olson notes,

> Though both the majority and the autocrat have an encompassing interest in the society because they control tax collections, the majority additionally earns a significant share of the market income of the society, which gives it a more encompassing interest in the society's productivity. The majority's interest in its market earnings induces it to redistribute less to itself than an autocrat distributes to himself.[15]

Olson strengthens his point by applying the same logic to the common democratic experience of super-encompassing majorities in systems of representative government. When one focuses on blocking innovation and not solely on redistribution of tax revenues, Olson's point is strengthened even further, because the great bulk of the gains from innovations lies in the future and tends to accrue to large and unorganized swathes, if not to virtually the entirety, of the population. In contrast, the much smaller losses from innovation tend to fall more immediately and on far more concentrated, known, and easily organized segments of the population, e.g., already established producers who do not adopt the innovation or whose capital is specific to the pre-innovation form of production and which thus falls in value.

The problem of succession of power means that the time horizons of autocrats tend to be not longer, but *shorter* than those of encompassing majorities.[16] Although electoral cycles suggest time horizons for political leaders that are shorter than those of investors, the time horizons of democratically elected leaders are still likely to be longer and more encompassing than autocrats who fear losing power to a rival, partly because the losing politician is generally still able to run for office again in future. Not fearing imprisonment, exile, or execution also works to lengthen the horizon of politicians in democratic polities.

The dispersion of knowledge played a key role in the scientific revolution that had a transformative impact on European societies. Joel Mokyr has focused attention on the emergence of a "culture of progress."[17] A Republic of Letters dispersed across many political jurisdictions, with regular communication among its members, meant that no entity was able to suppress the emergence of new ideas.[18] What facilitated the emergence of a Republic of Letters was not simply investment in education, as we are often told, for the stultifying Chinese mandarinate was nothing, if not highly educated, but the difficulty faced by established authorities who tried to prevent, but failed to prevent, the emergence and spread of new ideas. The growth of a Republic of Letters contributed to, but was not the essential ingredient in, the emergence of a culture of progress. What else was needed was a liberal revaluation, which drove the extension of the presumption of liberty to every class and creed, to every color and language, to everyone. The resulting culture of progress welcomes value-creating innovation, as well as freedom to work, capital accumulation, investment, freedom of contract, freedom of entry and exit, and the other central elements of economic development.

In 1920, historian J. B. Bury distinguished two theories of progress that correspond to the two approaches described here, that of the authoritarian "developmental state," on the one hand, and what Deirdre McCloskey calls "innovism," on the other.

> Theories of Progress are thus differentiating into two distinct types, corresponding to two radically opposed political theories and appealing to two antagonistic temperaments. The one type is that of constructive idealists and socialists, who can name all the streets and towers of "the city of gold," which they imagine as situated just round a promontory. The development of man is a closed system; its term is known and is within reach. The other type is that of those who, surveying the gradual ascent of man, believe that by the same interplay of forces which have conducted him so far and by a further development of the liberty which he has fought to win, he will move slowly towards conditions of increasing harmony and happiness. Here the development is indefinite; its term is unknown, and lies in the remote future. Individual liberty is the motive force, and the corresponding political theory is liberalism; whereas the first doctrine naturally leads to a symmetrical system in which the authority of the state is preponderant, and the individual has little more value

than a cog in a well-oiled wheel: his place is assigned; it is not his right to go his own way.[19]

Importing social technologies

Even very-low-income countries have seen increases in lifespans, health, communications, and more to levels much higher than those attained by residents of the wealthy countries of only fifty years earlier, without having adopted many of the principles of liberal democracy and of "innovism." An obvious example is the mobile phone, which was until recently only available to the very wealthy in rich countries and is now ubiquitous—and incalculably better, incorporating video cameras, translators, entertainment, GPS maps, dictionaries, fitness programs, and far more—in very poor countries. The reason is that production technologies are comparatively easy to transport from one country to another, while social technologies are not generally transplanted so easily.[20]

It is our thesis that people working in their own countries are more likely to be able to introduce—or more generally, to adapt or evolve—new social technologies that are conducive to development. Distant actors in Washington, London, Geneva, Paris, Tokyo, New York, or other centers of the international development industry have less knowledge of the facts on the ground, of the opportunities for change, and of the politics of coalition building than do local actors. And when it comes to social technologies, local actors also are far more likely to know what can be imported, what needs to be adapted, and what existing indigenous institutions provide services analogous or equivalent to those familiar to foreigners in their home countries. As Ghanaian economist George B. N. Ayittey quipped, when foreign officials observed African tontines and savings clubs, they referred to them as "primitive communist accumulation," whereas in the United States, they are called "savings and loan associations."[21]

Among the legacies of colonialism in Africa was the external imposition of rulership that made the take-up of liberal democratic institutions and norms especially difficult. Policies of "indirect rule" designated preferred Africans as agents of the colonial power and essentially made them unaccountable to the African people over whom they were given power, which was backed up by colonial armies. As Olúfẹ́mi Táíwò noted in *How Colonialism Preempted Modernity in Africa*, modernity and modern notions of dignity were suffocated in Africa:

Where the modern legal system was anchored on individual responsibility, the colonial legal system was suffused with laws requiring collective responsibility; where the modern legal system allowed the manifestation of subjective will in action without undue restriction, the colonial legal system hemmed in native subjective will with myriad restrictions, including, especially, spatial ones; where the modern legal system was founded upon respect for the integrity of the person, the colonial system legitimized or required forced labor that was, at bottom, a denial of subjectivity; where the modern legal system sought to cloak itself in legitimacy founded on the consent of the governed through the latter having a say in the constitution of their government, the colonial legal system made it a felony—sedition—for those who asked that they not be ruled by a government in the constitution of which they had no say; where the modern legal system had a built-in presumption of innocence for an accused, the colonial legal system had a built-in presumption of guilt until proven innocent for native accused because, according to the image of the native that dominated the thinking of the colonial administrators, Africans were congenital liars.[22]

When the colonial powers left, to one extent or another, the states they left behind were inheritors of systems of substantially unaccountable rulers. Indirect rule in Africa can be compared to the Spanish imperial practice of ruling entirely through Spanish-born agents, which left a varied, but lasting, legacy across the former Spanish empire. Contrast that with the statement of modern democratic dignity from the Leveller leader Colonel Thomas Rainborough in the Putney Debates:

> For really I think that the poorest he that is in England hath a life to live, as the greatest he; and therefore truly, sir, I think it's clear, that every man that is to live under a government ought first by his own consent to put himself under that government; and I do think that the poorest man in England is not at all bound in a strict sense to that government that he hath not had a voice to put himself under.[23]

Overcoming the legacies of colonial administration and indirect rule is one of the most important challenges of post-colonial countries. The attempt to operate institutions that were left behind by foreign occupiers was, unsurprisingly, not very successful. The attempt to import foreign development agendas has been more of the same—less brutal, but no less a failure. As Ayittey concludes: "Enough development by imitation. The continent is already littered with putrid corpses of failed imported systems."[24] Embracing democratic dignity means that local people lead change, whether it is undoing the harmful legacies of colonialism or creating locally rooted systems of accountability and securing for their own people the blessings of the presumption of liberty and the dignity of self-government.

Democratic (civic) dignity

Political scientist and classics scholar Josiah Ober has identified four kinds of dignity—*meritocratic, elite peerage, civic,* and *human*.[25] The first two are restricted categories that are rooted in aristocratic social orders. The third—*civic dignity,* the dignity foundational to democratic governance— is the focus of our inquiry, although it is strongly interwoven with human dignity, as well. Focusing on civic dignity brings out the political and legal aspects of dignity, which involve not only one's expectations of respect for oneself—the respect accorded to one by others, but also the respect that one accords to others, just as bourgeois dignity accords respect to others and expects it in return.

Being able to hold one's head up and to face others as their legal equal is at the heart of dignity, whether characterized as bourgeois or civic. It is relational and not merely internal or self-contained. An enslaved person may act in a dignified way, or maintain his or her dignity, but not be respected by others. A person in such a state typically will still desire that others respect her or his dignity; indeed, it's one reason oppressed and brutalized people sometimes magnify their dignity, precisely to demonstrate to themselves and to others that they are better than the humiliating treatment they receive.

In a society characterized by civic dignity, dignity is publicly, as well as privately, recognized. As Ober describes it,

> Dignity certainly involves self-esteem, and we may retain an irreducible core of inviolable personal dignity as self-respect no matter what we suffer at the hands of others. In practice, however, living with dignity involves the regard in which we are held by others, and how we are treated by them. Our dignity is manifested in how we behave toward others, and in how they behave toward us. The dignity relevant to democracy is, in substantial measure, a matter of the respect and recognition we publicly accord to one another, through our words and our actions.[26]

That kind of dignity enjoyed by the *demos*, the common people, characterized the first political communities to bear the name *democracy* and it is that characteristic of civic dignity that sustained them. It is worth underscoring that the demos did not include the entirety of the human population. In that respect classical democracy was in many ways an early prototype of modern democracy and should in no way be romanticized as an ethical or political ideal. The principles took millennia to be applied consistently and required the advent of liberalism, thus, of liberal democracy, for its fruition in the modern world. Despite their manifest flaws, early prototypes still contain important lessons for later versions, and it is to those that we look when studying the democratic prototypes of antiquity.

The Athenian orator and democrat Demosthenes, in his prosecution of Meidias for publicly assaulting him and seeking to humiliate him, after making his case, concluded his address to the Athenian jury with a reminder of what it meant to be a citizen of a democratic polity:

> Just think. The instant this court rises, each of you will walk home, one quicker, another more leisurely, not anxious, not glancing behind him, not fearing whether he is going to run up against a friend or an enemy, a big man or a little one, a strong man or a weak one, or anything of that sort. And why? Because in his heart he knows, and is confident, and has learned to trust the Polity, that no one shall seize or insult or strike him.[27]

That confidence in one's dignity was not due to the physical power of one person or his ability to defend himself in combat, but due to the confidence all had in the laws and to the widespread willingness to defend the dignity and rights of others. Demosthenes reminded the Athenian jurors that

> it is not that you alone of the citizens are drawn up under arms, not that your physical powers are at their best and strongest, not that you are in the earliest prime of manhood; it is due to no cause of that sort but simply to the strength of the laws. And what is the strength of the laws? If one of you is wronged and cries aloud, will the laws run up and be at his side to assist him? No; they are only written texts and incapable of such action. Wherein then resides their power? In yourselves, if only you support them and make them all-powerful to help him who needs them. So the laws are strong through you and you through the laws.[28]

The civic dignity of the ancient world is different in many respects from that of modernity, but the origins of civic culture provide some lessons and some standards for the role of dignity in grounding active citizenship in support of the public good, that is to say, of the framework for the mutual pursuit of our various goods. As Aristotle described the popular understanding of democracy,

> (1) Now the basic premise of the democratic sort of regime is freedom. It is [1317b] customarily said that only in this sort of regime do men partake of freedom, for, so it is asserted, every democracy aims at this. One aspect of freedom is being ruled and ruling in turn. (2) The justice that is characteristically popular is to have equality on the basis of number and not on the basis of merit; where justice is of this sort, the multitude must necessarily have authority, and what is resolved by the majority must be final and must be justice, for, they assert, each of the citizens must have an equal share. The result is that in democracies the poor have more authority than the well off, for they are the majority, and what is resolved by the majority is authoritative. (3) This, then, is one mark of freedom, and it is regarded by those of the popular sort as the defining principle of the regime. Another is to live as one wants. For this is, they assert, the work of freedom, since not living as one wants is characteristic of a person who is enslaved. (4) This, then, is the second defining principle of democracy. From it has come [the claim to merit] not being ruled by anyone, or failing this, [to rule and be ruled] in turn. It contributes in this way to the freedom that is based on equality.[29]

Government by discussion is historically grounded in the culture of civic dignity. In practice, democratic Athens exemplified civic dignity in the practices of *isegoria* (equality of speech), *isonomia* (equal application of laws), and *isokratia* (equality of political power). Those principles have long been spread across the globe. They are not the property of any one culture but the framework for development for all. Modern dignity demands democracy.

In his famous speech on ancient and modern liberty, Benjamin Constant insisted that modern liberty embraced what we have called (following Deirdre McCloskey) bourgeois dignity when he defined it as

> the right to be subjected only to the laws, and to be neither arrested, detained, put to death or maltreated in any way by the arbitrary will of one or more individuals. It is the right of everyone to express their opinion, choose a profession and practice it, to dispose of property, and even to abuse it; to come and go without permission, and without having to account for their motives or undertakings. It is everyone's right to associate with other individuals, either to discuss their interests, or to profess the religion which they and their

associates prefer, or even simply to occupy their days or hours in a way which is most compatible with their inclinations or whims.

He concluded his definition, however, with what we have called (following Josiah Ober) civic dignity: "Finally it is everyone's right to exercise some influence on the administration of the government, either by electing all or particular officials, or through representations, petitions, demands to which the authorities are more or less compelled to pay heed."[30]

Bourgeois dignity and the presumption of liberty are incomplete and unstable without civic dignity and active democratic politics. We quoted this warning from Constant earlier, but it is so important that we consider it worth quoting again, because his warning is so relevant to contemporary debates about autocratic "managed (pseudo) democracies" vs. liberal democracy.

> The danger of modern liberty is that, absorbed in the enjoyment of our private independence, and in the pursuit of our particular interests, we should surrender our right to share in political power too easily. The holders of authority are only too anxious to encourage us to do so. They are so ready to spare us all sort of troubles, except those of obeying and paying! They will say to us: what, in the end, is the aim of your efforts, the motive of your labors, the object of all your hopes? Is it not happiness? Well, leave this happiness to us and we shall give it to you. No, Sirs, we must not leave it to them. No matter how touching such a tender commitment may be, let us ask the authorities to keep within their limits. Let them confine themselves to being just. We shall assume the responsibility of being happy for ourselves.[31]

No matter how many emoluments and false promises are offered by autocrats, their rule is no improvement over liberal democracy. And no matter how tender the commitments of outsiders, they cannot develop other people. Those who strive to become prosperous must not leave their development to others. Outsiders may help, but they must keep within their limits. The development of poor communities and of poor countries is in the hands of the poor. They are the agents of their own development.

Notes

1   Morton H. Halperin, Joseph T. Siegle, and Michael M. Weinstein, *The Democracy Advantage: How Democracies Promote Prosperity and Peace* (New York: Routledge, 2010), Kindle Edition, location 828.

2 Halperin, Siegle, and Weinstein, *The Democracy Advantage*, location 895. One advocate of autocratic statism, behavioral psychologist B. F. Skinner, considered evidence of this sort beside the point because "the real mistake is to stop trying." He argued that

> if planned economies, benevolent dictatorships, perfectionist societies, and other utopian ventures have failed, we must remember that unplanned, undictated, and unperfected cultures have failed too. A failure is not always a mistake; it may simply be the best one can do under the circumstances. The real mistake is to stop trying.
>
> (B. F. Skinner, *Beyond Freedom and Dignity*
> (New York: Vintage Books, 1971), p. 148)

3 Halperin, Siegle, and Weinstein, *The Democracy Advantage*, location 4319, Appendix C.
4 Halperin, Siegle, and Weinstein, *The Democracy Advantage*, location 4326, Appendix C.
5 World Bank, Metadata Glossary, https://databank.worldbank.org/metadatag lossary/gender-statistics/series/NY.GDP.MKTP.CD.
6 Other studies undermine the common belief that "leaders" are responsible for positive economic outcomes. For example, Stephanie M. Rizo and Ahmed Skali analyzed even larger data sets on "economic growth, political regimes, and political leaders over the 1858–2010 period" and found that

> Growth-positive autocrats, which are those leaders whose countries experience larger than average economic growth, are found only as frequently as one would predict based on chance alone. This finding is robust to several alternate definitions of political regimes, and also to alternate measures of economic success. Thus, we find no evidence to suggest that autocratic leaders are successful at delivering economic growth in any systematic way. In contrast, we show that growth-negative autocrats are found significantly more frequently than chance would predict.
>
> (Stephanie M. Rizo and Almed Skali, "How Often Do Dictators
> Have Positive Economic Effects? Global Evidence, 1858–2010,"
> *The Leadership Quarterly*, Vol. 31, 2020, pp. 1–18, 2)

7 Halperin, Siegle, and Weinstein, *The Democracy Advantage*, location 851.
8

> Commitment problems are not only present in politics but also in all areas of social life. Almost all economic transactions have a temporal dimension. Traders typically deliver goods today but receive payment tomorrow. A commitment problem arises if customers promise to make a payment tomorrow but, when tomorrow comes, it is not in their interest to make the payment. In this case, they renege on their promises and fail to make the payment. Therefore, there is ample room for commitment problems in social and economic relations.
>
> (Daron Acemoglu and James A. Robinson, *Economic
> Origins of Dictatorship and Democracy* (Cambridge:
> Cambridge University Press, 2006), p. 134)

9 Douglass C. North and Barry Weingast, "Constitutions and Commitment: The Evolution of Institutions Governing Public Choice in Seventeenth-Century England," *The Journal of Economic History*, Vol. XLIX, No. 4, December 1989, pp. 803–832.

10 Ronald J. Gilson and Curtis J. Milhaupt, "Economically Benevolent Dictators: Lessons for Developing Countries," *The American Journal of Comparative Law*, Vol. 59, No. 1, Winter 2011, pp. 227–288, 229. As they note, the allegedly benevolent motivations may have been a matter of "sheer luck," which would make it a rather weak foundation for a development strategy.

11 It is worth noting the contentious claim of Gilson and Milhaupt that "from the 1990s to the present, Chinese growth has been state led. Reforms in the second phase focused on improving the performance of state-owned or affiliated enterprises and the expansion of foreign direct investment" (p. 260). According to a careful examination of the accounting of State-Owned Enterprises (SOEs) in China, including the subsidies granted to SOEs, which receive preferential tax treatment, do not pay land rents or resource rents, and pay lower interest rates to state banks, Chinese economists Sheng Hong and Zhao Nong concluded that SOEs actually lose money and "play a negative role in income distribution." Sheng Hong and Zhao Nong, *China's State-Owned Enterprises: Nature, Performance and Reform* (Singapore: World Scientific Publishing, 2013), p. 124.

12 Global Index of Economic Mentality, preliminary findings, www.atlasnetwork.org/assets/uploads/misc/GIEMREVISED4.pdf.

13 Manuel Hinds, *In Defense of Liberal Democracy* (Watertown, MA: Imagine Books, 2021), pp. 79–83.

14 Headlines from *Die Welt, Le Point, Folha de São Paulo*, and *The Washington Post*: "Europas Taxifahrer streiken gegen Uber" www.welt.de/wirtschaft/gallery128968543/Europas-Taxifahrer-streiken-gegen-Uber.html; "Taxis contre Uber: « On est dans une situation de concurrence illicite » www.lepoint.fr/editos-du-point/laurence-neuer/taxis-contre-uber-on-est-dans-une-situation-de-concurrence-illicite-20-07-2020-2384856_56.php; « Alvo de críticas de taxistas, Uber abre escritório em São Paulo," www1.folha.uol.com.br/tec/2014/08/1500063-alvo-de-criticas-de-taxistas-uber-abre-escritorio-em-sao-paulo.shtml; "Cab companies unite against Uber and other ride-share services," www.washingtonpost.com/local/trafficandcommuting/cab-companies-unite-against-uber-and-other-ride-share-services/2014/08/10/11b23d52-1e3f-11e4-82f9-2cd6fa8da5c4_story.html.

15 Mancur Olson, *Power and Prosperity* (New York: Perseus Books, 2000), p. 16.

16

> Our basic interpretation of the evidence suggests that limited governments allow faster city growth because they tend to impose lower and less destructive tax rates. One effect, however, might point in the direction of suggesting that lower tax rates would be found under absolutist princes. Absolutists might have a longer time horizon than merchants if their businesses have relatively short lives while princes' realms are passed on to their children. As a result, absolutist princes who

belong to stable dynasties might care about present and future economic prosperity because it increases the future tax base. If absolutists care more about the long run than do merchants or estates, they would tend to impose lower tax rates and nurture economic growth. While attractive theoretically, this argument appears to be wrong empirically. It is a mistake to think that princes establish stable dynasties. In Europe the time horizons of princes are short.

> (J. Bradford DeLong and Andrei Schleifer, "Princes and Merchants: European City Growth Before the Industrial Revolution," *Journal of Law and Economics*, Vol. XXXVI, October 1993, pp. 671–702, 699)

They test their thesis that the time horizons of autocrats are short due to uncertain succession by considering one of the strongest and longest-lasting monarchies in Europe: that of England. Examination of the list of English rulers for five hundred years showed that "there was only a 22 percent chance that the English throne would pass peacefully down to the legitimate grandson (or other heir of the second generation) of any monarch," p. 700.

17 Joel Mokyr, "Progress, Useful Knowledge, and the Origins of the Industrial Revolution," in, *Institutions, Innovation, and Industrialization*, eds. Avner Greif, Lynne Kiesling, and John V. C. Nye (Princeton: Princeton University Press, 2015), pp. 33–67.

18 Mokyr describes the condition for the creation and dissemination of useful knowledge as "political fragmentation within an intellectually unified market," Joel Mokyr, "Culture, Institutions, and Modern Growth," in *Institutions, Property Rights, and Economic Growth*, eds. Sebastiani Galiani and Itai Sened (Cambridge: Cambridge University Press, 2014), pp. 151–191, 176. See also Joel Mokyr, *A Culture of Growth: The Origins of the Modern Economy* (Princeton, NJ: Princeton University Press, 2017),

> the European Enlightenment … involved two highly innovative and complementary ideas: the concept that knowledge and the understanding of nature can and should be used to advance the material conditions of humanity, and the belief that power and government are there not to serve the rich and powerful but society at large.
>
> (p. 341)

19 J. B. Bury, *The Idea of Progress: An Inquiry into Its Growth and Origin* (New York: Dover Publications, 1955), p. 236.

20 The distinction is at the center of Thráinn Eggertsson's *Imperfect Institutions: Possibilities and Limits of Reform* (Ann Arbor, MI: University of Michigan Press, 2005).

21 George B. N. Ayittey, "African Peasants and the Market System," *Humane Studies Review*, Vol. 5, No. 3, April 1988, p. 5.

22 Olúfémi Táíwò, *How Colonialism Preempted Modernity in Africa* (Bloomington, IN: Indiana University Press, 2010), p. 186. The harmful legacy of indirect rule and the stifling of indigenous forms of accountable government is

described in detail by George B. N. Ayittey in *Indigenous African Institutions* (Ardsley-on-Hudson: Transnational Publishers, 1991).

23 In A. S. P. Woodhouse, ed., *Puritanism and Liberty: Being the Army Debates (1647) from the Clarke Manuscripts with Supplementary Documents* (London: J. M. Dent & Sons, Ltd., 1992), p. 53.

24 George B. N. Ayittey, *Africa Unchained: The Blueprint for Africa's Future* (New York: Palgrave Macmillan, 2005), p. 334.

25 Josiah Ober, "Democracy's Dignity," *American Political Science Review*, Vol. 106, No. 4, November 2012, pp. 827–846.

26 Ober, "Democracy's Dignity," pp. 831–832.

27 Demosthenes, "Against Meidias," *Orations XXI–XXVI*, trans. J. H. Vince (Cambridge, MA: Harvard University Press, 1935), 221–222, pp. 147–149. We have substituted "Polity" for "State" in Vince's translation to avoid an annoying anachronism. We also use "he" and "his" because, at that time, such expectations were those of men, and not of all of them, although women in such societies tended to have more rights and more dignity than in others where the degraded status of the men permitted them to degrade and humiliate women all the more.

28 Demosthenes, "Against Meidias," 224–225, p. 149.

29 Aristotle, *The Politics*, trans. Carnes Lord (2nd ed., Chicago: University of Chicago Press, 2013), VI, 2, pp. 172–173. Fustel de Coulanges famously claimed that "The ancients knew … neither liberty in private life, liberty in education, nor religious liberty. The human person counted for very little against that holy and almost divine authority which was called country or the state," Fustel de Coulanges, Numa Denis Fustel de Coulanges, *The Ancient City* (New York: Doubleday Anchor, 1956), p. 222. That claim, at least with regard to the Athenian democracy, is effectively rebutted by Mogens Herman Hansen, *The Athenian Democracy in the Age of Demosthenes* (Norman, OK: University of Oklahoma Press, 1999), and by Kurt Raaflaub, *The Discovery of Freedom in Ancient Greece* (Chicago: University of Chicago Press, 2004).

30 Benjamin Constant, *The Liberty of the Ancients Compared to That of the Moderns* (1816; Indianapolis, IN: Liberty Fund, 2011), p. 6, https://oll-resources.s3.us-east-2.amazonaws.com/oll3/store/titles/2251/Constant_Liberty1521_EBk_v6.0.pdf.

31 Constant, *The Liberty of the Ancients*, p. 17.

6 Indignity of development aid

Simon Bland, who worked in Kenya for what was, at the time, the UK's Department of International Development, once gave journalist Nina Munk a succinct picture of development's failures in the region: "Broken water pumps, half-finished healthcare clinics, abandoned housing blocks, roads that lead nowhere, dams that have collapsed. Africa is strewn with the remains of well-meaning development projects. The problem is when you walk away, what happens?"[1] Those types of failures are not confined to Africa. Reflecting on the aftermath of the 2004 tsunami, a Sri Lankan official was quoted in *Aid on the Edge of Chaos* as saying, "I don't know which was worse, the first wave of water or the second wave of aid."[2]

In 2017, World Bank economists Michael Woolcock and Kate Bridges asked, "Why do development agencies persist with approaches that are routinely acknowledged as problematic?"[3] It's a good question. The failures of traditional aid are well documented and diverse voices have called for reform. So, why hasn't it happened? To better understand the answer to that question and to get a sense of the type of change needed, we next explore *why* aid has failed.

In November 2019, Harvard University's Nathan Nunn published "Rethinking Economic Development," in which he provided a summary of what has been learned about aid's impact on developing countries. We highlight here four main areas of concern.[4]

The bulk of foreign aid has been tied to spending practices favoring the donor country. The US government stands out especially, with the highest proportion of tied aid, which acts effectively as promotion of favored industries and firms. The tying of aid to goods and services produced in donor countries raises their costs "by 15–30 percent on average and by 40 percent" in the case of food.[5]

Foreign aid feeds corruption. A large proportion of aid goes missing. Thirty percent is not uncommon and there are documented cases where

DOI: 10.4324/9781003229872-7

100 percent of aid dollars never reached their intended destinations. Aid increases domestic rent-seeking and encourages destructive maneuvering. Economic growth does not make up for the corruption aid enables; the relationship of foreign aid to economic growth is elusive at best.

"Foreign aid does not fuel growth-promoting investments (or growth itself) but instead crowds out domestic savings and increases consumption of foreign products."[6] (We should note that increased consumption of foreign products would not be a bad thing by itself if those foreign products were purchased by domestic production.)

Foreign aid can exacerbate the potential for conflict. Even food aid has been sold off to increase military preparedness. One study found that, on average, "the year following an increase in US foreign aid into a country, there is an increase in killings, repression and torture by the state."[7]

Add to this list the very real concern that foreign aid undermines government accountability to its citizens in budding democracies. In recipient countries, elected officials and their ministries face perverse incentives as they cater to the demands of outside powers. Often they have to devote much of their time and attention to complying with aid-related administrative requirements and shuttling to meetings outside of the country.

Consider the case of Tanzania, a country in Africa for which foreign aid over the last ten years has ranged between 30 percent and 70 percent of the government's budget.[8] Imagine the impact such an outsized contribution has on political leaders and their accountability to their own citizens. It's not only a drain on time. The consequences can manifest themselves in alarming ways. In Sierra Leone, for example, officials once organized a party to celebrate the news they had once again landed at the bottom of the UN Development Programme's list of worst countries in the world, thus ensuring another year of aid largesse.[9]

Even when aid comes with few strings attached, recipient country governments have often failed to use funds in the best interests of their citizens. Linda Polman, a Dutch journalist who spent fifteen years covering humanitarian crises, has documented a pattern of mismanagement and corruption by unaccountable elites who used aid funds to advance their own ambitions. Her book, *The Crisis Caravan,* is an eye-opening tour through the moral dilemmas that challenge conventional assumptions about what outsiders can really do to help. From Darfur to Goma, Kabul to Addis Ababa, aid has proven to be highly susceptible to the opportunism of the most egregious, criminal-minded actors within recipient country power structures.[10]

Decolonizing development

Emma Mawdsley, who wrote a 2020 book about the unhealthy dynamics dominating donor and recipient country relationships, is not optimistic that governments of wealthy nations will soon change their ways. Instead, she looks to ordinary people and to civil society groups in recipient countries to demand that their governments break the aid cycle.[11] Calls for civil society leadership and increased grassroots influence over aid power dynamics are starting to mount. For example, the international NGO *Peace Direct* gathered 158 activists, academics, and development practitioners in November 2020 to discuss the status of donor dominance over the development agenda. The results of that discussion were summarized in a fifty-six-page report that called for a renewed commitment to valuing local knowledge over outsider priorities. Per the assessment of those participating,

> Many current practices and attitudes in the aid system mirror and are derived from the colonial-era, which most organisations and donors in the Global North are still reluctant to acknowledge. Certain modern-day practices and norms reinforce colonial dynamics and beliefs such as the "White saviour" ideology visible in fundraising and communications imagery used by INGOs, to the organisational structures of INGOs in the Global South and the attitudes of some White international aid workers working in Global South.[12]

The report's focus on issues of race converges with broader themes on racial equality currently rippling across the Global North (a shorthand term for the traditional set of donor countries). Even more recently, in February 2021, the *New York Times* editorial board published their view on those trends with the title, "Foreign Aid Is Having a Reckoning."[13] To illustrate their argument, they draw a parallel between the Black Lives Matter movement in the United States and growing indignation among people of color living in the Global South who are tired of foreign elites intervening paternalistically in their countries. Under the slogan "Decolonize Development," the movement is working to shift decision-making power away from the Global North.

The *Times* describes the work of Degan Ali, an activist and NGO leader in Kenya:

> Ms. Ali believes that if global institutions were more fair when it comes to lending money and removing barriers to trade, African countries wouldn't need so much aid. She wants to make the

top-down, foreign-dominated system of handing out assistance a relic of the past.

According to Ali, "The first step is to immediately cease the marketing of people in the Global South as passive 'beneficiaries' of aid who need 'white saviors.'"

Growing dissatisfaction with development aid is helping to highlight the indignity that unseen individuals suffer at the mercy and (in)competence of distant sources of power. MacArthur Genius award winner Mauricio Miller, whose efforts to revolutionize poverty work in America led to an appointment within the Obama administration, argues that this power imbalance is universal when it comes to outsiders taking over the lives of poor people. In the context of social services, he advocates a radical non-interventionist approach in his book, *The Alternative: Most of What You Believe about Poverty Is Wrong*. The new paradigm Miller envisions "requires us to recognize that the everyday initiative of the many plays a more critical role than the grand gestures of those we designate as heroes."[14] Or, as Emma Mawdsley puts it, in the context of international development, "Western foreign aid is inherently demeaning and humiliating, founded as it is on a set of colonial and post-colonial hierarchies that assume the superiority of 'Western' ideas, models and norms, and the right to intervene."[15] That we would perpetuate a costly set of programs that, in the end, fail to demonstrate much positive impact and, at the same time, foist new indignities on vulnerable communities speaks to the intractable mess the aid industrial complex has become. Indeed, why does it continue when we know it is ineffective and does harm?

Resistance to change

Pablo Yanguas, in *Why We Lie about Aid*, offers a very human explanation for why the development community is loath to change its ways:

> Proponents of aid, in turn, are usually the very same people whose livelihoods and very sense of professional identity depend on its continuation: their involvement in the aid ecosystem makes them almost blindly supportive of larger budgets, and it is unclear whether their claim to speak "for the people" actually holds up to scrutiny.[16]

The false idea that, for poor countries, unelected outsiders are appropriate decision-makers, fashioning strategies for development on behalf of indigenous populations, has been justified by the mistaken notion that development precedes the emergence of democratic norms. That denial of the self-determining human dignity of a country's people has only emboldened the rampant paternalism that permeates development practice today.

The scourges of paternalism are so pervasive and hard to reverse precisely because it is so easy for outsiders to believe that they are best equipped, with their formal educations, degrees, and resources, to make a positive difference. Development professionals may entertain new ideas for improving aid, but too often they stop short of seriously considering alternatives that would challenge their own leadership roles in the process. That paternalist mindset has been baked into an overly simplistic and dehumanizing model that leads experts to overestimate their ability to evaluate the rightness of other's economic decisions.

In *Escaping Paternalism: Rationality, Behavioral Economics, and Public Policy*, economists Mario Rizzo and Glen Whitman investigate the intellectual roots of today's prescriptive solutions to social problems and expose a fallacy in common mental models. It's the mistake of believing that our existing models of human behavior are sufficiently representative of the human experience that they can reliably reveal to us what a person *ought* to do to optimize her utility, regardless of context. One reason that approach leads to error is that it assumes that important variables, such as someone's preferences, can be accounted for in the model. The problem is that preferences, or what people would reference to explain their own decisions, do not really exist independently of the decisions we want to predict. They are constructed in the process of negotiating and adapting to changing circumstances. Conceptualizing them as preexisting information we can collect and analyze is a mistake that has had serious negative consequences.

Many development theorists, like the central planners of old, confuse information with knowledge. Information can be written up in reports, set out in tables and graphs, and transmitted, accumulated, and analyzed. Knowledge involves far more, including perception, experience, practice, discourse, and interpretation.[17] Paternalists of the modern sort tend to exalt information, which they can collect about the objects of their study, and they dismiss the knowledge they cannot collect. That "expert mindset," in turn, reinforces the paternalist impulses of policymakers who see themselves as vindicated in advancing their own ends. According to Rizzo and Whitman, those "policymakers will tend to promote some combination of their own preferences, socially approved preferences, or special-interest preferences—none of which are synonymous with the real preferences of people targeted by paternalist laws."[18]

Rizzo and Whitman argue for a much more useful "inclusive rationality" applied to a "paternalism-resisting framework" rather than a "paternalism-generating framework" for public policy.[19] This broader view helps us see that as outsiders we should not dismiss other people's behavior as irrational just because it challenges our own assumptions about what they should think, want, or do. That is not to pretend that every human decision is optimal. Practically speaking, we all make mistakes we regret. The important question is not, "How can we better figure out what other people ought to be doing?" The important question should be, "Under what conditions are people most likely able to discover and act on decisions that match their own emerging definitions for success?" As outsiders, we need to learn to operate within a less paternalistic framework and begin to craft a different role for ourselves in supporting development. Development economist William Easterly put it concisely, "Development may have to give up its authoritarian mindset to survive."[20]

One local NGO think tank leader, Arpita Nepal of Samriddhi Prosperity Foundation, told us about the parade of outsiders who have come to Kathmandu to help women become economically independent. One of their solutions was to teach low-income women sewing skills with the idea that, because a sewing business could be conducted in the home, low-income women could start earning extra income to provide for themselves and their families and, at the same time, become less dependent on their husbands.

As Arpita recounted, suddenly many women were offering sewing services, but few could find any customers. Of course, if there had been a market for home-based sewing services, and maybe there was, the intervention had managed to flood it. When it comes to testing a market hypothesis, it's better to rely on entrepreneurs, who have reasons to be more alert to opportunities than foreign "development experts." Entrepreneurs can test the market iteratively at a small scale to learn what works in their context. The knowledge that matters is the knowledge of the individual woman herself, exercising the dignity of self-determination, not the presumptions of outsiders, who are informed only by their good intentions.

Rarely do such errors in outsider judgment come to full light. Most of the time aid project failures are obscured not because the people responsible for the intervention are dishonest but because *they don't usually know they failed*. Most programs measure success by their outputs, rarely by their outcomes. Ben Ramalingam, a researcher and advisor to OECD's Development Assistance Committee, wrote in his 2013 book, *Aid on the Edge of Chaos: Rethinking International Cooperation in a Complex World:*

Development and humanitarian work … is an export industry, and an exceptionally blunt, supply-oriented one at that. It gathers up poverty, vulnerability, and suffering from the South, packages them for sale in the West, and exports off-the-peg solutions back in relentless waves of best-practicitis.[21]

For Ramalingam, the problem with the historical approach to aid is that it offers linear solutions for nonlinear problems, rather like using a step-by-step recipe book to fall in love. Add precisely measured ingredients in the right ratio, stir for ten minutes, pour into a pan, and bake at 220°C for forty minutes. Or, as Ramalingam put it, "It has also been argued that aid agencies, despite good intentions, are boxed into a self-reinforcing 'collective illusion' centered on an engineering philosophy."[22]

To take a famous case, the Millennium Villages Project (MVP) was a much-heralded $300 million effort that ran in ten countries in sub-Saharan Africa from 2005 to 2015. The project was conceived and led by Jeffrey Sachs, an economist from Columbia University in New York who enjoyed quasi-celebrity status in the West. Sachs argued that many aid interventions failed because they were too narrow in their aims and too anemic in their funding. He advocated a "big push" strategy whereby he hoped to demonstrate that spending a lot of money on all of the symptoms of underdevelopment at once would cause low-income communities to leap beyond the multi-layered "poverty trap" that otherwise kept any single intervention from making much of a difference. (Recall John Kenneth Galbraith's description of "self-perpetuating" poverty that is "something which one must accept" and his adamant agreement with the assertion that "meaningful change must come from the outside.")[23] In villages across Africa, the MVP provided technical expertise and funding to tackle everything from agriculture to education, infrastructure, and public health.

The journalist Nina Munk spent six years covering the MVP and detailed the many stories of its failure in her unflattering book, *The Idealist: Jeffrey Sachs and the Quest to End Poverty*. She describes an indefatigable crusader, an outsider, blinded by his own insistence that his ideas should work, if only everyone would listen and follow his guidance. Toward the end of her analysis, Munk reveals the pervasive disconnect so many do-gooders face between their own technical knowledge and the vast, local knowledge they ignore. She writes, "Jeffrey Sachs's observations on the ground were necessarily limited—by the pressures of time, by language, culture, education, background, preconceptions and ingrained models of thought."[24]

For example, in Uganda, MVP planners had persuaded the local village of Ruhiira, comprising 7,000 people, to switch from growing matoke, a banana-like crop, to maize in order to increase crop yields. The harvest was plentiful, but they could not sell the excess corn. Bad roads made transport cost-prohibitive and there was nowhere to store it. As a result, the corn rotted in the open and attracted pests. One Ugandan woman, a widow with nine children, was driven to complain in desperation, "Maize is everywhere! Under the beds, in the living rooms, in the kitchens—everywhere! And the rats are everywhere too."[25]

In August 2018, the UK's Department for International Development (now a part of the Foreign Office) released the first independent evaluation of the MVP. Though it looked for silver linings wherever possible, the report concluded that "there is no evidence that people living in the MVP areas have escaped the poverty trap" and that "what has been achieved could have been attained at a lower cost."[26] Behind such reports are hundreds of thousands of people whose lives have been deeply affected by the MVP gamble. Munk quotes one woman in Dertu, Kenya, who, frustrated by the inability of outsiders to deliver on their promises, told her, "It is only God and us who know the kinds of problems we have here."[27] Few people would defend the MVP today. It has fallen out of fashion and, we should note, many aid workers on the ground were critical of Sachs's project early on. Still, it's not clear that today's projects can claim to be so different from MVP insofar as they remain solutions designed and led by outsiders who continue to dominate decision-making around how best to intervene next.

Pitfalls of top-down paternalism

In 2018, researcher Dan Honig investigated the relationship between paternalist control and project failure in *Navigation by Judgment: Why and When Top-Down Management of Foreign Aid Doesn't Work*. Honig compiled a massive database of 14,000 aid projects and their outcomes, representing work in 178 countries over the period of 1973–2013. In addition to revealing the poor performance of the vast majority of aid projects (only one percent of project indicators even focused on the ultimate impact of the projects),[28] Honig also considered whether International Development Organizations (IDOs, as he referred to them), such as United States Agency for International Development or Department for International Development (again, now part of the Foreign Office) could see their projects perform better if they ceded more authority from the central office to field agents on the ground who are closer to the action. Honig concluded that the answer depends on several factors, principally two: the degree of environmental predictability and how verifiable the nature of the project's outcomes lend themselves to be.[29] In short, it all depends.

Honig put his finger on the boundary between what fits within the engineering problems paternalists can solve and the unseen possibilities that emerge in a decentralized system. In the end, Honig concludes that the aid industry has not solved—or even sufficiently come to terms with—its local knowledge problem. Within the paternalism-generating framework Honig knows best, his analysis leads him to suggest the answer lies in better navigating what is known as the principal–agent problem.

Every relationship in which one party must perform to the satisfaction of another implicates this problem and much of management science is, at its root, about solving it. Frederick Winslow Taylor, perhaps the world's first management consultant, argued in the nineteenth century that a manager's role is to determine how workers should do their jobs, train them to do them, and then hold them accountable to the prescribed method. Today, we know how limiting that approach is, given that it presumes the manager, or principal in this dyad, has all the knowledge necessary to succeed in the role Taylor describes and that the worker, or agent, has virtually no insights or knowledge to offer. Beginning in the twentieth century, participatory and democratic values began to temper Taylorism in the workplace.

During World War II, psychologist Kurt Lewin and anthropologist Margaret Mead were tasked with increasing the efficient use of rationed foods among households to free up more meat supply for the armed forces. They conducted an experiment among two groups of Iowan housewives. The control group sat through a lecture from an outside expert who urged them to use less meat with compelling arguments about "nutrition, scarcity, and patriotism." The experimental group received similar information but was then invited to discuss the problem together as a group to decide what to do differently. Empowered to lead, the latter group was much more successful in achieving the change they all sought.[30]

According to Mead, "[Lewin's] special gift for understanding American ideals of democracy led him to include in these first research plans his clear recognition that *you cannot do things to people but only with them* [emphasis added]."[31] Today, Lewin's and Mead's intellectual progeny refer to this insight with the mantra, "People support what they help create." Not only that, what they create tends to work better, as a "better fit" for their circumstances, not the "best practice" experts would expect them to adopt.

Perhaps this is where Honig's analogy to development practice breaks down, along with any hope of fixing foreign aid's top-down problem from the inside out. People living in low-income countries do not work for IDOs. They are not cogs that aid workers can adjust in a wheel. Increases in their standard of living are not products that we can watch roll off an assembly line. Even if every aid agency improves its man-agement practices, it won't matter because the entire business model is wrong. If we confine the approach to development within a paternalism-generating framework that relies on answers generated from the engin-eering mindsets of outside experts, we will fail. What is needed to expand the frontier of possibilities for human beings is the dignified exercise of their own self-determination. They can show us what is possible.

Ramalingam cites Roger Riddell, a British development expert who spent his career in Africa and, in 1987, wrote *Foreign Aid Reconsidered*.

> Despite reinventing itself throughout history, the aid industry retains many of its old problems—by not facing up to these systemic problems, those who would seek to transform aid are in fact busily streamlining and improving a system that is known to be flawed.[32]

Systems thinker Russell Ackoff put it this way,

> The righter we do the wrong thing, the wronger we become. When we make a mistake doing the wrong thing and correct it, we become wronger. When we make a mistake doing the right thing and correct it, we become righter.[33]

The challenge to reforming development aid is accepting that our own roles must change in deference to the important leading roles that the poor play themselves.

Notes

1 Nina Munk, *The Idealist: Jeffrey Sachs and the Quest to End Poverty* (New York: Doubleday, 2013), p. 135.
2 Ben Ramalingam, *Aid on the Edge of Chaos* (Oxford: Oxford University Press, 2013), p. 89.
3 Michael Woolcock and Kate Bridges, "How (Not) to Fix Problems That Matter: Assessing and Responding to Malawi's History of Institutional Reform," World Bank Group, December 2017, p. 2, https://openknowledge. worldbank.org/bitstream/handle/10986/29111/WPS8289.pdf?sequence=1.
4 Nathan Nunn, "Rethinking Economic Development," *Canadian Journal of Economics*, November 2019, Vol. 52, No. 4, pp. 1349–1373.
5 Nunn citing Clay, E. J., M. Geddes, and L. Natali (2009) "Aid untying: Is it working? An evaluation of the implementation of the Paris Declaration and of the 2001 DAC recommendation of untying ODA to the IDCs," Danish Institute for International Studies, p. 1351.
6 Nunn, "Aid untying: Is it working?" p. 1352.

7 Nunn, "Aid untying: Is it working?" p. 1354.

8 "Net ODA received (% of central government expense) – Tanzania," Development Assistance Committee of the Organisation for Economic Co-operation and Development, Geographical Distribution of Financial Flows to Developing Countries, Development Co-operation Report, and International Development Statistics database. Data are available online at: oecd.org/dac/stats/idsonline. IMF central government expense estimates are used for the denominator. https://data.worldbank.org/indicator/DT.ODA. ODAT.XP.ZS?locations=TZ.

9 Angus Deaton, *The Great Escape* (Princeton, NJ: Princeton University Press, 2013), p. 302.

10 Linda Polman, *The Crisis Caravan* (New York: Picador, 2010).

11 Emma Mawdsley, *From Recipients to Donors: Emerging Powers and the Changing Landscape of Aid* (London: Zed Books, 2012), p. 3.

12 "Time to Decolonise Aid: Insights and Lessons from a Global Consultation," www.peacedirect.org/wp-content/uploads/2021/05/PD-Decolonising-Aid-Report.pdf.

13 *The New York Times* editorial board, "Foreign Aid Is Having a Reckoning," February 21, 2021. www.nytimes.com/2021/02/13/opinion/africa-foreign-aid-philanthropy.html.

14 Mauricio Miller, *The Alternative: Most of What You Believe about Poverty Is Wrong* (Morrisville, NC: Lulu Publishing, 2017), p. 125.

15 Mawdsley, *From Recipients to Donors*, p. 6.

16 Pablo Yanguas, *Why We Lie about Aid* (London: Zed Books, 2018), p. 39.

17 Peter Boettke, *The Struggle for a Better World* (Arlington: Mercatus Center at George Mason University, 2021), p. 163.

18 Mario Rizzo and Glen Whitman, *Escaping Paternalism: Rationality, Behavioral Economics, and Public Policy* (Cambridge: Cambridge University Press, 2020), p. 19.

19 Rizzo and Whitman, *Escaping Paternalism*, p. 20.

20 William Easterly, *The Tyranny of Experts: Economists, Dictators, and the Forgotten Rights of the Poor* (New York: Basic Books, 2013), p. 350.

21 Ramalingam, *Aid on the Edge of Chaos*, p. 128.

22 Ramalingam, *Aid on the Edge of Chaos*, p. 80.

23 Interview of John Kenneth Galbraith by John Newark in *Aurora Online*, in *Interviews with John Kenneth Galbraith*, eds. James Ronald Stanfield and Jaqueline Bloom Stanfield (Jackson: University of Mississippi Press, 2004), p. 156.

24 Munk, *The Idealist*, p. 203.

25 Munk, *The Idealist*, p. 128.

26 C. Barnett et al., "Impact Evaluation of the SADA Millennium Villages Project in Northern Ghana: Endline Summary Report," Brighton: Itad., 2018, https://opendocs.ids.ac.uk/opendocs/handle/20.500.12413/14060.

27 Munk, *The Idealist*, p. 52.

28 Dan Honig, *Navigation by Judgment* (Oxford: Oxford University Press, 2018), p. 24.

29 Honig, *Navigation by Judgment*, p. 26.
30 Marvin Weisbord, *Productive Workplaces* (San Francisco: Jossey-Bass, 2012), p. 98.
31 Weisbord, *Productive Workplaces*, p. 98.
32 Ramalingam, *Aid on the Edge of Chaos*, p. 15.
33 Ramalingam, *Aid on the Edge of Chaos*, p. 15.

7   Dignity and institutions

We know that aid needs to change. The questions are *how* should it change, followed by how committed are we to change even if change challenges our investments in the status quo? In *How to Manage an Aid Exit Strategy*, Derek Fee makes the salient point that if countries are going to succeed in getting beyond aid, as some recipient leaders have begun to call for openly, it will certainly help if local capacity to govern effectively is ready to ease the transition.[1]

As a practical matter, Fee emphasizes the promise of improving domestic resource mobilization, or tax collection, to offset aid revenues. In addition to reducing budget shocks, Fee points out that, despite current deficiencies in collection performance, particularly in Africa, domestic resource mobilization can be a much more stable and predictable source of government revenue than volatile aid flows.[2] It should also be obvious that a more competent tax collection regime, following the democratic principles of low rates and a wide base, would make the lure of aid less tempting and would strengthen government accountability to its citizens. The focus then going forward, in part, is how to increase local capability to govern effectively. That, too, calls for not the imposition of foreign-derived "best practices," but for experimentation and evolution.

Even engineering problems can be solved through experimentation and evolution. In the 1980s, the Unilever corporation wanted to improve the nozzle used in making soap. In-house engineers were tasked with improving the nozzle, but no one managed to come up with a workable improvement. Finally, managers recruited the help of Steven Jones, an evolutionary biologist who was working at the time in one of the company's power stations.[3] Jones had no design skills, but he knew something about evolution. He focused less on designing an outcome and more on designing the process that would yield a desirable result. He took the current nozzle design and made ten random variations. He then tested those variations and discarded all but the top performer. He

DOI: 10.4324/9781003229872-8

then made ten new random variations and tested those, repeating this process forty-five times, or forty-five rounds of testing ten entirely new variations. What he ended up with was a vastly improved nozzle design that no one designed and that is still in use today.

Failure of cargo cult or copycat institutions

A focus on process to ensure optimal outcomes is not the same as designing an outcome. Much of development failure is a consequence of either too much focus on outcome design or misunderstanding the nature and role of processes in development. Strong institutions that facilitate increased standards of living are more about processes than outcomes, even if improved outcomes emerge. Institutions, as Easterly argues, are "complicated solutions to complex problems"[4] that evolved over time to become entities we evaluate as though someone had created them. Ramalingam reminds us that in a very practical sense "development should be seen as a process, a way of thinking about and navigating complex problems."[5] Appreciation for processes—"the rules of the game," as institutional economist Douglass North put it—leads to thinking about institutions in terms of not just their "strength" or "capability" but in terms of the enabling environments they facilitate (or jam up). Efforts to export the institutions of liberal democracy, the governance system most associated with developmental prosperity, sped up after the fall of the Berlin Wall. It's a story of wanting to get the institutions right, within the bounds of a paternalist mindset. In their 2017 book, *Building State Capability*, Harvard economists Matt Andrews, Lant Pritchett, and Michael Woolcock describe what was being exported: "Promoting 'good institutions' has, by and large, meant attempts to transplant Weberian-styled bureaucracies (and their associated legal instruments) throughout the developing world."[6]

According to Andrews and his co-authors, transplantation is a mistake, one that is embedded within the paternalist development paradigm that lures us into the kind of simplistic thinking they describe this way.

There is a powerful logic driving transplantation: If Weberian organizations underpin modern economic, administrative, and political life in high-income countries, isn't the shortest distance between two points a straight line? If we know what effective and capable state organizations look like—if indeed there is a "global best practice"—why not introduce them as soon as possible? Why reinvent the wheel? Programmatic approaches to "good institutions" routinely conflate form and function. The form of "institutions"—from constitutions to commercial codes to agencies overseeing land administration to procurement to how schools look—is easy to transplant. Countries can adopt the legislation that establishes forms: independent central banks, outcome-based budgeting, procurement practices, public–private partnerships in electricity generation, regulation of infrastructure.[7]

As evidence of the transplantation failure and to sensitize us to its unintended consequences, political scientists Ivan Krastev and Stephen Holmes point to the rise of authoritarian populism in donor and recipient countries alike as an intuitive and indignant rejection of foreign-recommended and funded liberal constraints on domestic politics. In their view, the post-Cold War period marks an extension of the post-colonial past in which Western governments, in many cases with the cooperation of developing country governments, sought to achieve liberal hegemony through the active top-down spread of liberal institutions.

The resulting rejection of liberalism by substantial parts of the population of some countries (Hungary and Poland certainly come to mind, as well as Russia, in all of which cases authoritarian leaders have promoted the rejection of liberalism) has to do, in part, with the way it was branded as a "gift" from "the West" that carried the outcome design-bias that prevailed among transplant experts who attempted to orchestrate such a global dissemination of copycat best practices. For this reason, Krastev and Holmes refer to the post-Cold War period in development as the Age of Imitation. When unfit copycat versions of Western institutions failed to function properly, as they were always destined to do (since they were designed outcomes that were dismissive of indigenous process), the indignity of chasing a foreign model that was offered as a superior "no-brainer" drove popular rebellion. The resulting foreign-imposed pseudo-liberalism failed to develop strong roots in some countries precisely because liberalism had been evangelized—and perceived—as a politics of imitation.

Krastev and Holmes explain, "the project of adopting a Western model under Western supervision feels like a confession of having failed to escape Central Europe's historical vassalage to foreign instructors and inquisitors."[8] They continue, "Even without coercion or enforcement, being regularly evaluated by foreign judges bereft of serious knowledge of one's country can fuel a politics of rage."[9]

It was inevitable, according to Krastev and Holmes,

> Because copycat nations are legally authorized plagiarists, they must, on a regular basis, seek the blessings and approval of those who hold the copyright to the political and economic recipes being borrowed

and applied second-hand. They must also unprotestingly accept the right of Westerners to evaluate their success or failure at living up to Western standards.[10]

Krastev and Holmes claim that today's illiberalism is

> rooted in a rebellion against the "humiliation by a thousand cuts" that accompanied a decades-long project requiring acknowledgement that foreign cultures were vastly superior to one's own. Illiberalism in a philosophical sense is a cover-story meant to lend a patina of intellectual respectability to a widely shared visceral desire to shake off the "colonial" dependency; an inferiority implicit in the very project of Westernization.[11]

The instinct to pursue liberal hegemony in this way is even more confounding given that the institutions of liberal democracy, anywhere they function at all, have emerged to protect processes that are inherently indigenous because they are by nature an expression of those they govern. That this mistake was made speaks to the power of the paternalist mindset that can see only solutions that require outside expert leadership for their implementation. Liberalism is about the dignity of humans making choices, which Krastev and Holmes argue is something all humans crave. A project of Westernization, especially one coordinated and implemented by foreign and domestic elites, is decidedly not liberalism.[12]

Edmund Fawcett, in his 2018 attempt to reclaim the true nature of liberalism, opens *Liberalism: The Life of an Idea* with this level-setting appeal:

> Polemical energy is wasted on showing that liberalism's aims and ideals are narrowly Western, secular-Enlightened, bourgeois-individualist, pro-capitalist or—to use a fashionable term of abuse—rootlessly cosmopolitan. None of these slurs or labels stick. No sect or party owns liberalism's aims and ideals. They serve every nation, gender and class.[13]

Like Krastev and Holmes, we are persuaded that liberal democracy is the governance model most likely to protect human dignity and human rights. But the question is not so much about whether *we* prefer one system over an alternative. The question is how the institutions of governance may be improved in the first place and whose preferences and interests matter most for influencing that process. The examples of disappointing post-Cold War experiments to spread liberalism help us see the folly of outsiders designing institutions on behalf of others. In fact, institutional design as a task in the abstract is also misleading. The key lesson from the last three decades is: if developing countries are going to strengthen their institutions, the roles of the people those institutions are meant to govern must overtake those of outsiders. Acknowledging their knowledge and participation in the process should appeal to our own democratic sensibilities. What's more, their own dignified participation has practical utility for institutional improvement. Efforts to take local knowledge seriously have already begun, as we will discuss next. Those efforts are encouraging, but they also reveal just how difficult the paternalist mindset is to shake off.

Elevating local leadership and capacity

In 2005, during an OECD meeting in Paris, more than one hundred countries reached a consensus on steps to shift away from overdependence on outsider knowledge. The resulting document is known as the "Paris Declaration on Aid Effectiveness" and can be summarized according to the following five key principles:

1 **Ownership**: Developing countries set their own development strategies, improve their institutions and tackle corruption.
2 **Alignment**: Donor countries and organizations bring their support in line with these strategies and use local systems.
3 **Harmonisation**: Donor countries and organizations coordinate their actions, simplify procedures and share information to avoid duplication.
4 **Managing for Results**: Developing countries and donors focus on producing—and measuring—results.
5 **Mutual Accountability**: Donors and developing countries are accountable for development results.[14]

The declaration was as much a call for recipient countries to lead as it was a challenge to curtail donor country paternalism. Three years later the declaration was updated at a meeting in Ghana as the Accra Agenda for Action (AAA) with an increased emphasis on recipient country leadership in pursuing democratic development planning with an eye to seeing their capability increase.

The AAA calls on donors to respect local priorities while encouraging developing countries to consult fully with their parliaments and civil society. Capacity development—to build the ability of countries to manage their own futures—is at the heart of the AAA, with an emphasis on ensuring that countries set their own priorities for where they need to build their capacity.[15]

The aspirations of AAA may well have inspired *Building State Capability*, referenced earlier. The book is both an argument for improving the competency and effectiveness of governments in developing countries and a model for pursuing that end. The solution Andrews and his co-authors offer is a bit of a mouthful: *Problem-Driven Iterative Adaptation*, or PDIA. What sets PDIA apart from outdated approaches to development is that it takes as its premise the insight that there is no one "best practice" for outsiders to teach when it comes to strengthening recipient country institutions. Instead, PDIA is a process for bureaucracies and ministries to discover their own "best fit" solutions. The approach is agnostic about government's role. However, as a matter of practicality, it does recommend, as a starting point, narrowing focus to only those functions that are critical for governments to get right in the short term. To help triage priorities, it offers a telling set of questions for government leaders to ask themselves when considering the wisdom of tackling ambitious government functions.

In short, it discourages policies or procedures that are:

- transaction intensive, requiring many government agents a lot of time to accomplish;
- discretionary, affording government agents too much ambiguity in decision-making such that decisions are inconsistent and unpredictable;
- onerous on citizens as opposed to supportive of their needs; and
- based on unknown technologies making successful administration less likely.[16]

The PDIA approach wants to steer clear of cargo cult thinking or what Andrews and his co-authors call "isomorphic mimicry," drawing a comparison to what some plants and animals do, such as moths, flies, and snakes, to imitate less vulnerable species. Instead, their approach would allow recipient countries to walk before they run. Accordingly, they start with a presumption of limiting government's ambitions. Just as importantly, their process helps us appreciate the idiosyncrasy of "best-fit" solutions—who's to say Denmark's land titling practices, for example, are the ideal everyone should adopt?—and the importance of self-determination in local contexts.

In the previous chapter, we discussed the importance of civil society and grassroots perspectives in development. The AAA covers that as well. It also challenges recipient governments to engage the people's representatives and civil society in the discovery of "best fit." Daren Acemoglu and James Robinson, known for their best-selling *Why Nations Fail,* in which they argue for a deeper appreciation of the role of quality institutions in development, more recently co-authored *The Narrow Corridor: States, Societies, and the Fate of Liberty.* In the latter work, Acemoglu and Robinson explain that successfully developed countries are those in which the capability of the state is well matched by a robust and engaged civil society that keeps it in check. Too much state capability without citizen involvement is undemocratic and demonstrates a failure to engage local knowledge. They emphasize the role of democratic institutions, such as free press, free association, and free speech, all of which facilitate pluralistic discoveries of solutions. In short, calls for improving state capability as part of an effective aid exit strategy must be complemented by the embrace of the universal ideals of liberal democracy, for without liberal democracy and civil society, strong states tend toward tyranny and poverty.

Randomized control trials

It is also worth covering one of the other recently heralded solutions to development's knowledge problem. In 2019, the Nobel Prize in economics was awarded to economists Esther Duflo, Abhijit Banerjee, and Michael Kremer for their development research. They argue that the only way to know what works in development is through careful application of a tool long used to investigate causal efficacy, the randomized control trial (RCT). By painstakingly working to clear out "noise"— factors that might influence but not sufficiently explain development phenomena—and isolating a control and treatment group, much as you would with a new drug in clinical trials, you can run an experiment in real time to see what interventions produce the best results. Those results, it is hoped, can contribute to a store of knowledge about what works in development—a resource that can further inform development practice more broadly. It's a "back to the drawing board" approach that insists that we can only know what we can prove scientifically using the techniques of randomized control trials and statistical inference and that only such validated knowledge should inform development policy. It is clearly a paternalism-generating framework, but at least it's more rigorous and scientific than much of what has guided development in the past. Let's see how it works in practice.

To take a well-known example, Duflo and Banerjee ran an experiment in India among schoolteachers to see whether certain changes in institutional rules would decrease absenteeism, a big problem for many developing countries hoping to see improvements in education.[17] The changes to the rules and incentive structure at the school worked in the sense that teachers began to show up at higher rates. But when they tried to apply those same rules and incentives, packaged as a generalizable solution for absenteeism, in other contexts, such as in a hospital where nurses were often truant, it failed.[18] The specific reason for the failure, as we understand it, came down to a lack of buy-in from hospital administrators. One suspects, in either a real or perceived sense, their role in institutional change took a backseat to the design experiments of the outside experts. Whether the misalignment here was willful or accidental, the effect is the same. "People support what they help create," both because the dignity they experience in the process earns their endorsement and because, as a function of their participation, they internalize and understand it.

Randomized control trials are designed to eliminate complexity in order to isolate a key variable. They can do that most reliably in cases where the variables are not themselves agents—such as human beings—who react and adjust their behavior interdependently and in unpredictable ways in real time. Early twentieth-century scientist and mathematician Warren Weaver called such cases "problems of organized complexity," which lie beyond the scope of traditional social science methods.[19] Human behavior is goal oriented and iterative, constantly taking in new information and drawing on and adapting to a complex admixture of values, beliefs, preferences, and impulses that influence decisions. In trying to understand the results of such behavior, Weaver said that we need a "third scientific advance" to address "problems which involve dealing simultaneously with a *sizable number of factors which are interrelated into an organic whole.*"[20] The choice of tools should be determined by the nature of the problem. We shouldn't assume that a tool that works well in understanding one set of problems is appropriate for understanding a very different set of problems.

If the purpose of the randomized control trial is to determine a finding that can be generalized and applied to other situations—a way to start making predictions about what works—it failed in the teachers-to-nurses case because the exercise of rooting out the "noise" in the system eliminated a factor that turned out to be significant. The network of social ties within the hospital influenced the shared norms that determined behavior. As a result, the nurses did not behave in the way the model predicted. In order to construct an RCT model for development (or any complex adaptive system comprised of agents) that is rigorous enough to provide a meaningful result, you essentially have to limit the use of that result to only that particular time and place. You might learn something about that particular situation, but it is unlikely you can scale that result as a best practice, or copycat institution, and spread it to other systems, no matter how similar or analogous they may seem.

If "people support what they help create," and their local knowledge is more likely to generate local improvements, then we must accept the loss of outsider control that represents. We may consider this, instinctively and arrogantly, a tragic loss, in the belief that people would be better off if they would just do what we, *the experts*, know is best for them. It can sound like heresy, or at least anti-science, to suggest that RCTs, considered by some to be the gold standard of social science, are of little or no use in some contexts. But heresy is often needed to shake up conventional wisdom, exposing its errors and forcing us to reexamine what we thought we already knew. One recent example of what we might call heresy has done just that by disrupting the perennial debate over nature versus nurture, and it now has many scientists rethinking much of what they had taken for granted.

Nature vs. nurture?

In the 1990s, a strange phenomenon was observed in the aquarium trade in Germany. A type of female crayfish had evolved, virtually overnight, to become self-reproducing, no longer needing males to generate offspring. An oddity, to be sure, but the real shock came from what scientists saw as a unique opportunity to further study the respective and highly debated roles of nature versus nurture. Given the nearly identical genetic make-up of the crayfish progeny, scientists were able to control for environmental influences among isolated groups.

With both nature and nurture undifferentiated in this way, the foundation of everything we thought we knew about the causes of variability among life forms would lead us to expect virtual uniformity in all observed physical and behavioral characteristics of the offspring. This is not what happened. Instead, generations of crayfish exhibited vast differences across multiple variables including size, habits, "personalities," and lifespan. Instead of maturing as identical copies, as our known models would have us predict, the genetically and environmentally identical crayfish still somehow exhibited enormous diversity.

Journalist Michael Blastland details that quirky, but deeply informative, story in his 2019 book, *The Hidden Half: The Unseen Forces that Influence Everything*. "Having straitjacketed the two big causes of everything, what makes the results so disorderly? The short answer is: we don't know."[21] Blastland summarizes the exasperating responses of the scientific community who, to a person, were hard pressed to make sense of the findings. He puts a fine point on the wake-up call this news triggered throughout the scientific community. "This is what I like to call the shock of ignorance. It's a good moment, a forced recalibration. It reminds us how easily we can be satisfied with established ideas, and what amazement might lie around the corner."[22]

The book is a tour de force challenging the hubris of what 1974 Nobel Prize winner in economics Friedrich Hayek called "scientism" in the address he gave to accept the award. Echoing Weaver, Hayek said that scientism is the overestimation of what we know, and can know, using the latest methods and techniques of science. The reason for this misplaced confidence, Hayek explained, was the false belief that everything we are able to measure, setting aside what we cannot, is sufficient to generate reliable predictability for virtually any important question that captures our imagination.

Blastland is quick to preempt any Luddite, conspiracy theorist, or mystic from using his book as justification for thoughtless dismissal of expertise. On the contrary, Blastland's motivation is to improve the credibility of experts and the responsible use of science. He points to a new moment of "meta-science," inspired also by the recent crisis of reproducibility in mainstream academic journals.[23] It's a reckoning foreshadowed by Weaver's call for a third advance in scientific methodology. Blastland similarly joins calls for keeping the door open for "a third source of developmental difference."[24] Since we have little idea what this third source is, it may not be as neatly identified as nature and nurture have been in our scientific inquiry to date. Like nature and nurture, the third source is probably best thought of as a new category for a variety of things. Blastland thinks that for now we can just think of it as what we have traditionally called "noise."

Of course, noise is the catch-all term for any factors or potential influences that can throw a bit of sand into the gears of our scientific models. It's what Duflo et al. work so hard to control for in their experiments. Prior to the Blastland "bombshell," the assumption was not just that noise is unimportant—a nuisance to be chiseled out of the equation—but that the power of its influence when tidily controlled for is marginal at best. To the extent it remains unisolated in a model's design, its impacts on the results are assumed to be trivial. That is to say, the direction and magnitude of the findings are probably about right, regardless.

But Blastland thinks we've treated noise too conveniently to suit our assumptions.

> We need to face the possibility that big influences are not as orderly or consistent as we expect, that the way things turn out is bound less by observable laws, forces or common factors than by the mass of uncommon factors, the jumble of hidden, micro-influences.[25]

In Thomas Schelling's seminal book *Micromotives and Macrobehavior*, he explains the different types of scientific problems that complex systems represent. "Situations, in which people's behavior or people's choices depend on the behavior or the choices of other people, are the ones that usually don't permit any simple summation or extrapolation to the aggregates."[26] Complexity science has emerged to tackle this problem or, at least, to better understand it. The Santa Fe Institute, a leading research center on complexity, has defined complex systems as systems "composed of many interacting parts in which the emergent outcome of the system is a product of the interactions between the parts and the feedbacks between that emergent outcome and individual decisions."[27] When it comes to the noisy, complex behavior of human beings, aggregate methods for making predictions just won't work. They are agents, not patients.

Blastland applies the crayfish findings to the broader fields of complex adaptive systems.

> If even clones in the same environment—where the problem is as simplified and controlled as humanly possible—are not the same, owing to the power of intangible variables, how reliably can we expect to pinpoint the sources of difference between people, businesses, or policies, in all their infinitely messy complexity?[28]

According to complexity scholars James Miller and Scott Page,

> If heterogeneity is a key feature of complex systems then traditional social science tools with their emphases on average behavior being representative of the whole may be incomplete or even misleading. While differences can cancel out, making the average a good predictor of the whole, this is not always the case. In complex systems, we often see differences interacting with one another, resulting in behavior that deviates remarkably from the average.[29]

In agent-based models noise includes the interdependent behavior of decision-makers acting and reacting to each other in real time. It includes a third source—call it noise but this time afford it some dignity—of unpredictable variation that can disrupt our best designs. Blastland pulls no punches. "Knowledge must generalize wherever we want to use it, otherwise it's not knowledge."[30]

Of course, acknowledging that noise, for some situations, can play a big and unpredictable role in development outcomes does not, on its own, provide us the paternalist-resisting framework we seek. Still, we can start to learn more about complex system processes through agent-based models. Findings from these models can help us appreciate that even the smallest of changes to the experimental setup can produce wildly different results. For example, using a computer-simulated agent-based model to test the spread of fire as a function of forest density, based on one set of randomized starting points, a tree density of 57 percent results in 7.5 percent of the forest getting burned. Increase that density by one percentage point and 16.4 percent of the forest succumbs, a little more than a doubling of destruction. But increase the density to 60 percent, just two percentage points more, and 76.7 percent of the forest is consumed. Add another percentage point still and the result only jumps roughly five percentage points to 81.4 percent.[31] Start the experiment over with newly randomized starting points and the results can change. What this kind of modelling can help us appreciate more deeply is the kind of phenomena that centralized models of prediction are ill suited to map. It's humbling, but agent-based modeling can also provide rich insights.

Agent–based modeling for complex systems

Eric Beinhocker recounts early agent-based modeling performed by Brookings Institution's Joshua Epstein and Robert Axtell in the 1990s. Known as Sugarscape, the computer model they created had simulated agents following a few simple rules reflecting agent preference for a utility-maximizing mix of sugar and spice. Agents could find sugar and spice on their own or they could trade with other agents if and only if they could find willing traders and mutually agreeable prices (negotiated units of sugar and spice). Under the trade scenario, the "society" of agents got much richer as each enjoyed the freedom to respond to changing conditions with their own particular mix of search for sugar and spice and search for agreeable trading partners. What's more, using agent-level data on the prices that emerged (willingness to buy and sell), the model revealed "an almost textbook downward-sloping demand curve, along with an upward-sloping supply curve, even though Epstein and Axtell did not explicitly build anything about supply and demand into their model."[32]

   In addition to validating theories of economics, agent-based models deepen our appreciation for the roles individual agents play in determining outcomes. The lesson? Stop focusing on designing outcomes and pay more attention to processes, to getting the rules right, or at least improving them. That has very practical implications for the way development has run up against dead ends in applying paternalist strategies to complex systems. For example, on the topic of export promotion in developing countries, Easterly and his co-authors at the World Bank discovered how devastating demand shocks could be under a "picking winners" model—shorthand for state-led prioritization of industries to pump up export volumes—an outcome design.[33] Easterly and his co-authors suggest that export flows follow a "power law," meaning "that successfully picking a winner becomes less likely exponentially with the degree of success that is predicted." In addition to this, they find that "the higher relative exposure of developing countries to demand shocks"[34] means the consequences of a risky "picking winners" approach are even more severe the less developed a country or region is.

There's a helpful analogy for understanding power laws in John Miller and Scott Page's book, *Complex Adaptive Systems: An Introduction to Computational Models of Social Life.* They describe a pile of sand and ask the reader to imagine each grain added to the pile as a sort of micro-influence on the pile's size and shape. As any of us who have spent time building sandcastles on the beach with kids can attest, there is often a moment, a tipping point, when a structure collapses (to either shrieks of delight or tantrums and tears). When a grain of sand, if we could observe it so closely, is added to a pile that has reached its limit, the fallout is much bigger than one grain tumbling down. The size of the avalanche it causes, in units of sand grains, is non-linear to the trend of grain additions that preceded it. That tipping point is not easy to predict, certainly not at the unit of a grain of sand. Build the pile again and you won't see a collapse event follow the same pattern.[35]

Likewise, systems of complexity are not readily stripped down to their component parts, noise well controlled for, and modeled for reliable prediction. It's time to give up on designing outcomes for developing countries and focus our attention on process. Even here, though, our addiction to paternalism has proven disastrous for institutional change. Our road to rehabilitation requires a firmer understanding and appreciation for the dignity of individuals, acknowledging their knowledge, their desires, their plans, their insights, and their own efforts.

Notes

1 Derek Fee, *How to Manage an Aid Exit Strategy: The Future of Development Aid* (London: Zed Books, 2012), p. 65.
2 Fee, *How to Manage an Aid Exit Strategy*, p. 65.
3 Prof. Steve Jones at Royal Society, March 8, 2010, viewable on YouTube: www.youtube.com/watch?v=0ZlQybxkTGM&t=361s.
4 William Easterly, *The Tyranny of Experts: Economists, Dictators, and the Forgotten Rights of the Poor* (New York: Basic Books, 2013), p. 28.

5 Ben Ramalingam, *Aid on the Edge of Chaos* (Oxford: Oxford University Press, 2013), p. 362.

6 Matt Andrews, Lant Pritchett, and Michael Woolcock, *Building State Capability* (Oxford: Oxford University Press, 2017), p. 44.

7 Andrews, Pritchett, and Woolcock, *Building State Capability*, p. 45.

8 Ivan Krastev and Stephen Holmes, *The Light That Failed: Why the West Is Losing the Fight for Democracy* (London: Penguin, 2020), p. 9.

9 Krastev and Holmes, *The Light That Failed*, p. 73.

10 Krastev and Holmes, *The Light That Failed*, p. 73.

11 Krastev and Holmes, *The Light That Failed*, p. 74.

12 Krastev and Holmes, *The Light That Failed*, p. 5. This is especially galling to students of Central Europe who know the deep traditions of liberalism there. See, for example, József Eötvös, *The Dominant Ideas of the Nineteenth Century and Their Influence on the State*, trans. Elizabeth A. Drummond (1851–1854; New York: Columbia University Press, 1996).

13 Edmund Fawcett, *Liberalism: The Life of an Idea* (2nd ed., Princeton, NJ: Princeton University Press, 2018), p. xiii.

14 Organisation for Economic Co-operation and Development, "The Paris Declaration on Aid Effectiveness and Accra Agenda for Action," accessed October 14, 2021. www.oecd.org/dac/effectiveness/34428351.pdf.

15 Organisation for Economic Co-operation and Development, "The Accra Agenda for Action," p. 1, accessed October 14, 2021. www.oecd.org/dac/effectiveness/45827311.pdf.

16 Andrews, Pritchett, and Woolcock, *Building State Capability*, pp. 104–106.

17 Abhijit Banerjee et al., "Remedying Education: Evidence from Two Randomized Experiments in India," National Bureau of Economic Research. December 2005.

18 Abhijit Banerjee et al., "Putting a Bandaid on a Corpse: Incentives for Nurses in the Indian Public Health Care System," *Journal of the European Economic Association*, Vol. 6, No. 2–3, 1 May 2008, pp. 487–500, https://doi.org/10.1162/JEEA.2008.6.2-3.487.

19 Warren Weaver, "Science and Complexity," *American Scientist*, Vol. 36, 1948, p. 536, https://people.physics.anu.edu.au/~tas110/Teaching/Lectures/L1/Material/WEAVER1947.pdf.

20 Weaver, "Science and Complexity," p. 5.

21 Michael Blastland, *The Hidden Half* (London: Atlantic Books, 2020), p. 6.

22 Blastland, *The Hidden Half*, p. 7.

23 For more on this, start with John P. A. Ionnidis, "Why Most Published Findings Are False," *PLoS Medicine*, August 30, 2015, https://journals.plos.org/plosmedicine/article?id=10.1371/journal.pmed.0020124.

24 Blastland, *The Hidden Half*, p. 10.

25 Blastland, *The Hidden Half*, p. 11.

26 Thomas Schelling, *Micromotives and Macrobehaviors* (New York: W.W. Norton & Company, 2006 edition of 1978 volume), p. 14.

27 Definition taken from the curriculum at time marker 0:12 in a video lecture presented as part of Unit 1.6 for the course "An Introduction to Agent-Based

Modeling," with instructor Bill Rand in association with Santa Fe Institute, www.youtube.com/watch?v=DPpy_nZ1L54&t=12s.

28 Blastland, *The Hidden Half*, p. 12.
29 John Miller and Scott Page, *Complex Adaptive Systems* (Princeton, NJ: Princeton University Press, 2007), p. 14.
30 Blastland, *The Hidden Half*, p. 12.
31 Based on the author's use of Forest Fire from Models Library in NetLogo 6.2.4.
32 Eric Beinhocker, *The Origin of Wealth: Evolution, Complexity, and the Radical Remaking of Economics* (London: Random House Business Books, 2007), p. 91.
33 William Easterly, Ariell Reshef, and Julia Schwenkenberg, "The Power of Exports," The World Bank, 2009, https://openknowledge.worldbank.org/bitstream/handle/10986/4273/WPS5081.pdf?sequence=1.
34 Easterly, Reshef, and Schwenkenberg, "The Power of Exports," p. 19.
35 Miller and Page, *Complex Adaptive Systems*, p. 50.

8 Dignity and knowledge

To wean ourselves from the paternalist mindset, we need to embrace an alternative. We propose a mindset that respects human dignity. It may help to first disabuse ourselves of the presumption of our own cognitive superiority as it relates to solving the economic problems of the poor. Anthropologist Clifford Geertz, in his 1982 book, *Local Knowledge*, uses the familiar term common sense to help us think about the value of the informal knowledge people in poor places possess. From an anthropological perspective, Geertz argued against a tradition of equating underdeveloped societies with inferiority of mind. He highlighted the work of allies who had helped to build the case for human dignity by publishing research

> designed to prove that "simpler" peoples do so have a sense for the divine, a dispassionate interest in knowledge, a feel for legal form, or a for-itself-alone, appreciation of beauty, even if these things are not immured in the neat, compartmentalized realms of culture so familiar to us.[1]

Still, Geertz was worried that we hadn't gone far enough.

> Though all this has had a certain success, in that hardly anyone now conceives of primitives, insofar as they use the term at all anymore, as simple pragmatists groping for physical well-being through a fog of superstition, it has not stilled the essential question: wherein lies the difference—for even the most passionate defenders of the proposition that every people has its own sort of depth (and I am one of them) admit that there is a difference—between the worked-up shapes of studied, and the rough-cast ones of colloquial, culture?[2]

DOI: 10.4324/9781003229872-9

Geertz saw the idea of common sense as a promising subject for study to increase our understanding of its role in human decision-making and to subdue our own assumptions about the omniscience of the formal expertise we identify with our own culture.

The analysis of common sense, as opposed to the exercise of it, must then begin by redrawing this erased distinction between the mere matter-of-fact apprehension of reality—or whatever it is you want to call what we apprehend merely and matter-of-factly—and down-to-earth, colloquial wisdom, judgments or assessments of it. When we say someone shows common sense we mean to suggest more than that he is just using his eyes and ears, but is, as we say, keeping them open, using them judiciously, intelligently, perceptively, reflectively, or trying to, and that he is capable of coping with everyday problems in an everyday way with some effectiveness.[3]

Consider the following example of a Peruvian woman, Verónica Cañales, who runs a market stall selling hardware supplies in the city of Cañete. In her own words, she describes her journey of starting her own business and what she has learned along the way.

It's a little different that a woman owns a hardware store; it's not common. I have the knowledge because I worked in a hardware store before starting my business. I know the suppliers, the clients, how to run a hardware store, and how you can offer a quality product at a good price.

I start the day waking up at six o'clock in the morning and I get ready. I go to the market between eight and half past eight to ready the showcases. If there is something to prepare, I prepare it for the client who requested it beforehand.

I would give three tips to future entrepreneurs who want to have a business. The first would be perseverance. They shouldn't let themselves be defeated by anything. One of the hard things to do is to start. One has doubts about how to start, but once you do, you no longer have to look back. Afterwards that is what drives one to keep growing and moving forward.

The second, they should continue to learn about their business. One has to be up-to-date on the technical specifications of each tool. The items for hardware stores are very broad, but as you work with clients you learn what each product means. That will make the customers happy and will contribute to the community.

What I love about my clients is that they demand things from me. And so I demand more of myself to serve them better and to have products that satisfy them. Understanding what they want and also treat them with kindness, to be friends with them. This has been very important.

Have confidence in yourself. That's important to address the problems and challenges that you have day-to-day with a business.

One of the challenges of the hardware store is the issue of capital. The hardware store business requires a lot of capital to keep growing. But since I already knew the suppliers and they are my partners, my allies, and some are my friends, they allow me to have products, market them, and pay them afterwards.

One of the dreams I have is that the business will grow to having other stores, distribution to another level, nationwide, not only in the province. I see that the community that surrounds me is also developing. Here at the market I think that the hardware store and the other businesses can continue to grow. The zone of Cañete has a lot of potential.[4]

Can there be any doubt that Verónica has learned from her experience crucial aspects of her business that influence her daily decisions to keep it going? What she orders and in what quantities, how often, what new tools are available, what they are best used for, who would benefit from owning them, and how best to price them so her customers can afford them while ensuring she is able to continue operating? No highly educated, technical advisor or development expert could learn all of this knowledge in a classroom or from a book. Its idiosyncratic complexity is dependent on unique variables of time, place, and circumstance. If all of those decisions impact, for good or ill, the viability of her business, how can a development model omit such crucial knowledge in its conception of promising strategies for success? Development practice ignores it because it can't account for it. It doesn't know how to get it or measure it, so it calls it noise.

We may not have great terms for the type of knowledge we have undervalued to date, but we can maintain a proper respect for its importance if we take seriously the modern concept of human dignity and refrain from conceiving of individuals, families, and communities as mere objects of our designs. To better appreciate the role of individuals' knowledge and preferences in discovering "better fit" solutions for institution building, we must learn to appreciate the roles of those who know better the contextual starting points—the initial conditions—for their journeys. Those initial conditions include the nuances of the norms of behavior that are idiosyncratic to every time and place.

Taking norms seriously

For Pablo Yanguas, development is institutional change on a societal scale. "It is the transition from old rules to new rules, and the often-difficult path that lies between them."[5] The error of development to date has been a dismissal of even considering the importance of that path. The sociologist Walter Powell observed that

> much of the social science literature on institutions has the character of a play that begins with the second act, taking both plot and narrative as an accomplished fact. Very little research asks how a play comes to be performed or why this particular story is being staged instead of some other.[6]

What are the initial conditions that matter for institutional change? According to economists James Caton and Edward Lopez, "The existence of an institution represents a collective agreement concerning a model of interaction. An existing institution includes structures of rules that agents have either already internalized or have the incentive to internalize."[7] In other words, local knowledge is the authority on local norms.

Norms comprise a wide range of both informal and formalized social expectations regarding behavior. In the context of institutions, Scott describes norms in three categories—regulative, normative, and cultural-cognitive—and suggests that scholars tend to emphasize one over the other two depending on their field.[8] For example, rational choice scholars may gravitate to regulative conceptions of norms, focusing on the explicit and formal rules and regulations that govern society. For those scholars the instrumentality of norms is paramount.

Normative rules may be more informal but no less influential. These include the social expectations, obligations, and prescriptions governing behavior. Sociologists may focus on the meaning of normative rules and may demonstrate less interest in their utility or disutility. We are concerned both with the meaning and with the influence norms bring to bear on how people choose which behavior is appropriate in a given situation. Economists focus on the guiding role of prices, but norms can be just as important to economic behavior.

For example, in the mid-nineteenth century, the market for life insurance was in its infancy. Despite the affordability and soundness of the actuarial calculations, very few people bought policies. As it turned out, most people thought it was shameful to reap a windfall when a loved one died. It wasn't until decades later that this norm was turned on its head; when people began to reframe life insurance as a dignified way to financially protect your family in the event of one's death, then the market for life insurance took off.[9]

Cultural-cognitive norms represent the accepted frameworks for divining meaning and social rightness. Anthropologists may gravitate to those norms to highlight boundaries for behavior that represent fidelity to orthodoxy. Those norms can confound outsiders as pesky hurdles in their way to saving people from themselves, but they are no less influential and relevant to behavior than the formal laws that governments employ. The following is taken from journalist Nina Munk's book investigating the Millennium Villages Project (MVP):

> In early 2007, as buds appeared on the shrubs and the desert grasses grew high, Ahmed [an educated local man hired to administer MVP programs in the area] set out to convince the people of Dertu of the benefits of hay. "If you gather and dry the tall grass now," he explained, "you will have food for your animals the next time the drought comes." The people were not impressed by his ideas about drying the tall grass. "God has brought us this grass," one man objected. "It is not ours to cut."
>
> Like the people of Dertu, Ahmed is both Somali and Muslim. He'd grown up in these parts; he was the son of a herdsman; he was one of them. For all that, he was viewed as an outsider in Dertu. His pleated dress pants, his starched shirts, his trim beard—those things set him apart. And more than once it was pointed out that while he was Somali, he was descended from a different sub-subclan than the people of Dertu. That alone was a reason to mistrust him.
>
> In Saudi Arabia, Ahmed reasoned, devout Sunni Muslims cut grass; if God didn't object to Saudis cutting grass, surely He would permit the Sunni Muslims of Dertu to do the same. No one was moved by this logic. "It is God's gift," someone repeated. "The more you cut, the angrier God gets—it is a bad omen."
>
> "Time is running out," Ahmed said gently. "The fires are coming with the winds from Somalia, and those fires will consume all the grasses if you do not cut them first."
>
> An old woman named Mama Abshira confronted Ahmed, poking her finger in his face. He was interfering in their way of life, she said. Others jumped in. Soon everyone was arguing. There was a blur of confused shouting. "Please," begged Mama Abshira. "For heaven's sake, don't cut our grass."[10]

Scott suggests we may be better off with an approach that views all of these facets as contributing, in interdependent and mutually reinforcing ways, to a social framework within which institutions emerge. This expanded approach has us reconsidering "rational behavior" as a "variable, not an assumption."[11] None of this should be taken to suggest that we should judge all norms equally in their practical value for institution building. Nor should any of us pretend that we look upon every norm, cultural practice, or religious belief with moral equivalency. There are norms that clearly get in the way of improved economic solutions, as well as norms that offend our sense of right and wrong.

The importance of appreciating the reality of norms is in appreciating the influence they have and the role they play in institutional emergence. It may be that a particularly obstructive norm or belief loses its potency over time in the minds of those who have practiced or observed it, particularly as the various payoffs of reinterpreting the norm increase. Or it may be that alternative solutions are discovered that bypass or otherwise account for and incorporate the norm into the new solution. Ignoring or dismissing norms as noise is the big mistake we make as outsiders because our dismissiveness does nothing to diminish their power to influence the course development takes. Because their sensitivities to the mutability or immutability of the norms that govern their communities are likely to be the keenest, members of low-income communities are better positioned than outsiders to participate in institution building and social change. That is to say, participatory and democratic principles are more likely than foreign imposition to generate improvements.

Economic historian Avner Greif has focused our attention helpfully on how "beliefs, norms, and organizations inherited from the past will constitute part of the initial conditions in the processes leading to new institutions."[12] That holds at every level, from small groups to large corporations to transnational networks of standardized professional and legal behavior. In any complex system, those initial conditions must be the starting point of change. If we take them for granted, skipping to the second act of Powell's play, or misinterpret them, the change we seek is frustrated. Misinterpreting them as outsiders is a near guarantee. Consider the fact that many norms are tacit, unspoken, undocumented, and may not even register as conscious reasoning to locals. Why fight this outsider disadvantage by jealously maintaining a leadership role in institutional change? Better to look to where the superior knowledge lies, with local voices who, connected to their own pasts, are better positioned to, as Greif later notes, lead their "societies to evolve along distinct institutional trajectories."[13]

Voice and institutional change

Patrick Heller and Vijayendra Rao add color to this alternative approach to development in the introduction to their 2015 edited volume, *Deliberation and Development: Rethinking the Role of Voice and Collective Action in Unequal Societies*. They criticize mainstream development for its weak gestures toward honoring local participation and contrast it with authentic, transformative deliberation that "can result in changes in the constitutive meanings that guide action and inform preferences." They write, "the very idea of 'development' as something that is directed, planned, or orchestrated has come in for criticism," and with it a rejection of "magic pills" and "one-size-fits-all solutions." Instead, "Solutions have to fit the context … tradeoffs are enormously complex and the resulting need for experimentation is best supported by careful democratic deliberation."[14] Simply put, "the more a decision is secured through a process of rational discussion, the closer it comes to a 'common good' and hence carries greater legitimacy."[15] People support what they help create.

The regulative emphasis of our foreign aid and development practice to date has taken little notice of local norms and beliefs and, when it does, seeks to obliterate them by fiat. That's no match for the reality on the ground. According to Scott, "in stable social systems we observe practices that persist and are reinforced because they are taken for granted, normatively endorsed and backed by authorized powers. When the pillars are aligned the strength of their combined forces can be formidable."[16]

Enabling local people to harness local norms to become the wind in the sails of development should be our aim. No outsider will be in nearly as good a position to appreciate and draw on—or change—local norms. Local, iterative solutions will draw on those norms that matter most and in ways that align them to improvements for solving the various problems they face. That is the result that we should all wish to see achieved in development. Scott continues, "legitimacy is not a commodity to be possessed or exchanged but a condition reflecting perceived consonance with relevant rules and laws or normative values, or alignment with cultural-cognitive frameworks."[17]

In a nod to human dignity, Heller and Rao remind us that

> classical and contemporary theories of democracy take for granted the decisional autonomy of individuals as the foundation of democratic life. This capacity of rights-bearing citizens to associate, deliberate, and form preferences in turn produces the norms that underwrite the legitimacy of democratic political authority.[18]

In contrast to the rebellion against the cargo cult institutions promulgated during the Age of Imitation, Heller and Rao contend that "institutions built on the strength of a deliberative process are far more stable, legitimate, and likely to command loyalty."[19]

The diversity of local knowledge

Researcher Jeremy Shapiro tackled a similar challenge to Geertz's. He wanted to measure the difference between our assumptions about what we think people in low-income communities need and what *they* think they need and to test the efficacy of a sample of reputable aid interventions. He used a cash transfer model for comparison, a growing alternative to traditional aid. He explained the shift in thinking cash transfers represent:

> Whereas aid has historically focused on meeting needs of the poor as perceived by the aid community, cash transfers enable aid recipients to meet needs as perceived by themselves. This change belatedly mirrors a shift in the theoretical and philosophical underpinnings of international aid: from paternalistic colonial origins to a focus on the poor as agents in bringing about economic development.[20]

Shapiro and his team used proxy indicators to identify those in need from among a sample of Kenya's poorest counties. Specifically, they targeted unemployed adults as well as heads of households whose homes lacked manufactured materials in their construction. (How those in need are identified in the first place becomes an important variable to further scrutinize in a follow-up study.) Next, the team surveyed the low-income cohort of 3,008 people to find out what cash values they would each place on three distinct but related aid interventions: agricultural training, free fertilizer, and a one-time supply of twenty-five baby chicks.

The cohort was then randomly assigned to receive either one of the interventions or a cash transfer equivalent to the per-person cost of the intervention relevant to their region. Six months later, they assessed the recipients to discover the relative impacts of the different treatments on well-being. They found little difference between those who received interventions and those who received cash transfers and no discernible difference even among those who received their most valued intervention. They did find, however, that those who received cash transfers reported increased feelings of autonomy over those who received aid interventions.

For Shapiro, demonstrating that the poor are no worse than aid professionals at optimizing resources for development, even when setting aside overhead costs, is an important breakthrough for resolving the following question, as he describes it:

> Are development outcomes best achieved by enabling aid recipients to optimize according to their unique information and constraints?

Or is it better for the aid industry to implicitly or explicitly influence the decisions of recipients and the use of aid resources?[21]

Advocates of the "poor-but-efficient" hypothesis might argue the former while paternalists might say the latter. Shapiro might say a tie goes to the poor. It's a question that turns, fundamentally, on our own appreciation for, and fidelity to, a modern conception of human dignity.

In a follow-up paper published later the same year (2019), Shapiro drilled down further on the question of value variation by testing a wider range of fourteen interventions. He found high levels of heterogeneity in preferences and disparate levels of indifference between common aid interventions and cash—a reminder that, just like everybody else, low-income people are not homogenous groups.[22] Each has her own preferences and tradeoffs, and, consequently, tends to place very different values on various goods and services. What's more, Shapiro tested the valuations against commonly used proxies for need and found that there was no correlation between those whom outsiders would expect would need the intervention and the value placed on the intervention by the recipient. Taken together, those results should give us pause when using any proxy indicators of need to suppose we know what people in low-income communities want from us and should weaken any indignation we might at times share with the exasperated expert who asked, "Why don't they want what we know they need?"

To be sure, the findings do not necessarily suggest cash transfers are the best way to support meaningful development. But the findings are an example of what it means to take seriously the perspective of recipients and their preferences for what would make a difference in their lives. What matters is *their* knowledge of their time and place and their individual senses of what matters to them. That is the element that is so often absent in development strategy, and yet it is that which determines the impact of development work. Local preferences, knowledge, and norms, when not overridden by outsider control, can guide iterative adaptations in search of improvements to complex systems. An example from Mauricio Miller's experience of honoring individual knowledge may help to illustrate why intervening on behalf of allegedly "best practices" entails overriding local knowledge and the ability of others to adapt and to seek improved solutions.[23]

A young couple, Javier and Maria, were told by a mortgage broker, to their pleasant surprise, that they could afford to buy a home in their working-class neighborhood in Oakland, California. They were thrilled. As they prepared to secure the loan they shared their good news with their friends and family. Word spread to the staff of Miller's nonprofit, the

Family Independence Initiative (FII). Javier and Maria had been participating in an FII program designed to track their financial decisions.

The FII staff were concerned. They worried that Javier and Maria
were about to take on a predatory loan that they didn't fully understand.
That created a dilemma for Miller and his team. After decades of working
with low-income communities, Miller had concluded that outsider interference in people's lives, no matter how well intentioned, often did more
harm than good. One of the rules he had adopted was that if anyone on
staff tried to intervene with program participants' decisions they would
be fired. He had come to believe that professional social services actually
preclude or undermine solutions to poverty reduction that those living in
low-income communities discover on their own. But Javier and Maria's
planned mortgage was a big test of the new policy. It was hard to imagine
letting this young, struggling couple make such a monumental mistake.
So FII staff convened a team meeting to discuss whether to break the rule
just this once. In the end, they decided not to and just hoped for the best.

Javier and Maria got their loan and, sure enough, it was financially
untenable. Faced with ruin, Javier and Maria turned to their friends and
family and an idea was hatched. If everyone pitched in to renovate the
house, they could increase its value enough to refinance the home. It
worked. The community solved the problem themselves, and the experience of helping Javier and Maria recast homeownership as an obtainable
possibility. Soon more families started saving toward homeownership, and
throughout the community, several succeeded, something so many of
them had thought unthinkable. And they had internalized the lesson of
making sure the loan offered sustainable terms.

For outsiders, like the staff of the FII, it is hard to look at low-income
communities and not feel strongly about the choices they are making.
But Miller's insight into the negative impact of outsider influence
was critical to unlocking something most poverty programs lack. By
standing behind, not in front of, local knowledge, they allowed for iterative problem solving within the community, a process that is inherently
sensitized to the complexities of particular communities at particular
times and places.

It's an insight that's been appreciated by some in the social sector as far
back as Jane Addams, one of the earliest and most famous social workers
in the United States. Louis Menand described the big lesson Addams had
learned this way:

> She found that the people she was trying to help had better ideas
> about how their lives might be improved than she and her colleagues
> did. She came to believe that any method of philanthropy or reform

premised on top-down assumptions—the assumption, for instance, that the reformer's tastes or values are superior to the reformee's, or, more simply, that philanthropy is a unilateral act of giving by the person who has to the person who has not—is ineffectual and inherently false.[24]

Outsider solutions are, by nature, linear and planned. Who would have conceived of a plan whereby Javier and Maria would take a bad home loan, learn from their mistake, and, in forging a solution, strengthen social capital among their peer network and expand the awareness of what is possible for members of their community?

We also note that policies that are deliberately designed to increase homeownership rates present a classic case of unintended consequences. Such policies were central to the 2008 financial crisis. As Gretchen Morgenson and Joshua Rosner document in *Reckless Endangerment: How Outsized Ambition, Greed, and Corruption Led to Economic Armageddon*, "The partnership would achieve its goals by 'making homeownership more affordable, expanding creative financing, simplifying the home buying process, reducing transaction costs, changing conventional methods of design and building less expensive houses, among other means.'"[25]

Alphonso Jackson, acting secretary of the Department of Housing and Urban Development, claimed in 2004, "Offering FHA mortgages with no downpayment will unlock the door to homeownership for hundreds of thousands of American families, particularly minorities." One of Jackson's colleagues later added, "We do not anticipate any costs to taxpayers."[26] How did that work out?[27]

There is something fundamentally different about seeing a peer, someone you identify with, someone you see as like you, succeeding that changes your own perspective. Critically, choosing for oneself what innovations to adopt, when to adopt them, and how to adapt them to your circumstances is a key part of that process. It is the agency to choose for oneself, a tenet of human dignity, that is the secret to this success.

Positive deviance

This approach has a name. It is positive deviance and it was popularized in the 1990s by Jerry and Monique Sternin, who had gone to Vietnam to tackle infant malnutrition on behalf of the nonprofit Save the Children.[28] Like Miller, the Sternins tried something different. Instead of focusing on those most in need, they sought out and focused their attention on those doing relatively well within the community. Their question was not, *Who is suffering and needs our help?* Their question was, *Who, despite facing the same challenges and constraints as the others, is doing well and does not need our help?* They discovered several families whose children were not suffering from malnutrition, and they studied them. They discovered a range of habits and strategies that seemed to be making a difference. For example, families with healthy babies fed them several times throughout the day, not just three times. They also used the leftover broth from shellfish, not thought useful by anyone else, in their children's food.

It would be tempting to document these differences and to start a training program for families encouraging them to adopt these "best practices." Instead, the Sternins asked the successful families to cook with their neighbors to accelerate the effect of exposure to innovation within a network of active agents who take responsibility for their own lives and their own communities. That process honored the human dignity at the heart of innovation diffusion since it relied on the agency of peers to interpret and adopt innovation organically. It did not, as is often the case, rely on "professional" outsiders to intervene and "teach" something they had not experienced for themselves.

Oxfam's Duncan Green in his book *How Change Happens* explains positive deviance this way:

> The starting point is to look for outliers who succeed against the odds. But who is doing the looking also matters. If external "experts" investigate the outliers and turn the results into a toolkit, little will come of it. When communities make the discovery for themselves, behavioural change can take root ... positive deviance capitalizes on a hugely energizing fact: for any given problem, someone in the community will have already identified a solution.[29]

If we are to accelerate the effect of positive deviance and innovation diffusion within low-income communities, we need to concentrate on strengths, not weaknesses, and support the expansion of agency for the discovery and adoption of those innovations. This is, in fact, the way most human progress has occurred.

Beinhocker describes innovation from the individual's perspective in participatory (even democratic) terms,

> We use our brains as best we can in economic decision making, but then we experiment and tinker our way into an unpredictable future, keeping and building on what works and discarding what does not. Our intentionality, rationality, and creativity do matter as a driving force in the economy, but they matter *as part of a larger evolutionary process*.[30]

In retrospect, we like to tell ourselves a linear story about how breakthroughs came to be, and with that fiction we start down the problematic road of replicating that process by design. Our minds don't like stories of chance and intangible credit. We want to make sense of what happened so that we feel in control of events, in control of social progress. We fear that without an authority figure with the responsibility and the power to achieve breakthroughs we stand little chance of solving the problems we face today. But the opposite is true.

To increase the likelihood of breakthroughs requires enabling environments. We need to remove the unfreedoms, which Amartya Sen argues is the task of development. What outsiders often fail to recognize is that locals are solving their own problems incrementally—piecemeal—all the time, and they are doing it without external direction, in ways that work because they are iterative and emergent. As anthropologist Grace Goodell notes,

> A major virtue of piecemeal change for the purposes of economic development is that it is parsimonious, giving as much freedom of action and responsibility as possible to those closest to the problem, who have the most experience in that environment and can react the fastest. At the same time, it fosters continual finetuning.[31]

Continual fine-tuning is essential to development, but it's difficult for external planners to embrace because there is no obvious way to account for it in their designs. Goodell details the complex practice of producing and marketing eggs in the Philippines area of Santa Dalena, a process that had emerged prior to the government coming in and shutting it down since it didn't match the development plans of outsiders. She writes,

> No one in Santa Dalena began by saying, "What this place needs is an egg cooperative—here is how egg cooperatives should be set up." No agency came in with a big loan, a thousand chicks, and thirty ready-made UNICEF hen coops. Rather, through trial and error, need, initiative, convenience, and local effort the villagers went through the process of consolidating their own field of interaction for their own self-defined purposes, which is precisely what gave them their élan and expertise and enabled them to fend off the landlord's and bureaucrats' efforts to stop them. Throughout history autocrats and their technocrat henchmen continue to advance powerful economic arguments for imposing short-term "efficiency" which blocks these local foundations for long-term predictability, rationality, and bonding.[32]

Surprisingly, or perhaps not, the central government's plan was a mismatch for local conditions. The difference between the approaches is stark and reveals that outsiders need not be foreigners, per se; they can be fellow citizens. What makes an outsider an outsider is that they do not carry the burden of failure for the community in question. Why did the local solution work? Because it was a solution discovered through time-tested experience, navigated by those who stood to gain or lose based on the outcomes. A decentralized model that takes individual human dignity seriously allows for a vast number of simultaneous experiments, results, and adaptation. The best outcomes get replicated, not by any central authority, but by the wisdom of individuals free to navigate their networks and free to adopt what they like without seeking anyone's permission.

Notes

1 Clifford Geertz, *Local Knowledge: Further Essays in Interpretative Anthropology* (New York: Basic Books, 1982), p. 74.
2 Geertz, *Local Knowledge*, p. 74.
3 Geertz, *Local Knowledge*, p. 75.
4 Based on an interview of Verónica Cañales conducted in Mercado Mayorista, Canete, Peru, in October 2019 by Daniel Anthony. Printed with permission.
5 Pablo Yanguas, *Why We Lie about Aid* (London: Zed Books, 2018), p. 75.
6 Walter Powell, Kelly Packalen, and Kjersten Whittington (2012: 434) cited in W. Richard Scott, *Institutions and Organizations* (4th ed., Los Angeles: Sage, 2014), p. 113.
7 James Caton and Edward J. Lopez, "The Cognitive Dimension of Institutions," 15 July 2018. Available at SSRN: https://ssrn.com/abstract=3214278 or http://dx.doi.org/10.2139/ssrn.3214278.
8 Scott, *Institutions and Organizations*, p. 59.
9 Viviana Zelizer, "Human Values and the Market: The Case of Life Insurance in the 19th Century," *American Journal of Sociology*, Vol. 84, No. 3, November 1978, pp. 591–610.
10 Nina Munk, *The Idealist: Jeffrey Sachs and the Quest to End Poverty* (New York: Anchor Books, 2013), pp. 53–54.
11 Scott, *Institutions and Organizations*, quoting Swedberg on p. 15.
12 Avner Greif, *Institutions and the Path to the Modern Economy: Lessons from Medieval Trade* (Cambridge: Cambridge University Press, 2006), p. 17.
13 Greif, *Institutions and the Path to the Modern Economy*, p. 17.
14 Patrick Heller and Vijayendra Rao, *Deliberation and Development: Rethinking the Role of Voice and Collective Action in Unequal Societies* (Washington: World Bank Group, 2015), p. 5.
15 Heller and Rao, *Deliberation and Development*, p. 5.
16 Scott, *Institutions and Organizations*, p. 70.
17 Scott, *Institutions and Organizations*, p. 72.

18 Heller and Rao, *Deliberation and Development*, p. 9.
19 Heller and Rao, *Deliberation and Development*, p. 11.
20 Jeremy Shapiro, "The Impact of Recipient Choice on Aid Effectiveness," *World Development*, Vol. 116, April 2019, pp. 137–149, https://doi.org/ 10.1016/j.worlddev.2018.10.010.
21 Shapiro, "The Impact of Recipient Choice," p. 138.
22 Jeremy Shapiro, "Exploring Recipient Preferences and Allocation Mechanisms in the Distribution of Development Aid," *World Development Economic Review*, Vol. 34, Oxford, 2019, pp. 1–18.
23 Mauricio Miller, *The Alternative: Most of What You Believe about Poverty Is Wrong* (Morrisville, NC: Lulu Publishing, 2017), pp. 138–139.
24 Louis Menand, *The Metaphysical Club: A Story of Ideas in America* (New York: FSG, 2001), p. 311.
25 Gretchen Morgenson and Joshua Rosner, *Reckless Endangerment: How Outsized Ambition, Greed, and Corruption Led to Economic Armageddon* (New York: Times Books, Henry Holt & Co., 2011), pp. 2–3.
26 Lew Sichelman, "Bush to Offer Zero Down FHA Loan," *Realty Times*, January 20, 2004, http://realtytimes.com/rtpages/20040120_zerodown.htm.
27 See also Johan Norberg, *Financial Fiasco: How America's Infatuation with Home Ownership and Easy Money Created the Economic Crisis* (Washington, DC: Cato Institute, 2009) and Jeffrey Friedman and Wladimir Kraus, *Engineering the Financial Crisis: Systemic Risk and the Failure of Regulation* (Philadelphia, PA: University of Pennsylvania Press, 2011).
28 Monique Sternin, Jerry Sternin, and Richard Pascale, *The Power of Positive Deviance: How Unlikely Innovators Solve the World's Toughest Problems* (Boston: Harvard University Press, 2010), p. 19.
29 Duncan Green, *How Change Happens* (Oxford: Oxford University Press, 2016), p. 25.
30 Eric Beinhocker, *The Origin of Wealth* (Boston: Harvard Business School Press, 2006), p. 15.
31 Grace Goodell, "The Importance of Political Participation for Sustained Capitalist Development," *European Journal of Sociology*, Vol. 26, May 1985, p. 107.
32 Goodell, "The Importance of Political Participation," pp. 108–109.

9 Dignity and innovation diffusion

Recall the misguided solution to business empowerment in Nepal. An outside organization identified the problem as a lack of entrepreneurship among Nepalese women and devised a simple solution that failed to deliver. In contrast, a young entrepreneur named Rekha Dey decided to pursue a more affordable, environmentally friendly alternative to traditional home construction in India. In her own words, this is her story:

> My name is Rekha Dey. I have been working hard for the last twelve years to start my own business in bamboo. Finally, four years ago, I established my company, Wonder Bamboo Enterprises, under a partnership with Tanjun Associate LP. We make homes from bamboo.
>
> When I got married, behind my husband's house, there was a sort of bamboo farm. And I used to see how much people used it. Mostly it was used in making boundaries and roofing. There is not much work done in furniture and construction. So, I wanted to spend time in this area and do something innovative in it.
>
> Honestly, bamboo can save the environment. The whole globe is talking about global warming, climate change, environment sustainability. In India, it is a hot topic. To bring it into practice, we will have to take small steps. And from that point of view, bamboo interested me.
>
> Botanically, [bamboo] is a grass, a rhizome; it is not a tree. So, by cutting it, we are not harming the environment in any way. Conversely, it would be a waste if we did not cut it and it flowers after seventy years. And that's why, the more you grow bamboo, the better it is. Cut it after four years. It is best to cut bamboo after four years and use it for multiple purposes. And if it just lies there, it would be a problem.
>
> My dream is to take bamboo to a sophisticated furniture level like Ikea, where export-import is possible and India becomes an export-based country

DOI: 10.4324/9781003229872-10

by using bamboo as a raw material. I don't know how many years it will take. Whatever it takes, I think in this lifetime, I can get there.

This has been a long journey—from studying the bamboo and determining which species of bamboo is used for what purpose. The available bamboo in India comes in 145 varieties and each one has a different use. We are moving forward by taking small steps.

This will not happen in a day. But if we educate people about the multiple uses of bamboo in our daily life, you can stay in a house made of bamboo, you can make briquettes of bamboo, you can make furniture out of it. And if we use it widely, the zero-carbon footprint we talk of is achievable.

What is the demand? What can be done better? What are the gaps? Do we lack good designers? Who could design homes that are even six-floor houses made from bamboo? How can we get there? That was totally "self-research" for me.

When I registered my company on my own in June 2016 by going to Tinsukia [administrative headquarters of the Tinsukia district of the state of Assam], that was a challenging task. First of all, we went to Tinsukia to start a company, and we registered it. That was an experience in itself, because you have to go to the court.

In June 2016, in extreme heat, I went to Tinsukia. We, my husband and I, went to the court there and registered. It was my first time registering a partnership firm, and I did not know many of the legalities of it. When we registered our company in Tinsukia, we found out that you cannot commence your business just after registering the company. Even as this is 2019, and it has been barely three years, it is clearly embedded in my memory. We had to go through fingerprinting, photo, and scanning of documents. Then finally they gave me the certificate the third time I applied. In those three trips, all we achieved was a piece of paper of registration of sales tax which authorized one to do business.

It was like an everyday research, calling, inquiring about papers, which papers are needed. After the registration I came back and my first plan was to establish a bamboo treatment plant in our Tanjun-Wonder Bamboo workshop in Sarahanpur.

For that we researched and found out that the machines are available in two places—Gujarat and Indore. After surveying them, we came to the conclusion that we would purchase them from Dewas in Indore district.

We went there ourselves and surveyed. There were three or four providers. Since our requirement was very customized, we talked to one of the machine developers. We wanted to treat fifty poles in one go. If we did two rounds daily, we would have a per day treatment capacity of one hundred poles.

What I wanted was in my head, but how would that be cast in iron? We learned gradually how that is done. After going there and understanding all the technicalities, we placed an order. That was my first investment in the bamboo business. I did that very passionately because I knew that this business would require a few years' investment, and I was mentally prepared.

The capital for the initial investment was my personal savings. I didn't know from where the future investment would come from, but I knew that since I have started the journey, something would come along the way. I did not know how big a challenge it was to place an order for a machine in India at that time.

After registering the company, we went to the Sales Tax Office because it was the time of TIN (Tax Identification Number). It was compulsory to take a TIN number otherwise you could not trade in India. So, we went to Saharanpur, because the machine was to be installed at the workshop in Saharanpur District.

For that alone, I had to personally travel from Delhi to Saharanpur three or four times, and my daughter was barely six or seven years old then. I had to travel with her.

After that when we placed the order for the machine I did not know there was a C form, which allowed you a little rebate in tax. At that time, it was only available in hard-copy paper format. So we learned gradually.

After that we couriered the hard copies to Dewas and coincidentally that courier got lost. It was a proper government speed-post, no idea how it got lost. The next revelation was that that piece of paper was very important. So, if you lost it, you had to file an FIR (First Information Report). And where do you file the FIR? You must do that in the city where it was lost. Like this, every day we learned a new piece of information.

And then to file the FIR, I went to Dewas to the police station, I had to go there just for this. After going there we had to find out where the document had reached. It reached the GPO (General Post Office) in Dewas and after that there was no information. At GPO, we sought information, we couldn't find anything. Then we went to the police station, we filed an FIR, took a copy of the FIR. This is a matter of self-protection. If you have lost something and if it is misused tomorrow, then there would be fingers pointed towards you.

That summer, we traveled again and again and then came back to reapply for that form. Because without it, we could not get the tax-rebate. And that tax was a sizable amount. We reapplied for the forms. But in the meantime, the manufacturers of the machine made the delivery, and later we sent those papers.

You can see whenever someone starts a new business, and even now, and I think it will remain so forever, no one wants to do anything outside the legal system, outside the government rules. We all want to work within the framework of government rules. But when you experience it, you realize that it is a Pandora's box. You open one thing and something else comes up.

Everywhere you had to go personally and find out what they needed. We used to take everything with us, and we used to provide photocopies. I faced a lot of challenges, and they still come my way. I started in 2016, but the first consignment which I got in my entrepreneurial initiative was in 2017 when home-grown bamboo was acknowledged as rizome (grass) by the Indian government under the Forest Act.

Before then, whenever we discussed and negotiated rates in different states the traders used to tell us that these are forest products and there are different taxes on them. There are GP, TP, gate pass, transit pass. If you buy any forest products, obviously there are some tax regulations. That was applicable to bamboo as well, and at that time the cost-analysis that I did to determine at what cost we could do business was majorly mismatching because the cost of raw material was very high.

The traders used to inform us at the time of delivery that a lot of cash would need to be paid for taxes. We often could not estimate the amount in advance. So there used to be a fear in my mind that you have placed the order, paid the advance, but the cost could go so high that all your hard work resulted in nothing. So that is why I took time and I would say I am lucky that I started business only when the government accepted that bamboo is not a tree under the Forest Act; it is a grass and therefore there should not be any forest regulation taxes.

So, the first order we placed was after the change in the Act and we procured only home-grown bamboo because the traders there harvest it from different villages. Our bamboo comes from Kokrajhar district; some of it comes from other districts as well. But certainly cost wise, Assam bamboo is of good quality and also cheaper, and that's why we order it from there.

Since bamboo has been removed from the license-raj, it is a great blessing for entrepreneurs like us, because if you do not get the raw material for cheap and at a particular cost, your whole business becomes unviable. And all your hard work goes to waste.[1]

Rekha had a passion for how bamboo could be used as a building material and she devoted herself to learning the business. She faced many obstacles, including a burdensome regulation limiting the legal commercial use of bamboo due to its mischaracterization in the law as a tree. The regulation was a gift to Rekha's more established competitors, who benefited from the prohibition on Rekha's innovative entry into the construction space. Eventually, with the help of a local NGO think tank, Rekha was able to see bamboo reclassified correctly as a grass so that she could grow her business. Rekha already possessed the talent and know-how to succeed with her business, but the institutional environment prevented her from seeing her experiment through to fruition.

Regulatory barriers

An institutional environment that blocks the experimentation of Rekha and people like her can negate all the other efforts to solve the problem of poverty. The solution to poverty is a function of institutionally protecting the knowledge, autonomy, and initiative of individuals to experiment undirected and uncoerced. It requires honoring their self-determination and honoring their dignity. It was Rekha's knowledge and alertness that made possible the innovation of bamboo house construction, after local NGOs had successfully promoted the elimination of the law that miscategorized bamboo as a tree rather than a grass. How many "Rekhas" run into similar problems and understandably give up? Poverty reduction requires an open horizon of freedom for the very practical reason that no one can say from where the next innovations will come. Poverty reduction comes from multiple and diverse solutions to economic and institutional problems.

That is the utility of pluralism, and it mirrors the utility of human dignity as a social norm. Both principles are of great practical value. Pluralism, properly understood, anticipates the probability of discovering superior value in solutions that represent the combined influence of many voices. Respecting the dignity of all—rich and poor alike—increases the probability of discovering superior value (and the tautological guarantee of superior subjective value) in solutions that incorporate the individual's own point of view on questions related to that individual and her family, neighborhood, community, tradition, country, and so on.

Of course, determining which questions rise to the purview of the group—and of which group—is much debated at virtually all levels of social organization. In the context of development aims and the institutions that govern its success, we reiterate that such questions are best explored when all enjoy a presumption of liberty, within which market-tested innovation is most likely to take place. Pluralism and dignity are concepts that strengthen individual rights and democratic values. Menand points out that amid the various arguments for free speech, the practical one suffices: "We permit free expression because we need the resources of the whole group to get us the ideas we need."[2]

Scott makes another observation that suggests how we might think about a more promising future for development.

> Network theorists stress the importance of marginality to fostering innovation and learning processes. … Just as the locations where sea water meets fresh water are particularly supportive of varied forms of

marine life, so the areas of overlap and confluence between institutional spheres generate rich possibilities for new forms.[3]

Marginality, of course, can refer to anyone on the edge of a network, regardless of socioeconomic status, but given our historical failure to appreciate the value of low-income populations' roles in solving social problems, we suggest that a new approach to development requires the inclusion of those who are now or historically have been marginalized. In that context, recall that successful institutional change is a function of initial conditions—how people function now—and is made more promising by a participatory and diverse set of voices. A myopic and elite-dominated change process is unlikely to account properly for the vast stores of information, insights, and perspectives that low-income communities possess. A more balanced approach that empowers low-income communities to make their own choices without paternal meddling may humble outsiders, but it will also enrich the entire world.

The potential of "peasants" and informal markets

In a landmark study in the 1960s, Paul Deutschmann and Orlando Fals Borda compared the diffusion patterns, or rate of adoption, of agricultural innovations among peasant villages in Colombia to those demonstrated by farmers in much wealthier and more educated farming communities in Ohio. The patterns matched in significant ways. Low-income farmers in underdeveloped areas were just as likely to pursue improvements to their livelihood practice through thoughtful and judicious experimentation, and they were similarly sensitive to relative differences in exposure to new ideas and opportunities to apply them in practice. For example, farmers living in the Andes who had little access to mass media and who had to rely mostly on word-of-mouth to learn about new techniques were slower to adopt new innovations than others in their local cohort who diversified their information gathering through travel outside their village and more frequent access to newspapers, radio, and books.[4]

The lesson is that low-income groups are just as capable as wealthier, more formally educated cohorts when it comes to considering, testing, and adopting innovations they perceive as potentially improving their lot. At the same time, what slows their progress are the same factors that slow the discovery and diffusion of any innovation, namely, limitations on access to new ideas and constraints on freewheeling experimentation with those ideas. The Deutschmann and Fals Borda study inspired in the decades since an avalanche of similar studies on diffusion patterns, which further validate a near universal pattern of innovation diffusion as a function of network diversity, communication, and experimentation.

And yet, international development has operated as though the mountains of institutional change and diffusion research we have accumulated have been written in an alien language published in another galaxy. Instead, the same top-down approaches of the past have proceeded along lines almost opposite to, if not antagonistic to, what we have learned about the decentralized processes and autonomous participation needed to discover models of enduring change.

Scott highlights the work of David Strang, who reviewed an array of diffusion studies in 2010 and emphasized the autonomy of individuals observed in his research. In a "world of sovereign actors who decide whether or not to do something new," Strang stresses that while people pay attention to others and take their actions into account, they still behave relatively independently and exhibit sophistication in comparing practices and customizing them to fit their circumstances.[5] The part of the process where autonomous members of low-income communities exercise their prerogatives judiciously in validating or rejecting, adopting or adapting, innovating or maintaining the wide array of what their network exposure has on offer is what has been wildly underappreciated in development models.

Of course, the inclusion of marginal voices in aid and development is rhetorically very familiar to the ears. One of the most exhaustive efforts to capture the perspectives of low-income communities in development was conducted in the late 1990s for the World Bank. Expanding on traditional household surveys, the project known as Voices of the Poor sought to understand the perspectives of low-income communities through interviews and other analytical approaches. The results were published in three volumes, with the first two titles including *Voices of the Poor: Can Anyone Hear Us?* and *Voices of the Poor: Crying Out for Change*.

In the conclusion of the first volume, under the subtitle "Elements of a Strategy for Change," the authors stress the disconnect between the good intentions of outsiders who intend to serve poor people and the intentions and desires of the poor people themselves. "Institutional encounters often leave poor people disempowered, excluded, and silenced."[6] By the third volume, the concluding emphasis of *Voices of the Poor: From Many Lands* was on protecting the rights of poor people. The authors share the story of

> 21-year-old Fernando, who grew up in the *favela* of Sacadura Cabral in Brazil surrounded by crime, drugs, and abuse of power. … Fernando dreams of becoming a judge someday. He aspires to study law in order to empower himself and raise consciousness throughout

his community. In his view, education and awareness of rights are vital to the future of the *favela*. He said, "In a *favela* people have no idea of their rights. We have police discrimination; the policemen abuse us, and others use their knowledge to take advantage of us. So I want to know all about rights and obligations."[7]

The rights and obligations Fernando intuits as the answer to his neighborhood's problems are secured by the strong institutions we have been discussing, but the lack of connection he feels to even knowing about them speaks to the lack of participation of the poor in the process of institutional change. An outsider with a better institutional design cannot fix that, and there has been little evidence since the publication of *Voices of the Poor* that the international development community has reduced its role in co-designing institutional change in partnership with government elites.

No doubt, part of the reason the development community has not changed in this way is what Pablo Yanguas pointed to in terms of the existential nature of a reduced role for outsiders. The dilemma the well-meaning outsider faces is not so obviously resolved. What does a reduced role for outsiders look like short of becoming more passive or inactive in the cause of poverty reduction and development? The answer is not easily summarized in a line or two, but we believe it starts with some reflections from a leading African economist.

World-renowned Ghanaian economist and one-time Bono advisor George Ayittey has spent decades trying to turn development on its head. Despite serious health challenges, Ayittey visited our offices in August of 2016 with an ambitious project in mind. Ayittey's mastery of economics as a discipline is matched by his commitment to seeing Africa thrive. As the author of several important books published over two decades, including *Indigenous African Institutions, Africa Betrayed, Africa in Chaos*, and the best-selling *Africa Unchained*, Ayittey had another important book he wanted to write. He explained to us that one of the disadvantages Africans face in leading their own economic path to prosperity is that African students have access to only foreign economic textbooks. What was needed to bring economic principles to life for African students, he argued, was a robust textbook on *applied* economics written in the African context by an African economist using recognizable African examples and analogies.

Two years later, Ayittey's 400-plus-page *Applied Economics for Africa* was finished[8] and made available online, at zero price, to thousands of economics students, entrepreneurs, scholars, journalists, and policymakers across Africa. *Applied Economics for Africa* is not just a survey of economic principles. It is that, but it is also a rich tour of a lifetime of Ayittey's experiences and insights related to Africa's economic challenges and opportunities. He devotes several chapters to questions of development and holds many of the well-known culprits accountable for failure to date: colonialism, postcolonial governance, and foreign aid. Specifically, Ayittey argues that one of the harms done by colonialism, and perpetuated ever since, has been a severing of Africa's future from its past. Along the way, he says, Africans have been served a false narrative about their own history, one that either perpetuates the oversimplified myth of primitive hunter-gatherer societies with little to no evidence of economic institutions, or one that misinterprets traditional African societies as prototypically communal.

Instead, while acknowledging the rich diversity of African societies, Ayittey offers copious evidence to demonstrate a shared pattern of traditions inclusive of markets, property rights, and participatory demo-cratic norms. Ayittey seeks to reconnect Africans to their historical norms and practices in an effort to restore an otherwise broken chain of iterative evolution toward a brighter future of institutional development, one that Africans create and support.

Dictatorship, according to Ayittey, is as foreign to African culture as colonial power was in the previous century. As a general rule, trad-itional chiefs and kings did not have absolute or dictatorial control over their people. Most decisions were made by some form of consensus. Intergenerational households wielded broad, if not absolute, control over their property. Freewheeling marketplaces were common and robust, with no central authority determining location, prices, or preferred vendors. Much of that tradition was marginalized or destroyed by colonialism. Postcolonial strategies for development have been just as negligent, if not outright hostile, to authentic African traditions.

When Tom was in West Africa on a radio interview to discuss the economics of inflation, the topic of the day was the meltdown of the Zimbabwean economy. Tom's Nigerian colleague, who had been in Zimbabwe multiple times, said in response to the interviewer's praise of Robert Mugabe, "If Mugabe had wanted to help his country he could have become a king, instead of a president." To foreign ears that might have sounded odd, but African kings were traditionally limited in powers and focused on resolving disputes and securing peace in their commu-nities, and not—like many African presidents—holders of unlimited and arbitrary power, much less genocidal dictators.

In *Applied Economics for Africa*, Ayittey cites a police chief superintendent in the Zimbabwean capital of Harare who was explicit about his strategy for ending poverty by arresting informal merchants and confiscating their modest inventories.[9] The bizarre impulse to achieve development by banishing or outlawing everything that looks like underdevelopment is the opposite of what Ayittey says is needed to achieve growth. Ayittey argues that it is precisely the informal or transitional sector that represents the most promise for development, both because of its size—you cannot ignore it—and because it actually works, despite so many obstacles stacked against it. How much better could it work for the people making a living within it—and the rest of the country—if the industriousness and alertness to opportunity exhibited by its participants were afforded dignity, respect, and the protective services of legal institutions?

Defining development as not just growth, which can be wildly unequal, but as an increased standard of living for the average person, Ayittey criticizes most aid projects for either prioritizing urban settings, where the vast majority of low-income people do not live and where modernization efforts serve the sensibilities and preferences of elites, or for helicoptering into rural settings with foreign methods and "best practices" for agriculture that are often at odds with local knowledge and norms. Instead, with an emphasis aligned with what we have learned from positive deviance insights, Ayittey sees the solutions to poverty budding within the informal sectors led by the many anonymous movers and shakers who are likely to flourish by their own lights when properly afforded the dignity and institutionally protected freedom to pursue their own paths to prosperity.

The China non-model

In fact, this is how most modern miracles of development have been achieved. The so-called paradox of China's growth is only puzzling in the context of our failed model of exporting liberal democracy under the authority of foreign advisors. In a 2009 paper published in the *American Journal of Sociology*, Martin King Whyte asks why, as conventional wisdom would suggest, China could succeed as it has while seemingly failing to "get the institutions right"? By all accounts, starting with Max Weber's turn-of-the-century observations, China's traditional norms and values work against modern market innovation and economic growth. Described as "stressing reverence for the past, stability, and harmony rather than openness to change and the pursuit of individual self-interest," China's historical cultural attributes have been cited as evidence to explain its poor track record in the past.

What changed in 1978 is described in the last book the Nobel Prize–winning economist Ronald Coase wrote before his death. Written with co-author Ning Wang, *How China Became Capitalist* tells a story of institutional change that is very different from either the prescriptive Washington Consensus story or the state-led capitalism model China is superficially thought to manage.[10] It is a story of incremental decentralization, market experimentation, building from initial conditions, self-determination, and a profound shift in rhetoric. In short, China pursued what Yasheng Hunang, founder of MIT's China Lab, called "directional liberalism" starting from where they were, discovering what works, and codifying and scaling emergent successes as ad hoc policy. The rhetoric mattered, too, as economic historian Dierdre McCloskey has argued for the general case of innovation and development. Perhaps the rhetorical shift can be summarized with just two famous sayings attributed to Deng Xiaoping that, while brief, describe his policy.

> Cross the river by feeling the stones.
> To get rich is glorious.

The first can be seen as a simple but telling description of an incremental policy for institutional change. It is important to recognize that the leaders in the process were many millions of Chinese farmers and entrepreneurs, not the geriatric bosses of the Chinese Communist Party (CCP). The death of Mao—his greatest contribution to China's economic success—created space for the decentralized movement of *Baochan Daohu* ("contracting production to the household") to dismantle the disastrous communal farming system and then, in a remarkable example of ingenuity, to recapitulate the history of the modern firm, by means of *Dai Hongmaozi* ("wearing a red hat"), which created family-owned, and eventually shareholder-owned, firms under the guise of being communist labor cooperatives.[11] The changes were initiated at the grassroots, bottom-up, and Mao's successors, notably Zhao Ziyang and Deng Xiaoping, recognized a parade already underway and decided to get in front of it.

The second rhetorical example can be seen as a description of a changed attitude toward individual initiative, with not-so-subtle clarity around the new shared dignity that should be afforded those who pursue wealth and achieve it. Those simple slogans arguably describe the changes that took place in the years since. For example, town and village enterprises slowly enjoyed more control over their property, whom they could hire and what they could sell—all at freely negotiated prices. Control in most economic matters had been decentralized to provincial and local governments and they were incentivized, not with state-directed rewards, but with state restraint over confiscating the fruits of their success.

At the same time, state-owned enterprises were exposed to previously illegal market competition to ensure their attentiveness to productivity and quality. Those state-owned enterprises, which are held up by the CCP leaders as the crown jewels of the Chinese economy, are arguably—and unsurprisingly—a net drag on the productive enterprise of the Chinese people. As Sheng Hong and Zhao Nong of the now-shuttered (by government force) Unirule Institute of Economics in Beijing documented, once subsidies are taken into account, nominally profitable state-owned enterprises are revealed to be in reality loss-making enterprises. As they conclude after an extensive look into the accounting of state-owned enterprises, "SOES play a negative role in income distribution."[12]

There is no China model. What the Chinese did was allow bottom-up reforms and resist interfering with market-tested innovation while subsidizing loss-making firms to provide sinecures for the CCP elite. It is the open-minded approach to innovation based on competition that makes discovery of comparative advantages possible. Whyte observes that because China's rulers were politically constrained from turning their development problems over to Western foreign aid experts, they could allow the Chinese to pursue their own economic future. Unfortunately, with the ruthless concentration of power in the hands of one man, China is now on a path to subjugate the innovative and value-creating elements of Chinese society to the predation of the CCP elite.

As Prof. George Calhoun of the Stevens Institute of Technology noted of the rapid halving of the fortune of Tencent entrepreneur Jack Ma, the destruction of the Ant Group, and the increasing restraints being put on innovative and entrepreneurial enterprises, "Beijing is now doling out some of the most lucrative slices of Ma's business to new 'partners' of its choosing, including one of the most corrupt and financially shaky companies in all of China."[13]

No specific country, with its particular history, culture, institutions, regulations, and governance structure, provides "the model" for others to replicate. Each is at some evolutionary point in navigating an interdependent, idiosyncratic set of factors within the complex systems that make up social and economic phenomena. What we can learn from the various outcomes of relative degrees of success is what attributes of the process of change are more or less likely to facilitate innovation, poverty reduction, and an increased standard of living for the average person.

Adam Ferguson, a contemporary of Adam Smith, wisely observed that

> every step and every movement of the multitude, even in what are termed enlightened ages, are made with equal blindness to the future;

and nations stumble upon establishments, which are indeed the result of human action, but not the execution of any human design.[14]

We have become persuaded that liberal democratic institutions (civil rights, legal equality, property, presumption of liberty, free exchange, free expression, the rule of law) are critical to raising the levels of human flourishing. But that conviction alone does not tell us how to make the strengthening of liberal institutions more or less likely. Historically, it has led many down the path of copycat institution-building with disastrous results. With their focus on design, the outside "experts" have seen institutions exclusively as outcomes and have not bothered to consider the processes that generated them.

Liberal democracy, by definition, is a governance system that prizes individual voices and individual choices. How to pursue liberal democracy must also be a choice made by those who will be governed by the institutional expression of that aim. Those who have succeeded in strengthening institutions of liberal democracy that endure have led their change process, iteratively working to constrain state power from stifling the decentralized, experimental landscape needed to innovate toward solutions to poverty.

Notes

1 Based on an interview of Rekha Dey conducted in Dehradun, India, June 2019, by Gopikrishnan Nair and Ayushi Jain. Printed with permission.
2 Louis Menand, *The Metaphysical Club: A Story of Ideas in America* (New York: FSG, 2001), p. 431.
3 W. Richard Scott, *Institutions and Organizations* (4th ed., Los Angeles: Sage, 2014), p. 126.
4 Everett Rogers, *Diffusion of Innovations* (5th ed., New York: Free Press, 2003), pp. 269–271.
5 Scott, *Institutions and Organizations*, p. 156 citing David Strang, *Learning by Example: Imitation and Innovation at a Global Bank* (Princeton: Princeton University Press, 2010).
6 Deepa Narayan et al., *Voices of the Poor: Can Anyone Hear Us?* (Oxford: Oxford University Press, 2000), p. 273.
7 Deepa Narayan and Patti Petesch, *Voices of the Poor: From Many Lands* (Oxford: Oxford University Press, 2002), p. 492.
8 George B. N. Ayittey, *Applied Economics for Africa,* 2018, www.africanliberty. org/wp-content/uploads/Applied%20Economics%20for%20Africa.%20 African%20Liberty.pdf.
9 Ayittey, *Applied Economics for Africa*, p. 264.
10 Ning Wang and Ronald Coase, *How China Became Capitalist* (London: Palgrave McMillan, 2012).

11 The process is described in Kate Zhou's *China's Long March to Freedom: Grassroots Modernization* (New Brunswick: Transaction Publishers, 2009).

12 Sheng Hong and Zhao Nong, *China's State-Owned Enterprises: Nature, Performance, and Reform* (Singapore: World Scientific Publishing Co., 2009), p. 124.

13 George Calhoun, "The Sad End of Jack Ma, Inc.," *Forbes*, June 7, 2021, www. forbes.com/sites/georgecalhoun/2021/06/07/the-sad-end-of-jack-ma-inc/ ?sh=66847ce9123a.

14 Adam Ferguson, *An Essay on the History of Civil Society* (5th ed., London: T. Cadell, 1782), https://oll.libertyfund.org/title/ferguson-an-essay-on-the-history-of-civil-society#Ferguson_1229_388.

10 Development with dignity

If the solution to poverty is a function of human dignity exercised within an enabling environment of strong institutions, we need to construct a new development paradigm that ensures outsiders are helping and not harming. We can start by identifying the key entrepreneurial agents who lead enduring development.

When we think of an entrepreneur, we tend to think in terms of the somewhat exceptional. We think of an innovator who becomes famous for changing the way we do business or how we live our day-to-day lives. We think of a tech titan who becomes rich for her keen alertness to big profit opportunities, perhaps releasing a bestseller about rewriting the "rule book." There are practical, academic reasons to define entrepreneurship in narrow terms and much scholarly effort has wrestled with the boundaries of competing and complementary definitions.[1]

Universal and institutional entrepreneurship

Setting those academic debates aside, we propose, as a thought exercise, that in the context of development we should do more to recognize the entrepreneurial behavior that all human beings exhibit every day as they work to navigate the choices they face. Human dignity entails the prerogative to determine for oneself how best to live one's life, and that freedom liberates the enterprising attributes we associate with development. Call them—call all of us—universal entrepreneurs.

Vasily Grossman expressed the insight clearly in *Life and Fate*, his novel about the siege of Stalingrad, when Red Army Colonel Pyotr Pavlovich Novikov inspects the soldiers assembled under his command and realizes,

> Human groupings have one main purpose: to assert everyone's right to be different, to be special, to think, feel and live in his or her own way. People join together in order to win or defend this right. But

DOI: 10.4324/9781003229872-11

this is where a terrible, fateful error is born: the belief that these groupings in the name of a race, a God, a party, or a State are the very purpose of life and not simply a means to an end. No! The only true and lasting meaning of the struggle for life lies in the individual, in his modest peculiarities and in his right to those peculiarities.[2]

In our "modest peculiarities," we all share something in common; each of us is unique. And as we act to improve our situations in life, we are all entrepreneurs.

When Dinesh Dixit, a street vendor in India, decided to move to New Delhi to try his hand at selling bangles, he tested market hypotheses and adjusted his decisions based on the results. He found wholesale suppliers in distant places and selected an assortment of products based on his experience of what sold best and in what relative amounts. He accounted for alternative opportunities—some he had pursued for a time before abandoning them for street vending—as well as constraints imposed by time, transport, family, and government rules. He navigated all of those factors, making micro-decisions every day along the way to survive and, eventually, to thrive.

For some academic definitions, Dinesh Dixit qualifies as an entrepreneur, but when we think of entrepreneurship in the context of development, people like him are often left out. And yet, we would argue that the universality of entrepreneurial behavior found among humble people, particularly those operating in the informal sector, should prompt the development community to prioritize the dignity of every individual as an entrepreneur. It is *their* thinking, evaluating, projecting, and choosing behaviors that have the potential to blaze the idiosyncratic paths from today's poverty to tomorrow's prosperity. In that light, we further suggest that, as George Ayittey so clearly argued, our aspirations for development should be focused on unleashing the ingenuity of the informal sector, not as objects of our pity, but as powerful agents capable of leading progress.

Here again, William Baumol's landmark observations about the universal nature of entrepreneurship are key.[3] Conventional wisdom had considered entrepreneurship mainly in terms of its scarcity. Successful economies had more entrepreneurs; unsuccessful economies had fewer. The implication was that unsuccessful economies needed to somehow produce more entrepreneurs, which, in turn, led to many programmatic efforts to teach locals "how to be entrepreneurs."

Baumol recognized there was much more to this story. He posited that the total supply of entrepreneurs may vary some, but not much. The real variable is the relative productivity of entrepreneurial efforts as a function of the prevailing social norms and formal laws governing the local context. The most important question, then, is not, how can we get more entrepreneurs? The important question is, what effect do the society's rules have on whether entrepreneurial energy is spent productively? A society that affords its people latitude to experiment in the marketplace and protects the fruits of their efforts sees entrepreneurial energy spent on creating economic value for society. A society that restricts experimentation, looks down on commercial activity, and rewards political connectedness will see entrepreneurial energy spent on gaming that system accordingly.

Baumol points out that in medieval China, for example, dignity was not afforded to the merchant class, even to the rich among them. It was afforded to civil servants who faced ultra-competitive exams to earn coveted government posts. Merchants might become prosperous, but they would use their wealth to pay for tutors to help their children to become civil servants. Talent flowed to what Baumol called unproductive entrepreneurship, in this case an overinvestment in mostly studying philosophy and practicing calligraphy.[4] (Not that there is anything wrong per se with studying philosophy or improving one's calligraphy! It's just that such activities are likely better characterized as consumption than as production.) Worse, there is destructive entrepreneurship, which we recognize among bandits, ransomware hacking groups, and other criminal enterprises, which invariably impose harms far greater than the benefits they receive. It's also observed anywhere lobbying (and bribing) government officials for favors offers better returns than competing for customers in the marketplace. Much energy and talent are invested in connections, bribes, and closed-door maneuvering. Such destructive entrepreneurs exhibit plenty of creativity, talent, and industriousness, but they get rich at the expense of others, and typically in ways that impose far greater aggregate costs than the benefits they take. They don't add to the economic pie. They influence the way a smaller pie is allocated. Importantly, Baumol's theory of entrepreneurship has been demonstrated empirically in the years since his initial thesis.[5] If we want to see more net value–creating entrepreneurship, we need to change the way society treats entrepreneurs and the entrepreneurial behavior at work in all of us.

Understanding the latent promise of universal entrepreneurs, particularly those working in the informal or transitional sectors, requires that we appreciate that a big part of what stands between them and a more prosperous future are institutions and practices that degrade, humiliate, and control them; that replace the presumption of liberty with the presumption of power; and that place the burden on them to justify their innovations, rather than on state officials or on warlords to justify forbidding them. So many of those degrading, humiliating, and controlling practices were foisted on the poor by previous colonial masters, and then continued by the post-colonial inheritors of those institutions and practices. As a result, entrepreneurs must navigate landscapes of predatory, dysfunctional, and oppressive institutions. Reversing those trends and building stronger institutions from their initial conditions will take local vision and leadership.

Realizing the localization agenda

The global development community is slowly becoming more attuned to the critical role of local actors in driving development. The recognition of that role in development has been titled the "localization agenda." In July 2021, for example, newly appointed USAID administrator Samantha Power told the Senate Foreign Relations Committee that investing in localization will be key to the agency's long-term success.[6] We explore some elements of that agenda in this chapter to highlight both its promise and its pitfalls. As the international development community turns its attention and resources to supporting the "capacity-building" of the Global South to lead its own development, it should learn quickly how to wind down its own leadership role to get out of the way. This is not inevitable. In the same testimony, Power also suggested USAID would need *more* resources and personnel in-house to account for a more diversified set of local grantees who may not be adequately prepared to comply with the agency's onerous paperwork.[7] In this sense, we suggest the implications of true localization have not really sunk in. To better understand those implications, we next review contemporary localization models, with a focus on a type of local grantee candidate with which we are most familiar: the local, nongovernmental think tank.

In a 2017 working paper for the Gwilym Gibbon Policy Unit at Oxford, Guy Lodge and Will Paxton share their experience working to build capacity for local, nongovernmental think tanks in Zambia, Zimbabwe, and Rwanda.[8] Lodge and Paxton run Kivu International and, from their website, they describe their purpose this way:

> We believe the most effective way to achieve policy change is by supporting and strengthening local policy actors. They are best placed to develop policy solutions which will work in their political environment. They understand how change happens—and does not happen—in their context. Our role is to work with our partners by using their local expertise and knowledge, and our extensive experience of policy-making and policy-influencing, to help them to bring about the change they want to see.[9]

In their paper, Lodge and Paxton address the limits of outsiders in the context of the development community's growing recognition, as Pablo Yanguas argued, that ignoring the political realities of institutional change in development is naïve. At the same time, in a post-colonial world, reluctance to get involved in a recipient country is understandable. Lodge and Paxton observe that our commitment to prizing local leadership in determining development priorities has been weak, in part, because, in the end, aid agencies will always bend to political pressures in their own countries. To fulfill the aims of localization in spirit, the natural tendency then is to inflate the importance of less meaningful gestures such as increasing the presence of ex-pat staff "on the ground."[10]

Lodge and Paxton argue for a more complete transition to localization, citing think tanks as ripe candidates for donor support. They acknowledge, as we do, that local nongovernmental think tanks are not a silver bullet for solving development's localization challenge. Yet, they contend, local think tanks could play a much bigger role if donors would invest more in their potential.

A coalition of philanthropies, led by the William and Flora Hewlett Foundation, did just that. Recall the ten-year failed experiment of Jeffrey Sachs, the Millennium Villages Project, which invested big money—USD$300 million—in traditional, outsider-led technical solutions to poverty. About halfway through that project, in 2009, a very different project, the Think Tank Initiative (TTI), was launched. Over the next ten years, TTI would spend more than CA$200 million to support local think tanks with core annual funding, networking opportunities, and access to technical training. Citing a "critical lack of think tank capacity"[11] in developing countries, the idea was that local think tanks, each steeped in local culture and history, could achieve the institutional changes that lead to development. Taking care not to be too prescriptive, TTI chose to provide core funding, as opposed to project funding, so that local NGO think tanks in the Global South could flexibly determine how best to achieve their own visions for change.

On some measures, the project was very successful in that many of the initial fifty-two think tanks participating in the program reached new heights of organizational strength. (In the end, forty-three think tanks representing twenty countries in Latin America, Africa, and Asia remained qualified for ongoing support throughout the life of the project.) The experiences of both the philanthropies and the grantees involved offer all of us a rich set of insights on the practical challenges associated with pursuing a localization agenda in this way. Some of those challenges will be familiar to traditional aid donors, and it's for that reason that we see so much value in reviewing TTI's pioneering effort. Two themes stand out:

First, across two independent evaluations of the project, one at the five-year mark in 2013 and one at the project's conclusion in 2019, evaluators struggled to draw a clear connection between grantees' increased capacity and the policy impacts they were aiming to achieve. Second, few of the think tank grantees succeeded in preparing for a smooth transition to alternative revenue once the TTI had completed its ten-year funding commitment.

In the 2013 report, evaluators observed that 41 to 50 percent of funding went to research quality, 22 to 30 percent went to organizational development, and only 18 to 27 percent went to communications and outreach.[12] They recommended rebalancing the three allocations to better align with the project's ostensible aims. They also offered early warnings of ambivalence among TTI's executive committee—the body most empowered to make decisions regarding the program—about the tradeoffs between policy goal agnosticism and "a more instrumental view" where the donors expect the think tanks to "work more directly on specific policy issues that they [the donors] perceive to be important."[13] This may have had an impact on grantees' ability to focus fully on their own priorities without worrying that any misalignment with donor priorities would threaten future tranches of scheduled funding.

In addition, while non-earmarked funding was key to TTI's strategy—allowing Global South grantees broad organizational flexibility—evaluators suggested (perhaps anticipating risk of dependency on TTI funds) that going forward grantees should be required to develop transition plans for becoming sustainable after the TTI support concluded.

By 2019, the final evaluation report, undertaken this time by a new set of independent evaluators, validated the prescience of the previous report's concerns. In its opening pages, the authors confess, "It is difficult to discern clear outcomes" in terms of policy wins by grantees traceable to TTI and that "implicit assumptions or hopes that long periods of core funding could prevent future funding crises does not hold."[14] They continue,

> Only a few [of the forty-three] have achieved major progress on resource mobilization. Some are already struggling to deal with the end of TTI funding, falling back to past reliance on more consultancy work and/or a shrinking number [of] permanent senior staff.

As part of the program, TTI had offered matching support to grantees in addition to their annual funding, but that component was extremely modest (between CA$20,000 and CA$50,000 with only a 25 percent match requirement of grantees), and from our reading those funds appeared to be aimed not at incentivizing the development of diverse funding sources but to engendering collaboration among the members of the grantee network. In our view, that was a missed opportunity. Had TTI, from the outset, been much more aggressive in its matching structure by tying large portions of their own giving to grantees' fundraising successes, that could have inspired grantees to be more attentive to developing and pursuing long-term plans for diversifying their funding. They might have truly leveraged the resources TTI provided, and their independence from even the unwitting influence of any single funder would have been strengthened as well.

In our experience, it is not the case that think tanks in developing countries cannot find local funding sources. It is not easy, but it can be done and, what's more, it must be done. To spare think tanks the burden of diligent fundraising efforts robs them—would rob any of us—of the important learning and organizational strengthening that comes from winning a diverse portfolio of supporters. Just as importantly, the value of creatively seeking out and developing those types of relationships locally further galvanizes the influence of homegrown perspectives on think tank priorities, thus rooting grantee vision more squarely within a process that prizes authentic pluralism. Matching structures need not be 1:1 to be effective, but they should tie future tranches of support to an ambitious but attainable match amount. That ratio (and/or number of new donors) could even be determined collaboratively with the grantee.

Regarding TTI's design, the evaluators did ask, "Did the reduced pressure to focus on the 'bottom line' lead to acceptance of inefficient or unsustainable costing models?"[15] In our experience working with think tank grantees, we believe that the reduced pressure to focus on the "bottom line" can be a false comfort that does more harm than good in the long run. Like any of us, in any situation, grantees respond to signals and incentives and prioritize energies accordingly. If the goal is to increase the capacity of local think tanks, philanthropists must take care not to insulate grantee leadership from the ongoing imperative of fundraising. Diverse funding is important for independence, and the learning that comes from consistently honing a value proposition is an important feed-back loop that many "feast or famine" nonprofits never fully embrace. The need to demonstrate continuously that a group is creating net value and thus that it merits support is an important spur to excellence, as is the comparison of results with those obtained by other think tanks.

It's not clear whether TTI, in practice, consistently signaled their commitment to noninterference about grantee priorities. Andrew Hurst, the program director for TTI over the last five years of its run, published in 2020 his reflections on lessons learned in the *Canadian Journal of*

Development Studies. Hurst concluded that more needs to be done to figure out how to neutralize the negative effects of the power imbalance between donors and recipients:

> Everybody acknowledges that the "results agenda" is necessary, especially for bilateral funders who are accountable to tax payers and in the context of a growing donor focus on demonstrating value for money. However, most also acknowledge that this has distorted the development narrative and privileged simplified, technocratic views of "how change happens." This has made it difficult to defend messier, less linear change processes at the heart of development.[16]

Rightsizing power imbalances

We can sympathize with funders who, even when sensitized to the problem of too much outside interference from foreign donors, still want some clarity about aims and a reasonable means of ensuring accountability from grantees. We have observed that, for many, the alternative to outsider-dominated projects is to overcorrect by embracing another extreme: blind support of unaccountable recipients. That is also not helpful. We have seen the positive effects of a more balanced approach that addresses to a large degree the principal–agent problems discussed earlier. Outsiders can and should support the recipient's own vision for change and defer to the recipients' own best judgment on how to get there, but those recipients should still compete for that support by articulating, *ex ante*, what they are specifically hoping to achieve and what verifiable indicators will signal their success. In that way, outsiders learn from grant seekers what their vision is for change (rather than tainting the well with their own pet concerns), and then leave it to the grantee to define their own success. At the same time, they can still hold those grantees accountable according to the grantees' own proposed outcomes that the grantees provided at the start of the project or grant term.

Of course, donors can be deferential about grantee priorities while still being judicious when it comes to assessing the quality of the articulated strategy, chosen indicators, and the overall social value of the proposed outcomes. That is not to say that think tanks should be expected to possess such predictive or forecasting powers that anything short of the successes anticipated should be counted a failure. The uncertainty and complexity of institutional change should temper our expectations that project plans will always be completed exactly as anticipated. The real utility of this hybrid framework—in which recipients define success ambitiously and donors hold them accountable—is that it provides a signaling-and-incentive structure to think tanks within which they are more likely to innovate and to work to achieve documentable outcomes. The anticipated aims may be accomplished, or an alternative set of outcomes may be achieved and then defended at the end of the project term *in reference to and in the context of* the originally anticipated outcomes. Healthy and respectful relationships between donors and recipients will lead to mutual recognition of the valuable learning that comes from this approach. Future funding need not hang capriciously on strict fidelity to the original outcomes, as imagined at the proposal stage, but rather on the quality of learning and earnest commitment to true impact.

Under such a model, it is our experience that positive impacts are, indeed, achieved. What's more, the *ex ante* commitment to clear and specific outcomes lends great credibility to grantee claims of success when they do happen, a very welcome solution to what TTI evaluators—and many others before them—suppose to be a somewhat hopeless causality dilemma when it comes to crediting local actors with institutional change.

Hurst also emphasizes the distinct type of knowledge—practical knowledge—that think tanks are well positioned to help cultivate locally through social collaboration and which they bring to bear on institutional change. "An important dimension to ensuring legitimacy and positioning for use in the research process, was making connections to, and engaging with, citizens and communities."[17] For us, this is perhaps one of the most important lessons from the TTI project that can guide future efforts to advance the localization agenda. The more local NGOs of all types authentically represent the views of universal entrepreneurs in their communities, the more relevant their priorities will be for solving the institutional challenges they face.

In addition to advancing global learning on the practical implications of the localization agenda, the TTI also seems to have succeeded in expanding the leadership visions of think tank grantees. For example, think tank leaders Sukhadeo Thorat, Ajaya Dixit, and Samar Verma participated as grantees in the initiative and compiled a volume of essays that included several other participants in their region to tell the stories of the fourteen South Asian think tanks and what they learned from the experience. What the co-editors take from those stories is encouraging. As they put it,

> Problems of the Global South cannot be resolved with solutions from the North. It is time for Southern think tanks to step up—there is no need for Northern votes for Southern ideas. ... To remain

masters of their own voices, think tanks should responsibly be able to differentiate what they want to say, and what their fund-providers' policy agendas are.[18]

We could not agree more. Wisely, they call on local donors to step up to play their new part in this localization agenda shift as well. "If leading international donors of TTI can take a leap of trust in think tanks in developing countries, surely domestic philanthropies can rise to the occasion." The more local funding can join the cause of local think tanks, the stronger will be the think tanks' ties to local priorities and independence from major funding influences from abroad.

We fully acknowledge that our own familiarity with think tanks leads us, naturally, to emphasize the role they can play—and the limited role outside funders of think tanks should play—in development. However, it is not our contention that all roads should lead to think tanks as the answer. One of the key aims of this book is to stress the pluralistic, multi-causal nature of enduring institutional change. Our hope is simply to increase appreciation for the many diverse local actors that can and should enjoy a larger role in leading development, many of whom have been quietly operating in the background while foreign powers and experts debate their next development moves largely among themselves.

When it comes to identifying ideal nongovernmental development partners that are indigenous to the countries in which they work, many will have their own instincts and attachments. We are all fortunate that, in recent years, the options have increased considerably. According to David Lewis, Nazneen Kanji, and Nuno Themudo in their 2021 book, *Nongovernment Organizations and Development*, it is difficult to know for sure just how many NGOs are out there. What methods we do have for estimating their number would indicate a rapid rise since 1990 from some 5,000 organizations to upwards of 75,000 today.[19]

Given the proliferation of NGOs, and likewise that of local NGOs, it may seem daunting, even inefficient, to spread support across such a diverse and decentralized landscape. Of course, if institutional change is the best way to achieve productive, universal entrepreneurship, then we can focus development support on the subset of local NGOs, such as think tanks, whose models are geared toward institutional change and policy reform. According to the University of Pennsylvania's Think Tank and Civil Societies Program, there are roughly 8,200 think tanks in the world.[20] This is still a large number. While TTI made a significant contribution to our understanding of the opportunities and pitfalls of supporting capacity in the Global South, even their relative largesse was limited to, in the end, only forty-three organizations. At the same time, if freewheeling, decentralized experimentation and pluralism is such a powerful and resilient method for discovering innovative success, perhaps it is comforting to think that there need not be one uniform answer for how to support the Global South. If the past has taught us anything, we should get off the treadmill search for one big, simple solution to poverty and development. Instead, we can each pursue, in earnest and in a spirit of learning from each other, our very best hypotheses for effectively supporting institutional change leadership throughout the Global South and anywhere else democracy needs strengthening.

With that same spirit, we share the following set of ideas which have guided our own selection and support processes. First, if universal entrepreneurs are to be afforded their dignity as frontline innovators across the vast landscape of economic possibility, then not all institutional entrepreneurs (e.g., think tanks) ought to be considered equally helpful. Only those that are both inclusive of universal entrepreneur participation in process change *and* focused on properly defining the boundaries of legal restrictions on experimentation will lead institutional change in the direction of pluralistic prosperity.

In 2014, India adopted the Street Vendors Act, which provides legal recognition and improved ease of entry to the millions of people in India who earn their livelihoods by selling goods in the market. The legislation represents an incremental institutional change at the margins of the informal market. That change was made possible, in part, by local visionaries, a universal entrepreneur named Dinesh Dixit and an institutional entrepreneur named Parth Shah, each representing an important role in locally led change. Consider the following story of their change process presented in their own words.

Universal entrepreneur

> *My name is Dinesh Kumar Dixit. I sell bangles in Sarojini Nagar, Babu Market. I have been selling bangles since 1978. Back then, both Delhi Police and New Delhi Municipal Council (NDMC) used to impound my goods every time they came to the market.*
>
> *I had been struggling with these issues for years. Every time NDMC would impound my goods, I would make a written appeal to them—"This is the place you took my goods from, on this date," and I have saved a note for each such instance.*
>
> *It would crush my spirits that my goods worth thousands (of rupees) were being impounded and taken away. I used to get very upset. At that point in*

time, I was very distressed. Before 2014 no one would listen to us. They'd say you are unauthorized and you have no right! But when the 2014 Act came out, I felt empowered. I felt like now I have strength and with strength there has been a change in the way I think. Before 2014, I used to think, I am just a "patri wala" (street vendor). After 2014, I feel like we have this new strength in our bodies, and our voices can now be heard whether it be by the administration or the Parliament of India!

[In the act] there was a provision to create Town Vending Committees. This is where all the decisions are made. There was an election that took place. I applied to be a member of the committee and I had the highest votes! Now I raise my voice for the benefit of street vendors. After the 2014 Act we got our rights and our voices were elevated. Now, they listen to what we have to say, and they also implement it.

In New Delhi wherever there are street vendors, I go and see where they can operate. Then I talk to NDMC to allocate permanent places for these street vendors so they can earn their livelihood legally. In case there is an injustice, I take up that issue and they listen to me.

Street vendors realize that now they have a voice, the administration listens, and even Indian Parliament listens to us. I work hard day-in, day-out to get all of these street vendors a permanent place to work. They listen to me. I tell them this is how it is supposed to be done, they should get the licenses, all kinds of street vendors even those that roam around to make a livelihood. I will work for them as well to get them licenses issued so that they can have it on them and they will have an identity in the market [knowing] that TVC members did this work and now they can proudly lift their heads to earn a livelihood.

I am sixty-three years old, and whatever time I have left I want to spend it for the betterment of the society. I told the administration, it is no longer the time as it used to be, I am a TVC member. I used to be a "patri wala" (street vendor) now I am a TVC member and now my thinking has changed to do good for the society. That life [then] and this life now are totally different. Back then I used to be alone; now I am a million, billion voices, a people's representative.

There is society, so there are problems, and to solve these problems there is one Dinesh Kumar Dixit. I play my role in solving the issues. I sleep with my shoes on so that when someone calls for help, I don't waste time. I can be there for them immediately.

I feel like I used to be on the floor, now I am flying and touching skies. I have reached from "farsh" (floor) to "arsh" (sky). Previously, I used to sell goods worth a few hundred of INR (less than $2), now I have goods in my shop worth thousands. I feel like I have become a better businessman.

Institutional entrepreneur

> *I am Parth Shah, founder of Centre for Civil Society, a New Delhi-based think tank NGO.*
> *For the city of Delhi, there are 600,000 street vendors. On average, a street vendor pays about 200 rupees a month in bribes to the officers [to be left alone to operate their business]. That's about USD$4 a month that they pay in bribes. If you just multiply those two numbers, 600,000 by USD$4 per month, that's USD$2.4 million per month, which is collected from the poorest of the poor in the nation's capital. That gives you a very good insight into the cost of being informal.*
> *There are several advantages of being in the formal sector. You have access to easy credit. You're able to hire quality labor on contract. But the laws are so stringent that it's very expensive and very difficult to be in the formal sector in India. The formal sector is rather small compared to the informal sector in India. There are multiple challenges that they face in starting a business. The funding one would need in terms of getting certification from the government [is a challenge]. Secondly, there [used to be] a paid up capital requirement which they [must] put upfront, and quite often the amount of money that you have to pay is substantial.*
> *Until recently, the amount was about one lakh, 100,000 rupees that you had to put up. If you compare that with the per capita income in the country it is almost about 40 percent of the per capita income. Just to give you an idea what that amount means, the per capita income in the US is about $60,000. The capital requirement in India would imply that you would have to put up [the equivalent of] USD$25,000 or $30,000 upfront to register a business. That's a very heavy cost for a poor entrepreneur to bear in order to become formally registered as a business entity.*
> *The huge transformation in the life of just one person is an example that you can see. Multiply that by millions. And you can see the impact of a simple change in the law on real lives.*
> *The street vendors in the cities of India that you see are the homegrown bottom-up entrepreneurs who mostly come from out of town. They take tremendous risk in being settled in the city. They find a network of contacts to be able to start a business and fight the legal battles they have to fight every day.*
> *What personally inspired me to work on this topic was my own observation at one of the local markets where I was doing shopping with my family. Suddenly a police van came and as soon as we heard the siren of the van, all the vendors on the streets of that market began backing up and running "helter skelter." And I realized that the life of a street entrepreneur is so dependent on the whims of the regulatory system. At one moment, they are*

doing good business, the next moment they are all hiding and running from their own customers.

We had to fight this battle of legalizing street vendors at the local level. We ran a campaign in two cities of India—in Jaipur and Patna—and we met with the street vendors to understand the challenges they are facing. We worked with them to draft a particular kind of law that will change the status of street entrepreneurs, from being completely informal to being better recognized in the regulatory system.

You can see the example of the benefit of that in the story of Dinesh, who has been working there for more than forty years, and who always has been looked down upon by the system. And now he is elected to a Town Vending Committee, which is a committee that supervises and regulates the vending space in the city. He's now able to sit across the table from the same officers who used to beat him up and harass him and be able to challenge them in terms of how they think about the lives of people like him.

I think before the Jeevika ["Livelihood"] campaign to change the law, people like Dinesh would have no voice in the system. They were treated as something which is a pariah, as something which is not a good thing for society. All of those things suddenly changed, where Dinesh is sitting across the table from the government officers and able to talk to them and make them understand the challenges that he and millions of people like him are facing every day to earn an honest living.

Dinesh and his family for the first time have dignity, dignity as a human being, dignity as a street entrepreneur, dignity as a member of society, and are able to then conduct themselves being upright, not just in front of their own families and community but also in front of the government.21

From these and similar examples, we can see how a local think tank committed to iterative, institutional change can be a much more effective alternative to an outsider-led development design. When a think tank is sensitized to the importance of engaging and learning from real people living at the margins of society, their institutional change efforts can be both more positive and more long lasting. Our role as outsiders is to find those change agents and support their own entrepreneurial journeys.

The shortcomings of the "development through foreign aid" model have been recognized—and sometimes acknowledged by practitioners—for decades. In our experience, even sincere efforts to reconcile those shortcomings by tinkering around the edges of aid-project design or intervention-modeling have failed to address those shortcomings precisely because they do not get at the root of the problem: the entire paradigm is antagonistic, by construct, to the fundamentals of human dignity, to individual self-determination, to dispersed knowledge and wisdom, and to democratic participation.

It's time to think seriously about how to put foreign aid and out-sider intervention behind us completely. The philosopher Adam Smith was a pioneer of development economics, insofar as he took seriously the questions of both the *nature* and the *causes* of the wealth of nations. Some have suggested, however, that Smith could have been much more adamant about ending colonialism, that he, in essence, pulled some punches. William Easterly's research found evidence to suggest that, while Smith strongly opposed colonialism, he didn't make its end his sole or even his main focus, because at that time ending colonialism just seemed so unlikely.[22] It was a practice that was deeply entrenched and embedded in the status quo and had so many powerful interests invested in its perpetuation.

When it comes to foreign aid and international development, that may be the situation we find ourselves in today. The vast and com-plex interests—many, but by no means all, of them motivated by good intentions—that are caught up in our foreign aid establishment are enough to reckon with on their own, but the challenge of sunsetting for-eign aid practice is further complicated by foreign policy objectives that often enjoy the co-branding and complementarity of foreign aid activ-ities. Add to that inertia the fact that in popular culture, foreign aid and outsider-identified solutions for helping the world's poor are still gener-ally considered to be unquestionable moral obligations. But perhaps, like colonialism, foreign aid's appropriately canceled ancestor, this will be true until, suddenly, it isn't anymore.

The forces needed to reach that moment will likely include civil society in recipient countries pushing back as much as it will require rich countries taking to heart the lessons of our failure to spread democracy and prosperity from the top down. Adam Smith offered a more hopeful note for colonialism's end:

> Hereafter, perhaps, the natives of those countries may grow stronger, or those of Europe may grow weaker, and the inhabitants of all the different quarters of the world may arrive at that equality of courage and force which, by inspiring mutual fear, can alone overawe the injustice of independent nations into some sort of respect for the rights of one another.[23]

Local think tank NGOs that are committed to liberal democracy are among the best levers for achieving development. Outsiders can and should support their increased capacity and should hold them accountable to their own definitions for success. Of course, others will support development in different ways and that is probably a good thing. What we do hope to see more convergence around, however, is a better appreciation for the role universal and institutional entrepreneurs play in leading change in the places they live. It is their knowledge, self-determination, and democratic processes that hold the most promise for achieving development with dignity.

A big lesson for development practice is to recognize that complex adaptive systems are comprised of individual agents—human beings. A shared commitment to human dignity should remind us that those agents are autonomous and self-determining. As Nobel Prize–winning economist Angus Deaton has argued, "What surely ought to happen is what happened in the now-rich world, where countries developed in their own way, in their own time, under their own political and economic structure."[24] If we cannot find a helpful role for ourselves as outsiders, human dignity demands we stand down.

Notes

1 For a quick glance summary of the dominant theories and potential subdomains of entrepreneurship, see Steven Gedeon's "What Is Entrepreneurship?" *Entrepreneurial Practice Review*, Vol. 1, No. 3, 2010, pp. 16–35.

2 Vasily Grossman, *Life and Fate: A Novel*, trans. Robert Chandler (New York: Harper & Row, 1987), p. 230.

3 William Baumol, "Entrepreneurship: Productive, Unproductive, and Destructive," *Journal of Political Economy*, Vol. 98, No. 5, 1990, pp. 893–921.

4 Baumol, "Entrepreneurship," p. 901.

5 For one example, see Russell Sobel's "Testing Baumol: Institutional Quality and the Productivity of Entrepreneurship," *Journal of Business Venturing*, Vol. 23, 2004, pp. 641–655.

6 Adva Saldinger, "USAID to Push Localization, Counter China's Influence, Power Says," *Devex*, July 15, 2021.

7 Saldinger, "USAID to Push Localization, Counter China's Influence, Power Says."

8 Guy Lodge and Will Paxton, "Achieving Policy Change in Developing Contexts: The Role of Think Tanks," Gwilym Centre Working Paper, Nuffield College, Oxford, 2017.

9 See Kivu International web page "What We Do," www.kivu-international. org/what-we-do/, accessed June 27, 2021.

10 Lodge and Paxton, "Achieving Policy Change in Developing Contexts."

11 John Young, Volker Hauck, and Paul Engel, "Final Report of the External Evaluation of the Think Tank Initiative," Overseas Development Institute and European Centre for Development Policy Management, September 2013.

12 Young, Volker Hauck, and Paul Engel, "Final Report of the External Evaluation of the Think Tank Initiative," 2013.

13 Young, Volker Hauck, and Paul Engel, "Final Report of the External Evaluation of the Think Tank Initiative," 2013.

14 Ian Christoplos et al., "External Evaluation of the Think Tank Initiative (TTI) Phase Two, 2014–2019," NIRAS, April 18, 2019.

15 Christoplos et al., "External Evaluation of the Think Tank Initiative," p. 25.

16 Andrew Hurst, "Reflections from the Think Tank Initiative and Their Relevance for Canada," *Canadian Journal of Development Studies*, Vol. 42, 2020, p. 8.

17 Hurst, "Reflections from the Think Tank Initiative," p. 7.

18 Sukhadeo Thorat, Ajaya Dixit, and Samar Verma, eds. *Strengthening Policy Research: Role of Think Tank Initiative in Asia* (Los Angeles: Sage, 2019), p. 366.

19 David Lewis, Nazneen Kanji, and Nuno Themudo, *Nongovernment Organizations and Development* (2nd ed., London: Routledge, 2021), pp. 1–2.

20 James McGann "2019 Global Go To Think Tank Index Report," *Scholarly Commons*, 2020, p. 10, https://repository.upenn.edu/cgi/viewcontent.cgi?article=1018&context=think_tanks.

21 Based on interviews with Parth Shah and Dinesh Dixit conducted in New Delhi, March 2019 by AJ Skiera and Tarun Vats. Printed with permission.

22 William Easterly "Progress by Consent: Adam Smith as Development Economist," *The Review of Austrian Economics*, Vol. 34, 2021, p. 198.

23 Adam Smith, *An Inquiry into the Nature and Causes of the Wealth of Nations*, ed. W. B. Todd (Indianapolis, IN: Liberty Fund, 1981), Vol. 2, IV, vii, p. 626.

24 Angus Deaton, *The Great Escape* (Oxford: Oxford University Press, 2013), p. 312.

Appendix

Low income autocracy

Haiti: 1961–1985, 1988–1989, 1991–1993, 2000–2003
Honduras: 1961–1979
Indonesia: 1961–1998
Iraq: 1969–1978, 1991–1996
Ivory Coast: 1961–1998
Jordan: 1977, 1991
Kenya: 1969–2001
Korea South: 1961–1962, 1972–1974
Lesotho: 1970–1992
Madagascar: 1961–1990
Malawi: 1964–1993
Mali: 1968–1990
Mauritania: 1962–2018
Mongolia: 1982–1989
Morocco: 1967–2006
Mozambique: 1981–1993
Myanmar: 1962–2014
Nepal: 1961–1989, 2002–2005
Nicaragua: 1961–1978, 1981–1989
Niger: 1961–1990, 1996–1998, 2009
Nigeria: 1966–1977, 1984–1997
Oman: 1966
Pakistan: 1961, 1977–2007
Paraguay: 1961–1977
Philippines: 1972–1985
Rwanda: 1961–2018
Senegal: 1963–1999
Sierra Leone: 1967, 1971–1995
Somalia: 1969–1990
South Sudan: 2011–2012
Sudan: 1961–1963, 1971–1984, 1989–2011
Swaziland: 1973–1989
Tajikistan: 1991–2018
Tanzania: 1989–2014
Thailand: 1961–1967, 1971–1972, 1976
Togo: 1961–1990, 1993–2018
Tunisia: 1966–1995
Turkmenistan: 1994–2003
Uganda: 1986–2018
Uzbekistan: 1991–2018
Vietnam: 1985–2018
Zambia: 1972–1990
Zimbabwe: 1987–2008

Note: The data only includes those countries with both a GDP growth rate and a democracy score for the year. If either the GDP growth or the democracy score were missing, the data point was dropped from the analysis. In addition, countries were not counted that were categorized as "cases of foreign interruption," "cases of interregnum, or anarchy," and "cases of transition" by Polity IV. Finally, the countries that were dropped in East Asia are as follows: China, South Korea, Myanmar, Thailand, Cambodia, Vietnam, Indonesia, Malaysia, Philippines, and Timor-Leste.

Low income democracy

Bangladesh: 1972–1973
Belarus: 1994
Bolivia: 1982–2008
Cape Verde: 1991–2003
Comoros: 2006–2017
Dominican Republic: 1962
Fiji: 1970–1972
Ghana: 2004–2018
Guatemala: 1996–1998
India: 1961–1974, 1977–2018
Indonesia: 2004–2005
Kenya: 2002–2018
Lesotho: 1966–1969, 1993–1997, 2002–2018
Liberia: 2018
Madagascar: 1992–1997
Malaysia: 1961–1968
Mauritius: 1977–1983
Moldova: 2001–2010
Mongolia: 1992–2007, 2009
Myanmar: 1961, 2016–2018
Nepal: 2018
Nicaragua: 1995–2015
Niger: 1992–1995
Nigeria: 1961–1965, 1979–1983, 2016–2018
Pakistan: 1973–1976, 1988–1996
Philippines: 1987–2013
Senegal: 2000–2006
Sierra Leone: 2007–2018
Solomon Islands: 1990–1999, 2004–2018
Sri Lanka: 1970–1977
Sudan: 1965–1968, 1986–1988
Timor-Leste: 2012–2018

Note: The data only includes those countries with both a GDP growth rate and a democracy score for the year. If either the GDP growth or the democracy score were missing, the data point was dropped from the analysis. In addition, countries were not counted that were categorized as "cases of foreign interruption," "cases of interregnum, or anarchy," and "cases of transition" by Polity IV. Finally, the countries that were dropped in East Asia are as follows: China, South Korea, Myanmar, Thailand, Cambodia, Vietnam, Indonesia, Malaysia, Philippines, and Timor-Leste.

Full dataset autocracy

Afghanistan: 2014–2018
Albania: 1981–1989
Algeria: 1962–2003
Angola: 1981–1990, 1997–2018
Argentina: 1966–1972, 1976–1982

Full dataset autocracy

Armenia: 1996–1997
Azerbaijan: 1991, 1993–2018
Bahrain: 1981–2018
Bangladesh: 1974–1990, 2007–2008, 2018
Belarus: 1996–2018
Benin: 1965–1989
Bhutan: 1981–2007
Bolivia: 1961–1981
Brazil: 1965–1984
Bulgaria: 1981–1989
Burkina Faso: 1961–1976, 1980–2014
Burundi: 1963–1964, 1966–1991, 1996–2000, 2015–2018
Cambodia: 1997, 2017–2018
Cameroon: 1961–2018
Cape Verde: 1981–1990
Central African Republic: 1961–1992, 2003–2012
Chad: 1961–1977, 1985–1990, 1992–2018
Chile: 1973–1988
China: 1961–2018
Comoros: 1981–2001, 2018
Congo Brazzaville: 1963–1990, 1997–2018
Congo Kinshasa: 1965–1991, 2016–2018
Croatia: 1996–1998
Cuba: 1971–2018
Dominican Republic: 1966–1977
Ecuador: 1961–1967, 1972–1978
Egypt: 1961–2011, 2013–2018
El Salvador: 1972–1978
Equatorial Guinea: 1981–2018
Eritrea: 1993–2011
Ethiopia: 1982–1990, 2005–2017
Fiji: 1987–1989, 2006–2013
Gabon: 1961–2008
Gambia: 1994–2016
Ghana: 1961–1968, 1972–1977, 1981–1990, 1992–1995
Greece: 1967–1973
Guatemala: 1961–1965, 1974–1984
Guinea: 1987–2009
Guinea-Bissau: 1974–1993, 2003–2004, 2012–2013
Guyana: 1980–1991
Haiti: 1961–1985, 1988–1989, 1991–1993, 2000–2003
Honduras: 1961–1979
Indonesia: 1961–1998
Iran: 1961–1978, 1982–1996, 2004–2018
Iraq: 1969–2002
Ivory Coast: 1961–1998
Jordan: 1977–2018
Kazakhstan: 1991–2018

Full dataset autocracy

Kenya: 1969–2001
Korea South: 1961–1962, 1972–1986
Kuwait: 1996–2018
Lesotho: 1970–1992
Libya: 2000–2010
Madagascar: 1961–1990
Malawi: 1964–1993
Mali: 1968–1990
Mauritania: 1962–2018
Mexico: 1961–1993
Mongolia: 1982–1989
Morocco: 1967–2018
Mozambique: 1981–1993
Myanmar: 1962–2014
Nepal: 1961–1989, 2002–2005
Nicaragua: 1961–1978, 1981–1989
Niger: 1961–1990, 1996–1998, 2009
Nigeria: 1966–1977, 1984–1997
Oman: 1966–2018
Pakistan: 1961, 1977–2007
Panama: 1968–1988
Paraguay: 1961–1988
Peru: 1962, 1968–1977, 1992
Philippines: 1972–1985
Portugal: 1961–1973
Qatar: 2001–2018
Rwanda: 1961–2018
Saudi Arabia: 1969–2018
Senegal: 1963–1999
Sierra Leone: 1967, 1971–1995
Singapore: 1965–2018
Somalia: 1969–1990
South Sudan: 2011–2012
Spain: 1961–1974
Sudan: 1961–1963, 1971–1984, 1989–2011
Suriname: 1980–1989
Swaziland: 1973–2018
Syria: 1961–2007
Tajikistan: 1991–2018
Tanzania: 1989–2014
Thailand: 1961–1967, 1971–1972, 1976, 1991, 2006–2007, 2014–2018
Togo: 1961–1990, 1993–2018
Tunisia: 1966–2010
Turkey: 1971–1972, 1980–1982, 2016–2018
Turkmenistan: 1991–2018
UAE: 1976–2018
Uganda: 1986–2018
Uruguay: 1973–1984

Full dataset autocracy

Uzbekistan: 1991–2018
Venezuela: 2009–2012
Vietnam: 1985–2018
Yemen: 1993–2011
Zambia: 1972–1990
Zimbabwe: 1987–2008

Full dataset democracy

Albania: 2005–2018
Argentina: 1983–1988, 1999, 2000–2018
Australia: 1961–2018
Austria: 1961–2018
Bangladesh: 1972–1973
Belarus: 1994
Belgium: 1961–2018
Bolivia: 1982–2008
Botswana: 1997–2018
Brazil: 1988–2018
Bulgaria: 1990–2018
Canada: 1961–2018
Cape Verde: 1991–2018
Chile: 1989–2018
Colombia: 1974–1994
Comoros: 2006–2017
Costa Rica: 1961–2018
Croatia: 2000–2018
Cyprus: 1976–2018
Czech Republic: 1993–2018
Denmark: 1961–2018
Dominican Republic: 1962, 1996–2018
Ecuador: 1979–1999
El Salvador: 2009–2018
Estonia: 1999–2018
Fiji: 1970–1986
Finland: 1961–2018
France: 1969–2018
Gambia: 1967–1980, 1990–1993
Georgia: 2013–2018
Germany: 1990–2018
Ghana: 2004–2018
Greece: 1975–2018
Guatemala: 1996–2018
Guyana: 2015–2018
Hungary: 1992–2018
India: 1961–1974, 1977–2018

Full dataset democracy

Indonesia: 2004–2018
Ireland: 1971–2018
Israel: 1961–1980
Italy: 1961–2018
Jamaica: 1967–2018
Japan: 1961–2018
Kenya: 2002–2018
Korea South: 1998–2018
Kosovo: 2008–2018
Latvia: 1996–2018
Lesotho: 1966–1969, 1993–1997, 2002–2018
Liberia: 2018
Lithuania: 1996–2018
Luxembourg: 1961–2018
Macedonia: 2002–2018
Madagascar: 1992–1997
Malaysia: 1961–1968
Mauritius: 1977–2018
Mexico: 2000–2018
Moldova: 2001–2018
Mongolia: 1992–2018
Montenegro: 2006–2018
Myanmar: 1961, 2016–2018
Nepal: 2018
Netherlands: 1961–2018
New Zealand: 1971–2018
Nicaragua: 1995–2015
Niger: 1992–1995
Nigeria: 1961–1965, 1979–1983, 2015–2018
Norway: 1961–2018
Pakistan: 1973–1976, 1988–1996
Panama: 1989–2018
Paraguay: 2003–2018
Peru: 1990–1991, 2001–2018
Philippines: 1987–2018
Poland: 1991–2018
Portugal: 1976–2018
Romania: 1996–2018
Senegal: 2000–2006
Serbia: 2006–2018
Sierra Leone: 2007–2018
Singapore: 1961–1962
Slovak Republic: 1998–2018
Slovenia: 1991–2018
Solomon Islands: 1990–1999, 2004–2018
South Africa: 1994–2018
Spain: 1978–2018
Sri Lanka: 1970–1977

Full dataset democracy

Sudan: 1965–1968, 1986–1988
Sweden: 1961–2018
Switzerland: 1971–2018
Thailand: 1992–2005
Timor-Leste: 2012–2018
Trinidad and Tobago: 1962–2018
Turkey: 1961–1970, 1973–1979, 1989–2013
United Kingdom: 1961–2018
United States: 1961–2018
Uruguay: 1961–1970, 1985–2018
Venezuela: 1968–1998

Index

Note: *Italic* page numbers refer to figures and page number followed by "n" refer to end notes.

For Product Safety Concerns and Information please contact our EU
representative GPSR@taylorandfrancis.com
Taylor & Francis Verlag GmbH, Kaufingerstraße 24, 80331 München, Germany

www.ingramcontent.com/pod-product-compliance
Ingram Content Group UK Ltd.
Pitfield, Milton Keynes, MK11 3LW, UK
UKHW021425080625
459435UK00011B/164